ENJOYING CLARET IN GEORGIAN IRELAND

Enjoying Claret in Georgian Ireland

A history of amiable excess

Patricia McCarthy

OPEN AIR

Typeset in 10.5 pt on 13 pt Ehrhardt by
Carrigboy Typesetting Services for
OPEN AIR
an imprint of Four Courts Press Ltd
7 Malpas Street, Dublin 8, Ireland
www.fourcourtspress.ie
and in North America for
FOUR COURTS PRESS
c/o IPG, 814 N Franklin St, Chicago, IL 60610

A catalogue record for this title is available from the British Library.

ISBN 978–1–80151–013–4

Printed in Spain by Grafo S.A.

For Simon, Ross and Kate,
with my love

Contents

Abbreviations

IADS	*Irish Architectural and Decorative Studies*
IHS	*Irish Historical Studies*
IQR	*Irish Quarterly Review*
JCHAS	*Journal of the Cork Historical and Archaeological Society*
JGAHS	*Journal of the Galway Archaeological and Historical Society*
JRSAI	*Journal of the Royal Society of Antiquaries of Ireland*
NAI	National Archives of Ireland
NLI	National Library of Ireland
PRIA	*Proceedings of the Royal Irish Academy*
PRONI	Public Record Office of Northern Ireland
QBIGS	*Quarterly Bulletin of the Irish Georgian Society*
RIA	Royal Irish Academy
TCD	Trinity College Dublin
UJA	*Ulster Journal of Archaeology*

Acknowledgments

Before I began to research the subject of this book, I had some misgivings about my qualifications to do so. Much as I enjoy the occasional glass of wine, or sometimes more, I cannot pretend to be an expert. However, as my research on the subject increased, particularly on the social aspects of drinking wine in eighteenth-century Ireland, it seemed like an opportunity to put together a book that might be enjoyed by the average wine-drinker, if not the connoisseur. The stories connected with eighteenth-century wine-drinking are legion, and often very amusing, but I needed guidance from people who know about wine and its history, so through the author and historian, Turtle Bunbury, I was introduced to two prominent former members of the drinks industry in Ireland, Keith MacCarthy-Morrogh, late of Diageo, and David Miller, formerly of Findlater's. Apart from furnishing me with books of interest, they both read over early versions of chapters and sent me their comments, for which I am enormously grateful. Any errors that appear in later versions are entirely mine.

Two people whom I greatly admire, Dr Edward McParland, who supervised my PhD thesis at Trinity College Dublin, and Dr Bill Vaughan, late of the History Department, also at TCD, patiently worked their way through the early texts, giving me the benefit of their extensive knowledge of the period, and for which I am greatly appreciative. I have benefited from the writings of many scholars, such as Toby Barnard, Louis Cullen, James Kelly, Marie-Louise Legg, Conor Lucey, Charles Ludington, Máirtín Mac Con Iomaire and Martin Powell.

Many people have helped to bring this book to fruition, and my thanks to all of the following: Lilian Barton of Barton Guestier, Valerie Brouder, Turtle Bunbury, Daniel Calley, Andrew Carpenter, Anne Casement, Neil Cassidy, Brother Colman, Glenstal Abbey, Vandra Costello, Antoinette and Brian Dornan, Cathal Dowd Smith, Noelle Dowling, Charles Duggan, Jane Fenlon, David Griffin, Livia Hurley, Tim Jackson, Susan Keating, John Kirwan, Conor Lucey, Annette Mink, Jonathan and Robert Mitchell, the late Cathal Moore, Anna Moran, Rachel Moss, Danielle O'Donovan, Freddie O'Dwyer, Caroline Pegum, Brendan Rooney, Robert Towers, John Wallace and David Whelehan. Special thanks to my siblings, Catherine, Michael, Declan and John Murphy, for their moral support. Sincere thanks to Terry Foley for the cover design, and to Martin Fanning of Four Courts Press.

Enjoying claret in Georgian Ireland

MUCH OF THE BLAME FOR THE spread of drunkenness in eighteenth-century Ireland was laid, according to the Revd Samuel Madden, with the landed gentry. Madden, one of the founder members of the Dublin Society (now the Royal Dublin Society), wrote in 1738 that drinking had become so fashionable, that gentlemen competed eagerly to 'have the largest cellar and spend the most on hogsheads [of wine] every year'; and, like all fashions, this was spreading down the social scale as people sought 'the glory of drinking like their betters'.[1] Visitors found Dublin society less formal than that of London: one describing it as combining the polish of Paris with the 'wit, raciness, frankness, and hilarity of Hibernia', noting that the mix of gentry, professions and academia gave it a distinct urbanity.[2] However, others were shocked at the disparity between those who lavished money on eating and drinking with their friends, while the rest of the country suffered such poverty and, in the 1760s, one visitor, John Bush, found that Irish intemperance left him with feelings of disgust.[3] Edward Melville, an American visitor to Ireland, wrote from Bordeaux in 1805 about Irish disparagement of the French manner of drinking: 'The Irish say that three bottles of wine would serve forty Frenchmen at supper; an allowance which one honest Paddy would easily consume, and Paddy swears roundly, it is all stinginess makes the French so temperate, and stinginess with his generous nation is a crime of the deepest die.'[4] A poem published in 1742 describes some 'few modern Men of Taste':

> At length when you make shift to dine,
> His *worship* gives you sower Wine,
> He calls it *Bourdeaux*, or *Margoo*,
> Which you must drink until you spew,
> And if you stir he'll seize your *Trottle*,
> To keep you for another *Bottle*
> *'Dear Jack!* Don't leave me my dear Cousin
> Till you and I drink out the *Dozen*'.[5]

It was against this background and in the course of researching my previous book, *Life in the country house in Georgian Ireland* (London and New Haven, 2016), that the idea of writing about the amount of wine consumed by the upper classes in Ireland during that period took root. It should be stated at the outset, however, that this book is about the drinking of wine by those who chose to do so. It was not a drink that was enjoyed by the masses but it was common among upper levels of the middling sorts and the Catholic gentry, neither of whom were included in the political process. Not everyone drank alcohol, and of those who did, most probably drank it in moderation. In some ways this book is an extension of *Life*, which looked at how people designed and arranged their houses to facilitate their way of living. An important part of that was entertaining – eating and drinking – something that the Irish had done well for centuries, and that the Anglo-Irish ascendancy were happy to continue. After the political turmoil of the seventeenth century, house-building began in earnest and, due to the falling in of long-term leases between 1710 and 1730, landlords could increase rents. With money at their disposal, they furnished their new or re-furbished houses, laid out their grounds, and planned entertainments at which they could show off their tastefully decorated houses and, of course, the contents, which included wines from their cellars.

Nowadays wine cellars are not often used as such: most are filled with unwanted and unused items, and anything but wine. For centuries, basements have been the ideal location for wine storage, where there is less vibration, less light, and consistent temperature and humidity. Wine can now be stored in temperature-controlled cabinets, often within existing cellars, and this works very well but really cannot compete with the atmosphere of an old wine cellar with its heavy door, dim light, cobwebs hanging from the vaulted spaces, wine racks with dusty old bottles and numbered bins.

There is a vast amount of information available on the subject of wine, much of which has no direct relevance to the path I have chosen to pursue here, which is the social act of wine-drinking at a particular time in history. Any reader looking for advice on choosing wine will be disappointed. There is, however, no shortage of amusing and interesting stories connected with wine, from Jonah Barrington, Jonathan Swift and others, nor is there any shortage of those condemning the habit, like the earl of Orrery, Samuel Madden, the earl of Chesterfield and numerous others. While the lower classes consumed whiskey (which was being distilled, apparently, 'in every second house, in every town and village' in Ireland), without a doubt in Georgian Ireland, the amount of wine consumed by the upper classes was vast.

So much red wine from Bordeaux was consumed by Ireland's nobility and gentry in the eighteenth century that Jonathan Swift referred to it as 'Irish wine' in his letters, in the full knowledge that his correspondent would understand that he meant claret. That said, when Swift admitted that he preferred Portuguese to French wines, he felt 'bound to apologize' for such an unfashionable taste: 'I love white Portuguese better than Claret, Champaign or Burgundy: I have a sad vulgar appetite'. The wines of Bordeaux became known in Ireland and England as 'claret' from the old French 'clairet'– 'clear' and 'light-coloured'.[6] According to the wine writer, Jancis Robinson, most red wine in medieval France was the result of a short fermentation, no more than one or two days: this brief period of contact with the grape skins meant that the wines were pale and probably similar to today's rosés. So what grapes were used in its making? The four grapes of Bordeaux are Cabernet Sauvignon, the most important (80 per cent to 95 per cent of the crop), the remainder comprising Merlot, Malbec and Petit Verdot; at Château Mouton Rochschild the aim is to make a wine that is almost pure Cabernet, with only 5 per cent of Petit Verdot added to soften the severity of the former. Merlot and Malbec grapes are softer and more perfumed and add a smoothness that suits many clarets.

Claret was the preferred wine in England in the early eighteenth century but due to political and trade issues throughout the century, port became the alcoholic drink of choice there, where Samuel Johnston, having pronounced that 'a man would be drowned in [claret] before it made him drunk', rejected the claret handed to him by Sir Joshua Reynolds and memorably proclaimed, 'Claret is the liquor for boys; port for men; but he who aspires to be a hero must drink brandy'. Roundly ignored in Ireland, if they were even aware of the comment, it did nothing to dent the consumption of claret, as will be seen.

Chapter 1 looks at alcohol consumption in Ireland from a Celtic queen through to the Flight of the Earls in the early seventeenth century, followed by the later Flight of the Wild Geese after the Treaty of Limerick in 1691, when it was reckoned that 12,000 Irish Jacobite soldiers and their families departed Ireland. Making their way to the Continent, principally to France and Spain, many of these Irish families, Catholic and Protestant, established themselves as successful *négociants* in the wine business, with a ready market in their home country.

Chapter 2 discusses the use of wine cellars and how wine was stored. It was the Romans who created purpose-built spaces, often underground, which led to the creation of wine cellars in the basements of private houses, some of which will be looked at in this chapter. Here too is the story of the Irishman who obtained a royal patent to open the first bottle glassworks in the 1720s in Bordeaux, where a street is named after him. The advent of standard-sized bottles, the use of the cork as a stopper, and their storage in bins in the cellar, were revolutionary, enabling wine to mature for lengthy periods. Wine merchants in Ireland and their customers will be looked at, as well as other ways of acquiring wine – at auctions, by smuggling or, indeed, by stealth.

Hospitality was by no means confined to Dublin Castle; it was written into the DNA of the Irish, and adopted with alacrity by the Protestant ascendancy, as one tried to out-do his neighbour in the amounts of food and drink with which to impress their guests. This led at times to embarrassment and discomfort for guests, something that went probably unnoticed by the host, but was roundly condemned in letters and in travellers' accounts of the period as mentioned above. The importance of the dining room as the stage for hospitality is examined in Chapter 3, marked by the fact that the size of the of the room in newly-built and renovated houses increased in the early nineteenth century to facilitate greater numbers of diners. Much thought was given to the decoration, furniture and furnishing of the room, where dishes and cutlery were often monogrammed, and glassware sparkled. The importance of the butler's role in taking care of and serving wine is also looked at here.

Many visitors to Ireland in the Georgian period left records of their travels in the country by publishing accounts, by keeping a diary, or by writing descriptive letters, as Mrs Mary Delany did, in which vivid images of life in Ireland were conveyed. Many of these visitors were welcomed to the local 'big house' with open arms: owners were delighted to show off their houses and contents to their guests who in turn would inform their friends about what they saw. Chapter 4 concentrates on the contents of the dining room that were directly concerned with the serving and drinking of wine, including glass, silver and items of furniture, and a rather particular drinking table. It was the room where people spent hours eating, and men drank an inordinate amount of wine, especially after the departure of the ladies 'to their tea and gossip', as William Congreve put it.

In the course of research for this book, it was surprising to find how important toasting was at gatherings such as dinner parties. There was a stiff formality about toasts, a way of proposing and a way of accepting them: some people criticized the habit as being ridiculous. In Chapter 5 it will be seen that there was another, and very important, side to toasting – it was used almost as a game among men-only gatherings, at a time when clubs and fraternities were being formed where wine played a major part, with endless toasting as one tried to outdo another in both wit and drink. Many of these clubs were political in nature, where the 'glorious revolution' was one of the favourite toasts among Protestants while the Jacobites found ways to 'covertly' toast their side. The more sinister and potentially dangerous clubs are also looked at here, for example, the notorious Dublin Hellfire Club, and others for which lists of 'qualifications' for membership were drawn up. Women and their relationships with alcohol are also looked at. Little is known about the drinking habits of upper-class women, possibly because those who enjoyed alcohol, drank it quietly in their homes, but there were inevitably a few who did not.

Dublin Castle is the focus of Chapter 6 – the nucleus of social life in Ireland. It was evident that, however abstemious the viceroy, the amount of wine consumed at the Castle did not seem to vary from one administration to another. Wine was found to flatter, and to change minds. One viceroy actually died in Ireland from over-eating and over-drinking at the tender age of thirty-three. The same man, the 4th duke of Rutland, on being appointed, sent his chef to France to expand his knowledge of the *cuisine* in various kitchens of the nobility, and another member of his staff to source wines for the Castle's cellars. Wine flowed inside and even outside, in the courtyards, for the people of Dublin, to keep them happy.

To a large extent, we owe much of our knowledge about growing vines and making wine to medieval monks in Europe, particularly in Germany and France. No matter what was happening in the world, wine was required on a daily basis for religious services, at monasteries and other places of worship. As will be seen in Chapter 7, there were rules to be followed for making sacramental wine and there were wine merchants who specialized in this area who certified their wine as being suitable. We will look at the part played by religious orders, such as the Benedictines and the Cistercians in France, in the creation and tending of vineyards; at St Benedict's Rule regarding the drinking of wine by his monks; at an Irish saint who entertained his guests with a variety of wines, and the abbot who carried on a little wine business on the side.

It cannot be a surprise to find that health was a major issue as a result of excessive drinking, and this is the subject of Chapter 8. It was generally believed at the time that, when consumed in moderation, there were tangible, medicinal benefits to consuming wine. Gout, or as the earl of Orrery termed it, 'the Irish hospitality', was rampant, and numerous remedies were suggested and passed on. Most of these recommended even more wine. Every self-respecting lady-of-the-house had, to hand or in her kitchen, a notebook of recipes and remedies, many of which were utterly bizarre, if not dangerous, by our twenty-first-century standards, as will be seen. Excerpts from the private diary of Lord Clonmell (called 'Copper-faced Jack' due to his red face) show how much he desired to quit drinking but never quite made it, and Jonathan Swift similarly continued to drink though 'it is bad for my pain'. The chapter also includes a few recipes of interest.

One might ask why the Irish chose claret above other wines? There are historical links: Gascon wines had been imported into Ireland from medieval times; then, with the 'Flight of the Wild Geese' in 1691, thousands of Irish Jacobite soldiers and their families fled to France where they were incorporated into the French army and, significantly, many made their way into the wine business in Bordeaux, safe in the knowledge that there was a ready market in Ireland among their families and friends. But above all of that, the Irish simply enjoyed its taste: it was said that they had a 'love affair' with claret. Though Jonathan Swift referred to it as 'the Irish wine', this research has found that red wine from Bordeaux was rarely referred to as anything other than 'claret'.

CHAPTER I

'Their wine is chiefly claret'

THE DRINKING OF ALCOHOL has played a large part in the history of life in every country.[1] From the Middle Ages it was Ireland's major import. Because it was not safe to drink water, wine, beer and mead were part of the normal diet. 'Small beer' or 'small ale', so-called because it was quite weak, contained calories that were necessary to their diet. It has been pointed out that 'the name of the Celtic goddess Medb', who appears as the Queen of Connacht in the *Táin Bó Cúailnge*, means literally 'she who intoxicates' – a clear indication of the significance of alcoholic drink in Celtic culture. It is probably worth noting too, that Medb was associated with female sexuality and self-determination. Whiskey (also known as aqua vitae and usquebagh), originally taken for medicinal purposes, became so widely used among the population in Ireland, for reasons that were not always medical, that the English government in the mid-sixteenth century stepped in to impose some control by making a licence imperative for those involved in its production. The preamble to the statute stated that 'Aqua vitae, a drink nothing profitable to be daily drunken and used, is now universally throughout the realm of Ireland made', but the Act was not energetically enforced, though there was a suggestion to the lord lieutenant in the 1580s that it should be, as whiskey 'sets the Irish mad and breeds many mischiefs'. The worry for the English was that those who imbibed whiskey were 'the most rebellious part of the population'.[2]

A visitor to Ireland in the early seventeenth century, Fynes Moryson, wrote about the drinking habits in rural Ireland, '… when they come to any market town to sell a cow or a horse they never return home till they have drunk the price in Spanish wine (which they call the King of Spain's daughter), or in Irish usquebagh, and till they have outslept two or three days' drunkenness'. He adds that 'even the lords and their wives, the more they want this drink at home the more they swallow it when they come to it, till they be as drunk as beggars'.[3] On the subject of usquebagh, the antiquarian Sir James Ware noted that a recipe for making it was in the fourteenth-century Red Book of Ossory.[4] An annual tribute was paid to Brian Boru by the Vikings of Limerick at his residence on the River Shannon, of one ton or tun (equal to 252 gallons) of wine for every day in the year.[5] In an address in Irish to his countrymen from Rome in 1677, the Revd Francis O'Molloy referred to Dublin as 'the city of the wine flasks'. It was not difficult for a visitor to Ireland to find alcohol: in rural areas it was possible to purchase whiskey in any house, 'with which a man may get dead drunk for two pence' and there were alehouses in abundance.[6] Sometimes street names and place names would be a sure guide to finding wine – *Port an Fhíona*, the Irish name for Wineport in Co. Westmeath, means 'the landing place of wine'; there are Winetavern Streets, Winetavern Courts and Winetavern Alleys in Dublin, in Sligo and in Belfast (where there is also a street called Winecellar Entry); in Limerick, Scabby Lane was renamed Whitewine Lane.[7] In Cork city, Sober Lane recalls Father Theobald Mathew's campaign to promote total abstinence from alcohol which was launched nearby in 1838. Cork is also notable for another connection with wine. Between 1436 and 1644, it appears that, with the exception of only four years, every mayor of Cork was involved in the wine trade. The first mayor of Cork, appointed in 1273, was Richard Wine who, as tradesmen did at that time, took the name of his trade.[8]

Giraldus Cambrensis (Gerald of Wales), archdeacon of Brecon and author of *Topographia Hibernica*, who visited Ireland in the twelfth century, described the country as 'rich in pastures and meadows, honey and milk, and wine, but not vineyards … Imported wines, however … are so abundant that you would scarcely notice that the vine was neither cultivated nor gave its fruit there'.[9] In the second half of the seventeenth century, there were efforts in England and in Ireland to establish vineyards, as will be seen in Chapter 2. In 1826 at Carton, Co. Kildare, seat of the dukes of Leinster, the kitchen garden acquired a range of south-facing hothouses which included 'four vineries each 26 feet long'. Any produce of the vineries was ignored by the *Journal of Horticulture and Cottage Gardener* in 1863, in which they noted that Carton suffered from 'a want of that rarity and variety in the way of collections which we would naturally associate with such a magnificent place'.[10] Dessert grapes, however, were found to be thriving in the earl of Clare's garden at Mount Shannon in 1833 where they were trained along a south-facing brick wall. The fruit would have been for the estates' own consumption, that would include homemade wines and, probably, verjuice. The latter ('green juice') was made from the pressed juice of unripe, (usually) white grapes, creating an acidic liquid similar to a mild vinegar. Dating back to medieval times, it could be made from other unripe fruit like crab-apples and wild gooseberries. It was served with meat, fish and poultry and kept for both cooking and medicinal purposes.[11]

A brew-house was frequently part of the auxiliary buildings in country houses where beer and ale were made for the use of the household, including the servants. At Carton, for example, each servant who dined in the servants' hall received a pint of ale each evening; the cook in 1758 was allowed 2 pints of ale at 11 a.m., and 2 pints at 2 p.m., owing to the heat in the kitchen and, regarding 'small' beer, 'no person of the Family to be refused Small Beer as much as they shall drink till 6 o'clock, after which it may be refused till the bell rings for the servants' supper'.[12] In Dublin the Corporation gave permission for the construction of a brewhouse at the Blue Coat School in 1707 'whereby the number of the poor boys maintained therein may be encouraged by the frugal management of brewing their own drink'.[13] At Castletown, Co. Kildare, whiskey was supplied for the men who gathered ice in winter and packed it into the icehouse by the River Liffey. Alcohol was associated with the important events of life: christenings, weddings and wakes. For any of these occasions among the poorer classes it was a matter of pride that drink should be provided and, if the family could not afford it, there would be a whip-around amongst the neighbours and all would turn out to pay their respects. Fairs, patterns, markets and saints' days were part of the calendar that had long prevailed and were occasions that had always been celebrated in the community with drink, much of which was distilled locally, and the occasion usually ended in drunkenness.

For those with political ambitions alcohol helped when distributed to voters at election time; landlords like Lord Ely kept tenants on-side with Christmas parties at Castle Hume in Co. Fermanagh where in 1770, 120 of them enjoyed 19 gallons of rum, 6 gallons of whiskey, and 2 barrels of ale.[14] On the Wentworth holdings (south Wicklow and north Wexford), however, no tenant would drink anything at any public meeting but 'good claret, sack or punch'.[15] Voters expected to be diverted. At Kinsale, Co. Cork, in 1765, four parties were held simultaneously, reinforcing the social divisions, whereby eighty 'gentlemen' were accommodated at the town house of the Southwell family, and each given two bottles of wine: others had to fend for themselves, apparently. Colonel John Hore had twenty-four tables set up in his garden and served food, as well as lots of wine and beer, and in Longford town, Richard Edgeworth spent over £100 on fare enjoyed in three taverns: his main guests were the voters who returned him to parliament for the Longford borough in 1737.[16] In Maria Edgeworth's *Castle Rackrent* (1800), Thady, the faithful old retainer, was concerned at the 'loads of claret that went down the throats of them that had no right to be asking for it' in his master's election bid, for which the said master could ill-afford to pay.[17] And at Dublin Castle the hope was that lavish entertainments laid on for those invited, encouraged members of parliament to vote with the government; and the wine that flowed from fountains into the courtyard for the less privileged, helped to keep the populace, at least for some time, less restless. It is not clear whether the wine that flowed into the Castle courtyard was red or white or both, but it is almost certain that the wine that flowed inside the Castle was predominantly red, and from Bordeaux.

The close trading connection between England and France was established when, in 1152, Eleanor of Aquitaine married the-about-to-be King Henry II of England. Bordeaux, as part of the duchy of Aquitaine, became the centre of the wine trade between the two countries, with preferential tariffs granted to winegrowers, so that by the fourteenth century, a quarter of Bordeaux's wine was being exported to London. The Scots had been drinking red wine from Bordeaux from at least the thirteenth century, and its popularity continued, even after Scotland's union with

| Tun | Pipe, Butt ½ tun | Puncheon, Terian ⅓ tun | Hogshead ¼ tun | Tierce ⅙ tun | Barrel ⅛ tun | Rundlet 1/14 tun |

1.1 Wine cask units. The largest cask for wine is the tun, which holds *c*.954 litres; the hogshead contains *c*.240 litres of wine.

England in 1707 (which included equalization of taxes, including that on wine). There was now, however, a difference: the full-bodied claret drunk by English aristocrats made its way to Scotland, eventually replacing the inexpensive, 'thin', traditionally made claret the Scots had enjoyed up to this.[18]

The Irish continued their love affair with claret, as Lord Fitzwilliam's agent, Richard Mathew, observed, that 'we here in Ireland drinke but seldom portwine … the French claret has the ascendant here'.[19] Other wines, such as Tent (a strong Spanish red 'tinto'), Frontignac (a muscat sweet wine from Languedoc), and Malaga (or Mountain – a rich, raisiny fortified wine), were also consumed in Ireland. Claret, however, continued to be sought-after in England, but taxes became so high that only those with deep pockets could afford to drink it. It was, apparently, the 'vin ordinaire' of Bordeaux that was imbibed by the Irish: the more expensive Bordeaux wines being purchased by the ranks of wealthy Englishmen and, from time to time, Dublin Castle, as will be seen. In Ireland the doubling of consumption in imports of French wine, of which Bordeaux was the major part, mirrored the sharp rise in rents in the early eighteenth century which was to the benefit of landowners and led to increased spending on luxury goods, including wine. After 1745, when there was 'a general advance of the Irish economy … imports of French wine reached 6,019 tuns in 1753–4 and total imports of wine reached 7,993 tuns'.[20] French wine, according to James Kelly, commanded 60 per cent of the Irish market in the mid-1770s; by the early 1790s it had fallen to 40 per cent and, by 1815, it had fallen still further to 8 per cent.[21] Richard Hayes quotes statistics published in 1827 by the French consul to London, César Moreau, for the fifty years from 1771:

	French Wine in Tuns (imported to Ireland)
1771–80	27,802
1781–90	20,883
1791–1800	11,605
1802–11	4,876
1812–21	2,960

The amount of wine exported from France to Ireland between 1771 and 1789 was, according to Hayes, double the amount of French wine that was imported to England, Scotland and Wales combined.[22] Reasons for the decline in wine-drinking from the latter part of the eighteenth century will be discussed later.

It is not surprising that the amount of wine imbibed by the Irish was much commented upon by visitor and resident alike. In 1745, the fourth earl of Chesterfield (viceroy at that time) condemned the habit:

> Drinking is a most beastly vice in every country, but it is really a ruinous one in Ireland; nine gentlemen in ten in Ireland are impoverished by the great quantity of claret, which, from mistaken notions of hospitality and dignity, they think it necessary should be drunk in their houses; this expense leaves them no room to improve their estates, by proper indulgence upon proper conditions to their tenants, who must pay them to the full, and upon the very day, that they may pay their wine-merchants.[23]

The following year, Chesterfield, in a letter to an unidentified Irish friend, refers to his friend's son: 'I am glad my little trooper is well, I hope he remembers his promise to me of drinking no wine till I give him leave'.[24] Mrs Mary Delany commented in 1752: 'High living is too much the fashion here. You are not invited to dinner to any private gentleman of £1000 a year or less, that does not give you seven dishes at one course, and Burgundy and Champagne; and these dinners they give once or twice a week'.[25] It was a matter of concern to many others including the writer on sumptuary laws in the *Dublin Public Register or Freeman's Journal* of 2 October 1764, twenty years after Mrs Delany's comment: '(regarding dining) ... you have plenty of every Thing, a Variety of Wines, and are seldom permitted to stir, until you have swallowed an inordinate Quantity of French Claret ... that I look upon as highly prejudicial and destructive to this Country; and heartily wish there was as heavy a Duty laid on it here, as we have in England'.

The desire for claret had its roots in Irish connections with merchants in Bordeaux. The penal laws against Catholics and economic restrictions placed on Ireland by parliament – that affected Protestants also – meant that there were few economic opportunities in Ireland for those who were not born into land. Some joined continental armies, others studied for the Catholic priesthood, another option was trade. One area of trade that was both available and socially acceptable was to become a wine merchant: it cost a Limerick merchant, who traded overseas, 200 guineas to have a son apprenticed to a wine merchant in Bordeaux.[26] It made sense: Irish merchants had what French merchants wanted – butter, wool, fish and salt beef – and the nobility and gentry in Ireland and England drank a great deal of wine. Trade connections between Ireland and Bordeaux had already been established from the sixteenth century, and an Irish seminary was established there in 1603 for the education of Catholic priests.[27] Many Huguenot refugees who settled in Ireland came from Bordeaux after the Revocation of the Edict of Nantes in 1685, and maintained their contacts there by trading in wine; and, importantly, Irish merchants – among them the Bartons, a Protestant landed family – were the acceptable face of Britain in the eyes of the French; they had easy access to London; they were English-speaking and had pre-established trading networks in England.

These merchants knew what their wealthy Irish and English customers wanted. Over the course of the eighteenth century, they purchased the best wines when young, aged and blended them to their clients' preferences, and in the process created what is referred to as top-growth Bordeaux, which was of course expensive. The 'blending' of the wine was interesting. In 1764 the *Parlement* of Bordeaux, having been made aware of the practice of blending Bordeaux with other wines, issued an edict forbidding such a practice. A protest against this edict was led by Thomas Barton (plate 1.2), the most important of the Irish and English merchants, who pointed out that some years previously, 'a body of twenty-four Irish merchants and bottlers had complained that Bordeaux wines were mixed with Spanish', and they pointed out that there were 'at least a thousand wine merchants in Ireland who all mixed the wines of Bordeaux with the wines of Spain'.[28] According to Ted Murphy, the Irish merchants had reported the orthodox claret to be both 'deficient of body and destitute of flavour' and that they found it necessary to blend it to make it more palatable to their market.[29] The protest was so successful that the Bordeaux winegrowers experimented by adding 10 per cent of Benicarlo (a wine from Valencia in Spain) to a 'pot' of unfermented Bordeaux wine 'must' (this is the grape juice, together with the stems, skins and seeds), creating a new fermentation, which made the wine bright and clear, and put the merchants in Ireland out of business.[30] This was borne out by a conversation between a French visitor and a wine merchant in Galway at the end of the eighteenth century. The merchant complained of a downturn in his business, 'Before France knew how to make wine, we made it here', he claimed. The visitor was incredulous, and the merchant explained: 'In France the wine was simply the juice of the grape, and we brought it to Galway to make it drinkable. Unfortunately, the Bordeaux merchants can prepare it now as well as we did, and that has cut the feet from under us'.[31]

1.2 *Portrait of Thomas Barton* (1695–1774), *c.*1735 (artist unknown). Barton left Ireland for France in 1722 where he established himself in the wine business in Bordeaux in 1725. By kind permission of the Barton family, Bordeaux.

An account book in Barton & Guestier's archives shows how the 1788 vintage wines were blended. In his book, Edmund Penning-Rowsell explains:

> The company bought 56 *tonneaux* of Lafite 1788. Some was sold to Dublin and some to London. Then they bought another ten and three-quarters *tonneaux* of 'Lafite peur ('pure')', along with forty-one and a quarter *tonneaux* of Latour plus ten and three-quarters *tonneaux* of Latour 'peur'. Also bought were 13 *tonneaux* of a wine named Casterede, and 3 per cent of this was blended into the Brane-Mouton, Margaux, Larose, Leoville etc. Also 'Ermitage' 1788 was used half and half with Casterede for blending.

Also mentioned in the accounts is a purchase of Benicarlo (see above) that gave colour and body to wines.[32] The account books of another Irish merchant, Nathaniel Johnston – whose cellars, incidentally, in the Chartrons district of Bordeaux, held the equivalent of six million bottles[33] – leave no doubt as to what was done: the excellent Lafite 1795 was 'made up with Hermitage [it] was the best liked of any of that year'. Only the finer wines had Hermitage added as it was expensive, while the lesser wines had Benicarlo and Alicante added. Personally, Johnston's preference was for 'neat Lafite' of the 1798 vintage and, when dealing with the reputable London wine merchants, Barnes, he recommended that their claret be 'neat or very lightly made-up'.[34] The practice of blending, known as *assemblage* or *coupage* in France, continues today. An important decision in the production of wine is, which lots of the same wine can be blended to make up the final product? According to Jancis Robinson, it is almost a ritual in Bordeaux where many *châteaux* make their Grand Vin (that carries the name of the *château*) by selecting and blending only the best lots: the rejected lots may be blended to make a second wine, or sold in bulk to a *négociant* carrying simply the local *appellation*. Blending involves combining wines with different but complementary characteristics, for example, as Robinson explains, 'heavily oak-influenced lots aged in new barrels may be muted by blending with less oaky lots of the same wine ... [for] ordinary table wines, blending is an important ingredient in smoothing out the difference between one vintage and its successor'.[35]

Ludington points out that the claret consumed in England in the eighteenth century was different from that consumed earlier: 'during the Restoration [it] was generically named, haphazardly made, light in colour and body' while the claret enjoyed by the English elite in the eighteenth century was 'carefully produced, discernibly superior in quality and expensive' due to the high import tax there.[36]

On the subject of Benicarlo, in a letter from Castle Hamilton (where he was a guest) in 1734, Thomas Sheridan goaded his friend Jonathan Swift (plate 1.3):

1.3 Jonathan Swift (1667–1745), dean of St Partrick's Cathedral, Dublin. Engraved by Pierre Fourdriner (fl.1728–d.1758), after Charles Jervas (*c.*1675–1739), National Gallery of Ireland, NGI 10169 cc..

[Mr Hamilton] … has the best and fattest venison I ever tasted; and the finest boat, and the finest situation, and the finest house, and the finest hall, and the finest wife and children, and the finest way of living, I ever met. You live in *Dublin* among a parcel of rabble; I live at *Castle Hamilton* among gentlemen and ladies; you live among chaffed mutton, I live upon venison; you drink *Benicarlo* wine, I drink right *French Margoux* …[37]

In 1780, Arthur Young was in a minority when he criticized the quality of the claret in Dublin, describing it as inferior to that in England, but that the port in Ireland is 'incomparable … as to prove, if proof was wanting, the abominable adulterations it must undergo with us'.[38] According to one writer, luxury claret was rare in Scotland before the 1707 Act of Union, when Daniel Defoe remarked upon the Scots preference for the 'thin claret' as opposed to the stronger fuller-bodied type preferred by the English.[39] Back in the 1660s the diarist Samuel Pepys was adulterating his sherry: an entry in his diary records his first large purchase of sherry from Cadiz in wood, which he topped up with four gallons of Malaga wine to make it sweeter.[40]

It is no wonder that claret tasted differently depending on whether one was in Britain, Ireland or elsewhere. Jonathan Swift, who had his supplier bottle his wine, believed Irish-bottled claret was superior to that in England. 'I am resolved to have half a hogshead when I go to Ireland if it be as good and as cheap, as it used to be'.[41] In 1735, dismayed at a recent 20 per cent increase in the price of claret due to a poor season, and impressed with Spanish wine, he suggested in a letter to Sir Charles Wogan who was living in Spain, that he would 'direct Mr Hall, an honest catholick merchant here, who deals in Spanish wine, to bring me over as large a cargo as I can afford, of wines as like French claret as he can get'. He wonders if Wogan 'would descend so low as to order [on his behalf] some good quantity of wine that you approve of such as our claret drinkers here will be content with. For when I give them a pale wine, they say it will do for one glass, and then (to speak in their language) call for Honest Claret'.[42] On at least two occasions, Wogan sent Swift a cask of Spanish wine. The dean had a rather embarrassing experience with Hermitage. A friend in Rouen was lavish in his praise for a particular wine, and Swift promptly ordered 150 bottles for himself and recommended his Dublin friends to do likewise. Unfortunately, most of the wine turned to vinegar. Swift berated himself for not having purchased it through his supplier in Dublin, as he believed that 'good wine is ninety per cent of living in Ireland'. However, seven years later when he opened one of the few abandoned bottles of the Hermitage from his cellar, it tasted wonderful![43]

Statistics show that Ireland was the biggest and arguably one of the more discerning purchasers of Bordeaux wine in the world. A group of Irish visiting a London chophouse in 1761 upbraided the owner on being served poor quality wine, assuring him that they 'belonged to the kingdom that knew the difference between good and bad claret'.[44] An English tourist in Dublin wrote to his friend in Dover in 1769 giving his impressions of claret:

> Their wine is chiefly claret, the best of which, that the town produces, may be had at 2s. 6d. the bottle – the common price is 2s. – and to those who are unaccustomed to a claret of a greater body, it will soon become very pleasant, and the most agreeably palated wine he will meet in Ireland. 'Tis light, wholesome, and easy of digestion.[45]

The earliest-known mention of a wine by the name of the estate on which the wine was grown was in the cellar book of King Charles II in 1660 when the cellar master purchased 169 bottles of 'Hobriono' [Haut Brion] for a little over £180. This occurred within a month of the king's return from continental exile.[46] In 1663, Samuel Pepys casually mentioned that, at the Royal Oak Tavern in London, he 'drank a sort of French wine, called Ho Bryan, that hath a good and most particular taste that I never met with', and an advertisement in the *Tatler* of September 1710 advertises it as the 'new excellent French O'Brien Clarets, the very best vintage'.[47] According to Ludington, the new 'brand' of claret, called 'Margaux' ('Margoose'), was mentioned in two separate auctions in Britain in June 1705. This 'branding' of claret started a fashion with other wine producers, who began to use their names or the name of the vineyard itself in advertisements. In 1711, the *London Gazette* described the 'new' clarets as 'deep, bright, fresh, neat' – 'deep' and 'bright' relate to the wine's body and colour, 'fresh' to its age, and 'neat' to the fact that it was pure and unblended.[48]

The wine writer, Jancis Robinson, explains how this 'new claret' became so hugely popular in both Ireland and England at this time:

> In the second half of the seventeenth century, a new type of wine, of much higher quality and deeper colour, began to be produced in the *graves* [gravelly terrain] and on the sands and gravels of the Medoc to the north-west of Bordeaux. These wines, the provenance of specific properties, where close attention was paid to grape selection, improved methods of vinification, and the use of new oak barrels, became known by the beginning of the eighteenth century as New French Clarets, and the earliest and most famous of them were Haut-Brion, Lafite, Latour, and Margaux ... [These] best red Bordeaux are characterized by their subtlety and ability to evolve after years, sometimes decades, of bottle ageing.[49]

Curiously, the philosopher John Locke (1632–1704), on a visit to the Haut-Brion vineyard in 1667, found the reason for the superiority of this wine – 'a little rise of ground … white sand mixed with a little gravel; scarce fit to bear anything' but, he added, 'they say the wine in the next vineyard to it, tho' seeming equal to me is not so good'.[50] Unknown to himself, Locke had seized the concept of *terroir*, which refers to the natural environment of the site, comprising soil, topography and microclimate. According to Robinson, 'the holistic combination of all these is held to give each site its own unique *terroir*, which is reflected in its wines more or less consistently from year to year, to some degree regardless of variations in methods of viticulture and wine-making'.[51]

Stories abound about the amounts of wine consumed. Francis Andrews, provost of Trinity College and builder of the Provost's House on Grafton Street, enjoyed travel. He also enjoyed wine. For his solo ten-day journey from Madrid to Seville in the 1760s he packed ten bottles of claret and the same of Graves. When in Nice he had the foresight to send 'some excellent Hermitage and Champagne here before me & I daily expect a Hogshead of Claret from Bordeaux'. He described his Dublin cellar as 'extremely well furnished'.[52] In a diary kept by the Revd John Nixon of Killesher, Co. Fermanagh, he relates how after church one Sunday in 1769, two friends accompanied him to dine in his home: together they drank nine bottles of claret and two of port. In the evening they had tea, and then prayers, followed by a further bottle each of claret and port. The previous month he entertained sixteen friends to dinner, where they drank fourteen bottles of claret and four bottles of port. At supper the same group (now reduced to thirteen) consumed four more bottles of claret, two more of port and a bottle of whiskey.[53] At Newbridge House in Donabate, Co. Dublin, Archbishop Thomas Cobbe had a large goblet calculated to hold *three bottles* of wine. According to tradition, it was filled with claret, seven guineas were placed at the bottom, and he who drank it pocketed the money.[54] The owner of a bookshop, described as 'fond of his bottle', told of a hospitable literary friend, whom he liked 'because he poured his wine cellar down his bookseller'.[55]

A poem, *Sweet Chloe* by Edward Lysaght, a contemporary of Jonah Barrington's, reflects the subject's frustration with her loved-one's drinking:

> Sweet Chloe advised me, in accents divine,
> The joys of the bowl to surrender;
> Nor lose, in the turbid excesses of wine,
> Delights more ecstatic and tender;
> She bade me no longer in vineyards to bask,
> Or stagger, at orgies, the dupe of a flask,
> For the sigh of a sot's but the scent of the cask,
> And a bubble the bliss of the bottle.
>
> To a soul that's exhausted, or sterile, or dry,
> The juice of the grape may be wanted;

But mine is reviv'd by a love-beaming eye,
And with fancy's gay flow'rets enchanted.
Oh! Who but an owl would a garland entwine
Of Bacchus's ivy – and myrtle resign?
Yield the odours of love, for the vapours of wine,
And Chloe's kind kiss for a bottle![56]

While whiskey was the drink favoured by the masses, wine was the preferred drink of the well-to-do in Ireland. Until towards the end of the century, taking claret was a marker of social standing. In 1750 the Bishop of Elphin advised his daughter that it would not be fitting to offer a prospective housekeeper and steward an 'allowance of Tea or Claret'.[57] There was, and still is, an amount of snobbery attached to wine. In 1732–3 Sir Robert Walpole, the British prime minister, regularly purchased four hogsheads of Margaux, and a hogshead of Lafite every three months, spending £1,118 on (mostly French) wine in 1733.[58] He kept numerous casks of sweet Lisbon wine, i.e., Carcavellos, Bucellas, Malmsey, etc., in his cellar which he 'doled out to less fussy visitors, keeping his finest Clarets, Burgundies and Champagnes for his special friends'.[59] An article by Michael Glover in the *Independent*, 8 May 2013, reveals that 6,264 bottles of wine were drunk in Walpole's home, Houghton Hall, Norfolk, in 1730: this information apparently came from the wine merchant who counted the empties!

However, full marks for one-upmanship regarding claret must go to Mr Scott, the British Consul in Bordeaux. In his book, Edmund Penning-Rowsall tells of a dinner party given by Scott in *c.*1860, at which the wealthy mayor of Bordeaux, M. Duffau-Dubergier, was a guest:

> The crowning wine was the Mouton '28. It was greeted with great enthusiasm and the mayor at once asked 'Have you much of it left?' 'Alas, only a dozen bottles'. The mayor replied, 'Well, my dear fellow, I'm going to make you a proposition. Twelve bottles, twelve thousand francs'. 'You are asking an impossibility of me' answered Scott, 'but to show you how much I desire to fall in with your wishes, I'll agree to share it with you, and we'll say six bottles, six thousand francs.' 'My dear Scott', replied the mayor, 'if I buy wine at a thousand francs a bottle, it is on condition that I am the only man that can give it to his friends to drink'. Scott replied after a moment. 'Right; we'll say no more about it.' Then, turning to his butler he said: 'Bernard, decant us two more bottles of the 1828 Mouton.'[60]

CHAPTER 2

Wine cellars, merchants and links with Bordeaux

Iᴺ ʜɪꜱ ʙᴏᴏᴋ ᴏɴ ᴛʜᴇ ʜɪꜱᴛᴏʀʏ ᴏꜰ ᴡɪɴᴇ, published in 1775, Sir Edward Barry (1698–1776) (plate 2.1), a Cork-born medical doctor, recommends that some of the 'gentlemen of fortune who make improvement in agriculture their favourite practice', especially those 'in the most southern parts of the county of Corke', should plant vineyards and make wine, suggesting it would give 'rational and elegant amusement'.[1] Cultivating vines was a cause for patriotic concern for Robert Molesworth, on his estate at Breckdenston in Swords, Co. Dublin, in the early years of the seventeenth century, when he remarked that 'all the world sees the Scotch wine is admitted'; he was keen to prove that it was not impossible 'to get some from Ireland' as well.[2] In fact, well before Barry's book appeared, Richard Boyle, the second earl of Cork (1612–98), procured vine roots from England to plant at Lismore Castle, Co. Waterford; his interest in viticulture was possibly encouraged by various treatises on the subject published in the second half of the seventeenth century such as *The compleat vineyard* (1670) by William Hughes, and *The English vineyard vindicated* (1670) by John Rose, the king's gardener at St James's Palace, who, incidentally, sold vine roots to those who were interested.[3] Sir Richard Bulkeley (1634–85), MP for Baltinglass 1665–6, planted 900 grape vines on his Tallaght, Co. Dublin, estate, employing a 'Swiss vigneron' to aid his endeavour, claiming that the climate in Switzerland 'is nearer akin to England than either Italy or France', and encouraged by the vigneron's assurance that he 'should not fail of having grapes'.[4] Not surprisingly, the project failed. According to one writer there was a proposal to set up a society to encourage the cultivation of the vine in Ireland, 'where the soil … is excellent, and abounds … with a limestone gravel, which would admirably suit that species of culture, but the low temperature … and, especially, its extreme moisture, would present insuperable obstacles' to its success.[5] History does not reveal if wine was produced at Lismore, but there was, undoubtedly, a large supply of it in the castle's cellars.

On the subject of cellars, Barry states that 'wine is conveyed here [i.e., to cellars] with the sole intention of preserving and defending it from any changes but what is gradually acquired in advancing to its proper maturity'.[6] As far back as the first century ʙᴄᴇ, Vitruvius, the Roman architect and engineer, wrote about orienting different room types to specific light exposures. He recommended that the wine storage room should be located close to the oil press and kitchen, and the windows should face north. In the fifteenth century the Italian architect and author, Leon

2.1 *Portrait of Sir Edward Barry* (1698–1776) (artist unknown), physician and MP for Charleville, Co. Cork (1744–60); physician general to the forces in Ireland (1745–76); Regius professor of physic at Trinity College Dublin (1754) and president of the Royal College of Physicians (1749). Author of *Observations, historical, critical and medical, on the wines of the Ancients* (London, 1775). Courtesy of the Royal College of Physicians of Ireland.

Battista Alberti, stated that the wine cellar should be underground and enclosed, 'Even well-protected wine is ruined by exposure to any wind from the east, south, or west, especially in winter or spring, but under the Dog Star even Boreas disturbs it, the rays of the sun dry it up; the moon leaves it dull; movement throws a sediment and reduces the flavor'. He recommends that the cellar should be built 'somewhere solid, free from the vibration of carts'; it should be free from damp, 'dense vapors or smoke, and any strong-smelling vegetables, such as onions, cabbage, and wild or domestic figs', and the floor should be paved, 'leaving a small dip in the center to collect any leakage from the vats'.[7] Barry's recommendation regarding temperature was 'above that of thirty-two [degrees] in Fahrenheit's Thermometer and perhaps not much to exceed thirty-six'.[8] However, according to Hugh Johnson, 'Wine is not over-fussy: anything from 7–21 degrees C (45–70 degrees F) will do'.[9] Incidentally, Barry observed that the fermentation of some wines can be improved by 'being agitated on the sea': the American architect and urban planner, Daniel Burnham (1846–1912), successfully aged a barrel of Madeira by shipping it twice round the world on slow freighters. Madeira's winemakers found that when their wine was exposed to high temperatures and rough seas as it travelled to America and the Caribbean, it frequently spoiled, so in the mid-eighteenth century, after adding distilled grape spirit to stabilize it, they found, when some barrels returned still full, that the wine had improved substantially. Subsequently wine labelled *vinho da roda* (round trip wine) fetched a premium price.[10]

Just outside Rome, in Hadrian's Villa (AD 118–34), at Tivoli, wine was stored underground: it had a roof covering its southern side and cellar hatches facing north and east. The catacombs in Rome were also used to store wine and in Roman villas the wine cellars featured vaults supported by columns.[11] Tunnels and caves, dug into hillsides or mountainsides, were found to be ideal for storage due to their constant temperatures, and were sometimes lined with bricks. The French champagne house Taittinger, in Reims, has cellars eighteen meters below ground in fourth-century Roman chalk mines that connect with the crypt of the thirteenth-century Benedictine Abbey of St Nicaise, which was destroyed during the French Revolution (plate 2.2). According to a report in a Dublin newspaper on the Kingdom of Naples in 1734, the Jesuits (described as 'the great Merchants here') had a cellar that held 1000 hogsheads, 'and they have the best [wine], which they sell by Retail'.[12]

Thomas Dineley, who visited Ireland in 1680, notes in his *Journal*, that the houses of Limerick 'are tall built with black unpolisht marble with partition walls some of 5 foot thick, and have Battlements on the top, and the best Cellars, for so many, of any city in England or Ireland'. In large and medium-sized houses built in the eighteenth and nineteenth centuries the cellar, where supplies of alcohol were stored, was an essential part of the building, and many were quite extensive. John Sankey of 9 Merrion Square South (now 79 Merrion Square), described as 'Sheriff's

2.2 Engraving of the thirteenth-century Church of St-Nicaise de Reims. After the French Revolution, the abbey was plundered for its stone, and was eventually demolished in the nineteenth century. Its underground chalk quarries from the Gallo-Roman era remained virtually intact and are now used as cellars for Taittinger's champagne. (Image copyright G. Garitan 2012, public domain via Wikimedia Commons.)

Peer' and wine merchant trading at 77 Grafton Street, was declared bankrupt in 1796, when his stock in trade of 'a great Variety of Old Wines, in Wood and Bottles … of genuine Wines in high Order, of the first Growth and Quality', was auctioned at his home address (plate 2.3).[13] A large cellar was a selling point in an advertisement in *Faulkner's Dublin Journal* in 1758 for a 'handsome new House in Merrion-street' to be let or sold that had, apart from family accommodation, 'two Vaults that would each hold six or eight Ton of wine'. The Conollys of Castletown had a house on Merrion Street (probably with similar vaults), which was connected to the mews by a passage under the garden and, also in Dublin, a house on Henrietta Street that retains, besides a wine cellar in the basement (as was usual), *under* the rear garden, another wine cellar, lined with bins. In the basement plan of Kildare (later Leinster) House in Dublin (1745), there is a 'wine vault for hogsheads' and three smaller vaults for bins. An unexecuted plan (1792) for Townley Hall, Co. Louth, shows

OLD WINES.

By Order of the Assignees of John Sankey,
a Bankrupt,

TO BE SOLD BY AUCTION,

Precisely at 12 o'Clock,

On Thursday, December 29, 1796,

AT NO. 9, MERRION-SQUARE, SOUTH,

THE GENUINE STOCK IN TRADE of
said Bankrupt, which consists of a great
Variety of OLD WINES, in Wood and Bottle,
well worth the Attention of Wine Merchants,
and all others who wish to be supplied with
genuine Wines in high Order, of the first Growth
and Quality.

The Assignees will take approved Bills in Payment; and sell the Wines in small Quantities, for
the Accommodation of private Families.

An Office Desk, Counter, and a Parcel of
Scantling, will be sold by Auction at the above
Place and Hour.

2.3 Notice of sale of wines by auction at the home of John Sankey of Merrion Square, Dublin. Photograph courtesy of Conor Lucey.

one-third of the entire basement area designated for wine with two smaller cellars for beer; at Rockingham, Co. Roscommon (1809), the plans show seven cellars in the upper basement. Crom Castle, Co. Fermanagh (*c.*1833), enjoyed eight cellars: unfortunately, these plans do not indicate how many cellars for wine, and how many for beer, but an unsigned plan and elevations of a wine cellar, presumably by Edward Blore, the architect of the castle, includes the calculation that each of the thirty-two bins would hold 'about thirty dozen' bottles.[14] At Lissadell, Co. Sligo (1833), arrangements of the cellars were quite sophisticated: one was designated 'wine pipes', another 'French wine' and a third 'Wine', as well as those for beer and ale.

WINE BOTTLES

From about 1730, and with the advent of the cylindrical bottle, cellars were divided into 'bins', compartments of brick or stone in which bottles of wine could be laid down for maturing, lying one on top of the other, or in racks where they could be easily removed without disturbing others.[15] The role of the cork in this procedure should not be overlooked, as it was found to improve the flavor and extend the life of the wine by remaining moist and tight, keeping the wine in and the oxygen out. Prior to this bottles were stoppered with tapered wooden bungs, wrapped in cloth that had been soaked in wax or oil, that projected from the bottle. The brick bins in the cellar at Rathfarnham Castle in Dublin measure 30 inches high by 26 inches wide and 37 inches deep. In these bins the bottles were stored on their sides to allow sediment to gather on the lower side. This method allowed wine to mature for longer periods and, when required, could be carefully decanted, allowing the clear wine to be served. It was at this point that connoisseurship in wine began to flourish (plate 2.4).[16]

The binning of wine only became universal when the shape of glass bottles changed. Up to that time bottles varied a great deal in size and shape and were dark in colour, usually a greenish-brown that was almost black, but it was of no particular consequence because bottles were simply containers, filled at the cask, then brought directly to the table to be served. Because early wines were poorly made, and often adulterated with additives, quick consumption was necessary as they had a shelf life of less than a year before turning to vinegar. The shape of the bottle that we now know emerged gradually between the seventeenth and nineteenth century from what was called the free-blown 'shaft and globe' in the 1630s with a spherical body, a long conical neck and a heavy base with a pushed-in recessed 'kick' for stability, to the 1690s when the height of the neck shortened and the body took on an 'onion' shape (plate 2.5). In the 1720s the 'mallet' form of bottle (with sides tapering slightly outward towards the base) emerged, and this became common in the eighteenth century. These bottles could be stored, lying on their sides on

2.4 Bins in the cellar of Larchfield Estate, Co. Antrim. Photograph courtesy of Gavin Mackie.

2.5 Wine bottles dating to the 1650s discovered at Rathfarnham Castle, Dublin.
Photograph courtesy of Alva Mac Gowan/Archaeology Plan.

2.6 One of four wine bottles discovered at Rathfarnham Castle, Dublin, that have 'AL 1688' stamped on the bottoms, referring to Lord Adam Loftus, resident of the castle at the time. Photograph courtesy of Alva Mac Gowan/Archaeology Plan.

beds of sand where the moisture kept the corks from shrinking and good corks kept the wine from evaporating or being contaminated. There are examples of both the onion- and mallet-shaped bottles having handles attached which would indicate that they were used at the table. Gradually the mallet shape became taller and took on the cylindrical shape that we know today. Most bottles had an applied ring of glass just below the neck which secured the thread or wire used to hold in the stoppers. For the discerning, bottle seals with a family name, and date were sometimes impressed onto a disc of glass and fused onto the bottle. During the

2.7 Rembrandt Peale (1778–1860), *Portrait of Thomas Jefferson*, 1800, oil on canvas. White House Collection/White House Historical Association. (Wikimedia Commons)

recent excavation at Rathfarnham Castle the letters 'AL' and the date '1688' were embossed on a number of glass seals or discs, referring to Lord Adam Loftus (1625–91), first (and last) Viscount Lisburne, a descendant of Adam Loftus (1533–1605), archbishop of Dublin and lord chancellor of Ireland, who resided in the castle at the time (plate 2.6). These discs were fused onto the sides or, in the case of Loftus, on the bottoms of wine bottles. An anecdote regarding Loftus, a Catholic, relates that, having been created baron of Rathfarnham and Viscount Lisburne in 1686 by King James II, he took the other side in the Glorious Revolution, commanding an English regiment in 1689, when Marshal Schomberg wrote to King William, 'My Lord Lisburne's conduct is not good. He passes his life at play and the bottle; a little wine fuddles him'.[17] He had little time to enjoy his monogrammed bottles as he was killed by a cannon ball at the Siege of Limerick in 1691.[18]

The diarist Samuel Pepys was proud to see his 'new bottles, made with my crest upon them, filled with wine, about five or six dozen' in 1663.[19] One of Jonathan Swift's wine bottles in the National Museum of Ireland has a similar disc which has his name and 'Dean' and the year 1727. Likewise, the name 'Doneraile House' is on a wine bottle belonging to the St Leger family, in their house in Co. Cork. Thomas Jefferson, the third president of the United States (plate 2.7) (and an oenophile), was one of the earliest figures to insist that all wines ordered by him were bottled at source, and had his initials etched on each bottle. Up to then, his wine arrived in America from Europe in barrels that were frequently tampered with by 'rascally boatmen' of the Potomac and James rivers who tapped his barrels, drank some of his wine, then refilled them with water.[20]

PIERRE MITCHELL'S GLASSWORKS IN BORDEAUX

In France, bottles for wine were imported to Bordeaux from Hamburg and the Netherlands up to the beginning of the eighteenth century. Peter (or Pierre) Mitchell (1687–1740), whose father was a captain in an Irish regiment serving the French crown, settled in Bordeaux with his Irish wife, Jane Hicky, earning his living as a barrel-maker. Becoming aware of the need of the *négociants* to export their wine in bottles rather than in barrels, and of the great shortage of glassworks for this purpose, he moved, in 1723, to the Chartrons area of Bordeaux where he managed to obtain, not only a royal patent to establish the first bottle glassworks there, but also a ten-league exclusion zone from any competitors (plate 2.8). His success was due to a number of factors. Timing was one: as mentioned above, people were developing a taste for 'old wine', and wanted to 'lay it down' well-sealed, for the future; Mitchell used charcoal imported from England in his glassworks – up to this it was necessary for glassworks to be located near a forest for the essential supply of wood for the kiln and this had the unfortunate effect of using up Bordeaux's scarce supply of wood. Further, he employed glassblowers from England and northern France. His location at the port of Bordeaux was an obvious advantage, particularly in view of the burgeoning colonial trade.

The building that housed the glassworks was cone-shaped, similar to those he would have been familiar with in Ireland. It was described thus by a factory inspector in Bordeaux:

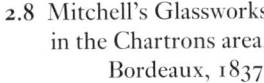
2.8 Mitchell's Glassworks in the Chartrons area, Bordeaux, 1837.

the baking oven, which is a square pavilion, built in the English style, so that the workers have enough air there. The roof is carried in direct elevation, and in the middle is the opening to serve as a chimney, the oven is built in the middle, its large mouth opening on the rising side and receptacles for the cooking of the material manufactured on one side … [21]

When a competitor settled near Bordeaux in 1726, Mitchell appealed to the Chamber of Commerce, but his appeal was rejected and he was told that his glasses and bottles would have to be made superior to those of his competitor.[22] He created the classic 'Bordeaux' or *bordelaise* bottle shape, still used for wines from the area, with its high square shoulders and straight flanks. Mitchell was also responsible for the Jeroboam, a glass bottle that holds 4.5 litres of Bordeaux wine.[23]

His business was obviously highly successful, receiving letters patent from the French monarchy in 1738 after which his business was known as the 'Royal Glassworks Bordeaux', located in what is now Place Mitchell. Meanwhile Mitchell was diversifying, acquiring vineyards, part of the manor of Arsac in 1724, and gradually expanding his holdings up to 1736 when he built the Château du Tertre (which, in the 1855 classification, established itself as a Margaux Grand Cru Classé) and, in 1740, the year of his death, he purchased two trading ships. By 1750, the glassworks was producing 200,000 bottles per year. His wife continued the business and, after her demise in 1761, their son Patrice, who married Elyse-Peggy (or Eliza) Lynch in 1774 in Dublin, carried on the business, becoming ennobled in 1777.[24] A street in Bordeaux, close to where Pierre set up his business, is called, appropriately, Rue de la Verrerie ('the street of the glass factory'). There too is another street named 'Mitchell' in his honour.

In Dublin, Rupert Barber, an artist who set up a glassworks at Lazar's Hill in 1750, was awarded a premium of twenty pounds that year by the Dublin Society for his decanters and bottles 'and other sorts of green glass ware; he being the first that has made that manufacture in the kingdom which before was imported from abroad'. According to Westropp it did not last very long.[25]

The problem of standardization, however, remained. Sir Boyle Roche, a member of the Irish House of Commons from 1775, proposed an act 'That every quart bottle should hold a quart' in response to complaints regarding the sizes of wine bottles.[26] Until then, as bottles were free-blown, the capacity varied. Then in 1821, Henry Ricketts of Bristol received a patent for a machine that manufactured identically sized bottles for 'Wine, Porter Ale or Cyder', and thus a standard size was created.

Up to the early nineteenth century, wine merchants sold wine from the barrel and bottled it for the client. There was a charge for the bottles, and the client would keep the bottles from the same barrel in a bin set aside for them. This was important in the event of the wine not being satisfactory to the client. The bins were generally numbered with, in some cases, a label indicating the type of wine. The bin labels were only rudimentally informative – 'claret', 'sherry', 'champagne' – but with letters large enough to be read by candlelight and almost always in upper case.[27]

BIN LABELS

The earliest bin labels were made of lead with white lettering, probably dating from the introduction of binning in the 1730s. Later in the eighteenth-century, earthenware and glazed pottery labels evolved, with black or blue lettering, in what became a fairly standard 'coat-hanger' shape. A hole at the top allowed them to be hung by or over the bin. Some were left partially unglazed to allow for more detailed information to be penciled-in. Labels with bin numbers rather than names were apparently not used until the beginning of the nineteenth century when the design for these evolved from the coat-hanger shape to small, circular discs made of pottery, lead, slate or wood.[28] Some years ago, three bin labels on slate were discovered in the wine cellar of a house on Merrion Square in Dublin (plate 2.9).

2.9 Two of the three bin labels of slate found in the basement of a house in Merrion Square, Dublin. Photograph courtesy of Conor Lucey.

Slate was convenient as it could have painted lettering or be left blank and chalked.[29] All three are roughly rectangular in shape with a hole pierced (off-centre) at the top; one reads 'CLARET. LANPHIER. SEPTEMBER 1789. 20 GUINEAS'. There is a band of foliate decoration across the top, under the hole, and more across the bottom. The second has a curved top and is labelled 'VERY STRONG BRANDY 1786' with a foliate motif each side of the year, while the third is also rectangle and marked 'CLARET LA[N]PHIER APRIL 1793'. In each case the words are painted in a gold-brown colour. There was a John Pennefeather Lanphier in Kilkenny 'of The White Hart Inn and other specified premises in the City' and with an address at Parkstown, Co. Tipperary.[30] With such an unusual name, there must be a connection, though how the labels came to be found in a Dublin house remains a mystery.

Paper labels on wine bottles, as we know them, had not made their appearance at this time, making binning something of a challenge, particularly as many varieties of wine were being produced. Thanks to Alois Senefelder (1771–1834), who invented lithography in 1798, it became possible to print paper labels in large quantities. The first labels were printed in Germany in the nineteenth century on white paper rectangles on which the name of the wine and the vintage year were printed. As time went by, the wine producers wanted labels that provided more information and even illustrations.[31] Since 1945, Château Mouton-Rothschild have brought together some of the most famous artists in the world, among them Picasso, Bacon and Miró, to create labels for their bottles, the originals of which are now exhibited at their château in Bordeaux.

CARING FOR WINE

Wine was generally ordered through merchants in Dublin or elsewhere, and delivered from their warehouse to the purchasers' cellars. In 1730, Lord Grandison's agent at Dromana, Co. Waterford, suggested that the earl 'get Mr George Fitzgerald to write to a proper person in … Bordeaux' to purchase wine for his cellar, suggesting that 'if the market encourages it, I will send butter [in exchange] for it'.[32] Bishop Edward Synge of Elphin had a wine cellar in both his palace at Elphin, Co. Roscommon, and his Dublin house in Kevin Street where his motherless daughter, Alicia, lived, with whom he was in constant correspondence. These letters are interesting in a number of ways: they give us an insight into the care of a wine cellar, the relationship between supplier and customer, and Synge himself who comes across as being particular, if not fussy, about the care of his wine and, at the same time, anxious that his choice of wines is met with approval. He respected the opinion of Alicia's governess, a Huguenot from La Rochelle, encouraging her to taste his wine and inform him of her opinion.[33] It seems he had a falling-out with the above-mentioned Dr Edward Barry when he and two companions dined with Synge at Elphin in 1749. It appears that Barry was invited to taste the wine in Synge's cellar though we are not informed as to his verdict. That evening, having departed earlier, '*Monsieur le Docteur*, unasked', returned and told the butler that he would stay for the night. Synge was furious: 'But I was determined he should not, and made Cary [his servant] carry him away. I suppose he is huff'd at this and am not sorry if He be. His Irish impudence deserv'd to be so mortify'd.'[34] Perhaps Barry was not sufficiently enamoured of Synge's wine.

The bishop's main supplier was Daniel Sullivan, whose warehouse was in Michael's Lane in Dublin. From Sullivan, Synge ordered claret, hock, champagne and French white wine, which would be delivered to his Dublin house in hogsheads, where it would be strained and sent to Elphin with bottles and corks, to be bottled there. It was a four-day journey and Synge was concerned that the wine be sent while the weather was cool, so that it would travel better. When the expected hock is delivered, he wanted it placed in the 'hogshead cellar, on the left side. There is but one hogshead there … it is so superlatively good'.[35] Corks were purchased from a Mr Waters, from whom he regularly bought two gross of the 'twenty-penny Corks' and he urged Alicia to 'get in pint Bottles and let them be boil'd well before they are put to rinse in cold water'. He seeks assurance that Sullivan visits to keep an eye on the cellar: 'Pray are he and his Cooper frequent in their visits to the cellar? And what say they about it? Make him write to me ...'

Cellars were designed to be well organized. When different merchants supplied wine to a client, each had a separate space within the cellar, so that, in Synge's case, Sullivan's cooper would keep an eye only on Sullivan's wine. Synge was also partial to port, and, on being informed that Arthur Lamprey of Big Ship Street 'dealt constantly with Lisbon wine', he instructed his daughter, 'Desire him to lay by a choice hogshead for me. If I like it on tasting I'll have it'.[36] In Drogheda, Co. Louth, the wine merchant Francis Brodigan, who traded with Samuel Delap in Bordeaux, supplied landowners in his area, including Blayney Balfour (whose grandson later built Townley Hall), members of the Brabazon family, and Sir Patrick Bellew.[37] Here, as with other merchants, it was not unusual to find two or more customers sharing an order, which made sense if they lived in the same general area. It was also not unusual to find that, for whatever reason, if someone required storage for his wine, friends would usually offer space in their cellar.

Between 1758 and 1761, the Rt Hon. Owen Wynne IV of Hazelwood, Co. Sligo, purchased three hogsheads of claret from a wine merchant in Derry – a substantial order but, as high sheriff in Sligo in 1758, he had to pay for, among other things, the entertainment of the judges. Other purchases by Wynne during this period were brandy and hock, bought at the rate of a dozen bottles at a time, and one purchase of eight dozen bottles of port.[38] Samuel Pepys noted the first 'great quantity of wine I ever bought'. He and three friends purchased two butts of sherry from Cadiz between them. The wine cooper divided the butts into four, which would give them each one hogshead (*c*.240 litres) 'and mine (Pepys') was put into a hogshead, and the vessel filled up with four gallons of Malaga wine'. Blending had the effect of sweetening the sherry somewhat, and is a topic which will be looked at later in this chapter.[39]

John Foster (1740–1828), MP for Dunleer, Co. Louth, was chancellor of the Exchequer of Ireland (1807–11) and last speaker of the Irish House of Commons (1785–1800). Despite his impressive appointments, Foster, whose estate at Collon, Co. Louth, had taken a heavy toll on the family's finances, was never in a position to build a mansion for himself and his family unlike other men of his rank, living instead in a fairly modest house on the estate.[40] He ran up numerous bills, including a number for wine: in 1786, Foster owed £1,474 to John Ferns, wine merchant, for wine purchased between December 1786 and August 1790; a letter from John Page at Dundalk asks Foster to pay as much of his account for £359 8*s*. 7*d*. to Page 'as he can': one item on this is for Foster's election dinner at £64 2*s*. and another is his 'Annual Wine account' at £231 in respect of wines purchased between 17 November 1813 and 7 June 1814.[41] To make matters worse, John Foster's niece,

Anne Burgh (the daughter of his wife's brother), was married to the prominent Dublin wine merchant Nathaniel Sneyd, who was also owed money. The latter wrote to Foster, addressing his letter to the chancellor of the Exchequer at Moran's Hotel, Dublin, in July 1810, asking him to settle his account for £321 for wine dating from November 1808; the company regret that Foster is displeased at their pressing for a settlement of the account, especially as he is 'so nearly connected with one of our firm'.[42]

Wine was a valued, often expensive, commodity, and the care of it needed to be regulated. In large domestic establishments, the butler had charge of it and retained the key of the cellar. The duke of Leinster was the owner of two large houses, Carton in Co. Kildare, and Leinster House in Dublin and, as the highest ranking nobleman living in Ireland, he was expected to entertain in accordance with his position in society. He had a list of 'Rules about Malt Liquor, etc. etc.' compiled for his servants, which included the following instructions:

> No cask to be pegged bored or tapped [methods of unsealing a cask] but in succession according to age.
>
> All casks should be stooped [placed at an angle] at night when there is a necessity for it that it may settle before morning.
>
> Whenever a cask is stooped another should be tapped of the same kind of Liquor.
>
> The cellars to be kept very clean and neat and washed out when there is occasion.
>
> The cellars to be kept locked the keys are not to be given to anyone to go and draw Liquor for themselves.
>
> It is not expected that the Keeper of the Keys of the cellars is to be always at home to deliver Malt Liquors upon Extraordinary Occasions but at Meal times he must not be absent.[43]

Indeed the butler was expected not just to hold, but to be, the key to the cellar. Mrs Beeton, writing on the subject in 1861, believed that the butler must understand 'the proper treatment of the different wines under his charge … his own reputation will soon compensate for the absence of bribes from unprincipled wine-merchants'; he should be competent 'to advise his master as to the price and quality of the wine to be laid in', and should 'make a careful entry of every bottle used, entered in the cellar-book; so that the book should always show the contents of the cellar'. She further remarks that 'nothing spreads more rapidly in society than the reputation of a good wine-cellar … and this a little knowledge, carefully applied, will soon supply'.[44]

In 1740, twenty-three-year-old Lord Dacre, Thomas Barrett-Lennard, decided to visit Ireland with his new bride to show her the town of Clones, his house and his estates in Co. Monaghan which, it appeared, he had never visited. He informed his agent, Todd, of his intention, whose response was not encouraging regarding the condition of the house which was called, like many large houses in Ireland at the time, 'the Castle'. Todd informed Dacre that it contained only 'one parlour and three bedrooms with fireplaces, and three other little rooms without fireplaces or any furniture'. The best thing in the house was, he said, 'a hogshead of old French claret, very good … in the cellar', adding 'I am sure all the people of Clones will rejoice to see you and your consort'.[45]

CELLAR BOOKS

In Dublin, the widowed Mrs Katherine Bayly kept a note of the way wine was laid down in her cellar in 1756: 'In the left hand bin, the oldest claret, 18 quarts; white wine in pints to the front, red, black and green seals; bottled ale next; and Mr Hartley's clarets at the back, in pints and quarts. Middle bin: in the corner, Mr Tew's claret, 3 dozen quarts and 4 dozen pints; hock, white wine, meath [mead?], currant wine, and on the floor, cider and four bottles of "my son's champagne".' She paid Gustavus Brooke eighteen shillings per dozen for 'mountain Malaga', a sweet fortified wine that was very popular in England.[46] It was a substantial amount of alcohol of which she was careful to keep note. Having a record of the cellar contents was important, and a number of cellar books have survived. They vary with information given but generally they document the name of the wine, when and from whom the wine was bought, how much was purchased and the price paid. Other information noted can include the vintage, the date when the wine might be drunk at its best, when it was actually drunk and under what circumstances, and tasting notes. Some note the names of those who enjoyed it. One of the most comprehensive cellar books is that of the second and third Lords Clonbrock, Luke and Robert Dillon of Clonbrock, Co. Galway. They numbered their bins one to fifteen, and the following show, as examples, the contents of Bins 1 and 2:

> Bin 1: 22 and a half doz 'of Claret bought in to lie from Sneyd in 1808. In Jan. 1813 began to drink the above. Finished Jan 1814'. On October 24th 1814: '23 doz Sneyd's claret stated to be prime chateau Margaux Vintage 1811. Cost 95 gns. Also 3 magnums of same. NB: 7 more magnums put in No. 2 and 2 into No. 7 – broached October 1819; finished January 28th 1820'.

> Bin 2: 'a Hhd [hogshead] 22 and a half dozen Claret same as No. 1. Jan. 1814 began to use this wine. Oct. 14th cleared out, 1 dozen 6 bottles remaining. Oct. 25, 1814, 23 doz Kinahan's Claret stated to be vint. 1807. Cost £100. Also 7 magnum of Sneyd's'.[47]

As can be seen, Sneyd was not the sole supplier of wines to Clonbrock: Dwyer's in Cork supplied port, and Kinahan's supplied a small amount of claret, but mostly port, sherry and hock. Sneyd's claret, however, remained the favourite. It is interesting to note that in 1846, six of Clonbrock's fifteen bins were for claret. Consignments of wine were also shared; for example: 'a pipe of sherry imported by Col. Hare' and 'Judge Daly's half pipe of Madeira'. Buyers were eclectic in their choice of wine merchant, as has been seen, sometimes due to a recommendation, to tasting at the house of a friend, or of news that a consignment of a desired wine had arrived at a particular merchant's premises. In 1729, James Bourke, MP for Naas, Co. Kildare, wrote to Henry Boyle at Castlemartyr, Co. Cork, offering to recommend a good Dublin wine merchant who will supply Boyle with good claret at a reasonable price.[48] At Emo Court, Co. Laois, John Dawson, second earl of Portarlington, recorded that between October 1824 and November 1826 he put down eighty-nine dozen bottles of claret, including twenty-four dozen 'Lafitte' claret (1819) and twenty-two dozen Latour 1822, supplied from three wine merchants, including Sneyd.

The cellar book of the Lenox-Conyngham family at Springhill, Co. Derry, in 1789 contained an impressive amount of alcohol:

> 2 Barrels of Porter, 1 Cag [16.5 gallons] of Rum, 1 hogshead of Port wine, and another half full, 1 hogshead of Clarret in bottles, 5 dozen of Sherry, 10 dozen French Clarret in bottles, 2 and a half dozen of Frontiniac, 3 Casks of Cyder, 2 barrels and 2 butts [126 gallons by 2] of Cyder, 67 bottles of Ale, 9 Barrels, 4 dozen bottles of Beer.[49]

Among the Ormond Papers is an account of stores and provisions which lists the wines kept but does not indicate the location: 'Canary, Sherry, White Wine, Clarrett, Mozell and Malaga'. 'Obryon' [Haut Brion] appears from 1701. In June 1703, a date that coincides with the arrival in Dublin of the duke of Ormond as lord lieutenant, there were nine hogsheads and fifteen gallons of claret in his cellar.[50]

IRISH LINKS TO FRANCE AND SPAIN

In 1718, Archbishop King observed that Catholics, 'being made incapable to purchase lands, have turned themselves to trade, and already engrossed almost all the trade of the kingdom'.[51] A substantial part of that trade was wine, where their links with continental Europe were hugely important. Many went to France with the Jacobite army after the Treaty of Limerick.[52] Some took out letters of naturalization, though for those who had joined James II in France after the Battle of the Boyne or for those who had served in the French army or navy, it was not necessary to do so. French citizenship was valuable to them because of a law in that country

2.10 *La Grande Nancy,* one of the trading ships belonging to Barton & Guestier.
Image courtesy of Barton & Guestier.

that prohibited merchants in Ireland or England from selling their goods in France directly; they required agents in France to act for them. Several Irish merchants had already settled in places like Nantes and Bordeaux, and the new arrivals entered into partnerships with them or began trading on their own behalf.[53] As wine was the chief export from Bordeaux to Ireland, these merchants brought over family members to train as merchants and join their businesses. In many cases, their relatives in Ireland set themselves up as merchants in their localities, confident of the quality of the wine coming from family members in France. To become apprenticed to a wine merchant in Bordeaux was not cheap: Michael

Stritch, a Limerick businessman, paid 200 guineas for his son's apprenticeship there.[54] In the early 1770s the Irish colony in Bordeaux could boast of fifty to sixty Irish merchant surnames. An indication of how successfully they integrated into French trading was that in the eighteenth century one-fifth of the members of the Bordeaux chamber of commerce was Irish.[55] The foundation of the first new Irish houses in Bordeaux (1715 to 1725) corresponded approximately, as Cullen says, to an upturn in the fortunes of the wine trade.[56]

Not all of the merchants were Catholic – the Black family from Belfast, the Bartons from Co. Fermanagh, the Johnstons from Armagh and the Lawtons from Cork, were among the smaller number of Protestants in the business. According to Ted Murphy, Abraham Lawton had some 2,000 customers and in some years accounted for as much as 20 per cent of the total production of wine in the Médoc.[57] Thomas Barton set himself up as a merchant in Bordeaux in 1725, trading first in cognac, then in claret, which became his most important export especially to Ireland. In 1728 he exported 2,700 barrels of wine, and by 1785 the company was shipping 125,000 annually (plate 2.10). He was the largest buyer of first growths, and was described in contemporary documents as the normal buyer of Lafite's crop.[58] By the time of his death he had amassed a considerable fortune. He married Margaret Delap, whose grandfather was a wine merchant in Sligo, and whose father, Samuel (mentioned above), had emigrated to Bordeaux. Hugh Barton, Thomas's grandson, took over the firm in 1786, and married another member of the Irish-Bordeaux community, Anna Johnston. In 1802 Hugh went into partnership with Daniel Guestier (Barton & Guestier); in 1821 he purchased Château Langoa, and four years later he acquired 50 hectares from the Léoville domaine, which he renamed Léoville Barton. He retained contacts with Ireland, purchasing Straffan House in Co. Kildare (later the K Club), commissioning architect Frederick Darley to design a new house in the style of a French château, where his family lived into the twentieth century (plate 2.11).

William Johnston settled in Bordeaux in 1729 with his Irish wife: they took out French nationality, became Roman Catholic and, in 1765, William and his son set up the firm known as William & Nathaniel Johnston.[59] The company established strong connections in the United States; in 1807 a family member sailed for New York with an introduction from General Lafayette to General McHenry, an Ulsterman who became secretary to George Washington. By 1809 the company had over 1,000 customers in the US.[60] Thomas Jefferson, the American minister (or ambassador) in Paris, while visiting Bordeaux in 1787, sought advice on stocking his cellar in Paris from Abraham Lawton.

Familiar Irish names in Bordeaux included John Lynch of Château Lynch-Bages, the Dillon family of Château Dillon and Château Margaux, Kirwan (of the 'Galway Tribes'), Phelan, Clarke, Boyd and Lawton, together with those whom Thomas Jefferson described in 1787 as 'the principal English wine merchants at

2.11 Portrait of Germain Rambaud, who was master of the cellar at Barton & Guestier in Bordeaux for sixty years (1755–1815). In recognition of his service to the company his portrait was painted by Gustave de Galard (1779–1841). Image courtesy of Barton & Guestier.

Bordeaux ... Jernon [Gernon], Barton, Johnston, Foster, Skinner, Cop[p]inger and MacCarthy'. All but Skinner were Irish.[61] Denis MacCarthy had a street named after him in Bordeaux, and owned two properties in St Estèphe, Château MacCarthy and Château MacCarthy-Moulas.[62] The Catholic Dillon family were particularly successful. In 1690 Lieutenant-Colonel the Honourable Arthur Dillon followed James II to France, where one son became the archbishop of Narbonne and a granddaughter became the marquise de la Tour du Pin. The 'Bordeaux Irish' kept up close contact with their families in Ireland. This was particularly true of the numerous families from Galway, for example, who became deeply involved in the wine trade in Bordeaux and who, through family ties in Dublin, shared in that trade which 'consumed two-thirds of the wine shipped to Ireland and roughly half of all wine shipments from Bordeaux to the British Isles'. The names became well-known – Joyce, Blake, Lynch, French, Darcy and Bodkin.[63]

Another Irish merchant, Francis Burke, took up residence at 41 Rue Borie in the Chartrons district of Bordeaux, in which he also ran his trading house. Until very recently, the building has been home to many well-known wine traders, such as Patrice Calvet. The house was built in the 1720s, apparently for Burke, and at present it houses the Bordeaux Museum of Wine and Trade, where two of the vaulted cellars contain the museum, and the former cooperage to the front of the building on the ground floor is the museum shop.

While most of the Irish established themselves in France – Bordeaux in particular – other Irish families, for example the Galweys (or Gallweys), spread themselves further. In the 1740s, John Galwey of Carrick-on-Suir (described as 'a very rich roman catholick') was appointed agent for the Ormond estates and provided with Carrick (now Ormond) Castle as a residence. The vast cellars in the castle had, as he saw, the potential for profitable use. There was one on each side below the entrance passage (which were filled in at some stage between 1750 and 1770 as the floors above were subsiding); more cellarage would have been available under the east and west towers, and under the old buildings south of the west tower.[64] Galwey entered the wine trade, possibly through his kinsman, Anthony Galwey, who was a wine merchant in Malaga and, in due course, John became 'the largest wine importer in Ireland'. Like many Catholics who could afford it, he sent his sons abroad for their education, later putting them in charge of his business interests overseas. One son, Anthony, settled in La Rochelle, while the eldest, John (1726–97), settled in Malaga.[65] John inherited his father's fortune, he 'kept up the retinue of a prince', was on intimate terms with the Spanish nobility and married Margaret, daughter of Thomas Quilty of Malaga, another merchant of Irish origin. He was admitted to Spanish nobility as *Hidalgo* in 1769. While there was a social barrier between the nobility and the mercantile class in Spain, so long as Irish merchants could prove that they ranked as 'noble' in their own country, it was possible to be so distinguished. *Hidalgo* indicated membership of the lower nobility of Spain. The word is a contraction of 'hijo de algo' – son of somebody (indicating status). Other members of the Galwey family were Henry, a wine merchant of Bordeaux, his cousin, Gerard, a wine merchant in Cork, Garret, who settled in Seville, and Henry, who founded the firm of Henry Galwey & Co., wine merchants, in Waterford in 1835.[66] In Lisbon, the firm of Morrogh & Gallwey were important merchants exporting dried fruit and wine, among other items, in the mid-1700s.[67]

George Boyd was first recorded as a Dublin wine merchant in 1753 and conducted his business at 44 Abbey Street from where was provided, not only Bordeaux wines, but also burgundy and champagne, to the lords lieutenant or viceroys at Dublin Castle in the 1760s.[68] In 1789 he entered into a partnership with another 'high-end' wine retailer, Charles Carrothers of Jervis Street in Dublin who owned, according to James Kelly, one of the two major houses in the city at that time that advertised the availability of 'first growth' wines of the houses of Lafite, Latour, Château Margaux and Haut-brion.[69] Jacques Boyd (brother of George) who, with another brother, formed the Bordeaux house of Boyd frères, married Evarina Barton in 1740, thereby creating an alliance with the largest Irish wine business in Bordeaux. The family later purchased a property in the Margaux district, the château of Boyd-Cantenac.[70]

These merchant families, as has been seen, carried on what became a feature of their networking – that of intermarriage. There was a preference for unions between families that were settled in the same area 'as it permitted the survival of the merchant house as well as social reproduction'.[71] The gains, among which was family stability – plus a son-in-law who had already some commercial expertise and contacts that he could bring to the firm – were on both sides and came to be generally known as 'rule by son-in-law'.

Trade had been carried on between Ireland and these countries from medieval times: the provincial Irish ports to which the ships came were notable for their agricultural hinterland, from where they exported wool, hides, tallow, salt meat and fish in return for large quantities of wine. The wine trade thus was based on an exchange of commodities at this time. Gerald of Wales, in the late twelfth century, noted that 'Poitou out of its own superabundance, sends plenty of wine [to Ireland], and Ireland is pleased to send in return the hides of animals and the skins of flocks and wild beasts'.[72] Waterford became the principal port for the importation of wine: its location on the south-east coast of Ireland was ideal as a first port of call for wine ships heading into the Irish Sea, and from where the merchants were enabled to distribute the imported wine via the Suir, Barrow and Nore rivers. Its importance as a distribution centre for wine is illustrated, according to Liam Murphy, by the fact that in 1300, 3,000 hogsheads of wine that had been imported into the town from Anjou in France were re-exported to the port of Skinburness near the Scottish border to supply the army of Edward I then fighting against the Scots.[73] In fact large quantities of Gascon wine, carried in ships from Bordeaux in the late thirteenth and early fourteenth century, were re-exported to royal armies in Wales as well as Scotland, for example in 1298, when the king ordered 1,000 hogsheads of wine for his expedition against the Scots; and in 1333, 400 casks were to be sent from Gascony to Dublin and 200 to Waterford for the king's Irish wars.[74] The trade records of Bordeaux show numerous shipments of wine in the sixteenth century to various Waterford merchants, to Richard Gould, the mayor of Cork and, in 1561, a Cork merchant acknowledged his debt to Etienne du Bourg, a merchant of Bordeaux, of '36 seasonable cow-hides of the best kind' in exchange for 3 tuns of wine.[75] Thomas Walsh, a Waterford butter merchant, established himself in Bordeaux in the 1680s, and later entered the wine trade: when James Brydges (later first duke of Chandos) was made earl of Carnarvon in 1714, he ordered six hogsheads of the best Bordeaux and one hogshead of white wine, from Walsh.[76] In 1711, over half the wine coming into the port of Waterford was shipped by thirty importers in that city, and ships from there sailed to La Rochelle, Lisbon and Malaga, while those coming from Bordeaux would sail on to Bristol, another important port with which Ireland traded.[77] Other Irish ports were Cork, Dublin, Limerick, Drogheda, Wexford, Galway, Youghal, Sligo and Coleraine.

On arrival at the port, it was necessary to pay the 'prise' or tax on wine, an ancient custom by which the king exacted one tun of wine from every ship that arrived with less than twenty tuns, and two tuns from ships laden with twenty or more tuns. Once the formalities were done with, the overland transport of the wine was often undertaken by pack horse: according to O'Neill, a sixteenth-century source mentions that 'the manner of carrying wine in Ireland is in little barrels on horses' backs'.[78]

PURCHASING WINE: IRELAND

There were numerous suppliers of wine throughout Ireland. It could be lucrative so long as one had the potential to build up a reputable business – that is, a reliable supplier on the spot in France, Spain or elsewhere from whom one could be sure of getting the right product at the right price. For the upwardly mobile it has been said that 'a man's wine merchant was more important than his banker if he wanted to groom the right sort of important and influential friends'.[79] Wine and its suppliers both at home and abroad was a topic of conversation among men, who often agreed, as has been seen, to share the cost of a hogshead or two. Bishop Synge's wine merchant Daniel Sullivan was not his sole supplier, but he was the regular and, indeed, the respected, supplier. It is interesting to look at other wine merchants in Ireland, and their relationships with clients.

The Dublin firm of Sneyd, French & Barton, whose business specialized in claret, dominated the wine trade in Ireland, and were one of the suppliers to Dublin

Castle. After the death of Edward Sneyd, his executors wrote to Thomas Conolly of Castletown in 1781 requesting the continuance of his custom 'as formerly on the best terms from the largest and most excellent stock of wines in this country'.[80] In 1809, Edward's son Nathaniel (*c.*1767–1833), MP for Cavan 1794–1800, who had succeeded him in the business, was asked to value the wines that Sir Arthur Wellesley had left behind, so that Wellesley's successor as chief secretary could make an offer for them, and in 1829, the British home secretary, Sir Robert Peel, recalled of Sneyd that his wine house 'was the first in Dublin when I was in Ireland (1812–18) and … I continued to have my wine from Mr Sneyd after I left'.[81] The company supplied wine to Viscount de Vesci at Abbeyleix, Co. Laois, not only claret between 1803 and 1806, but also port, red champagne, Madeira and Frontignac and, in 1803, they wrote to de Vesci to assure him of the quality of the claret ordered, 'a first growth of vintage 1800 of a parcel that has been most highly appraised by a number of our [friends?] to whom we have sent it'.[82] Other customers included the marquis of Abercorn, the second earl of Portarlington, and John Foster, speaker of the Irish House of Commons.[83] Together with other wine merchants, the company was a regular supplier of wine to the Cobbe family at Newbridge House, Co. Dublin.[84] Thomas Moore, the poet and songwriter, related in his memoirs how a Colonel Hull and two companions were returning overland to Britain from India; they had brought with them a supply of Sneyd's claret and, as they crossed the desert, they would 'finish a magnum or two every evening'![85]

A visitor to Ireland in 1807 left an account of the firm's wine vaults which he was invited to visit. Their premises were in Upper Sackville (now O'Connell) Street, Dublin, and he described a 'great number of long cellars'; in the first, he counted 120 bins, in each of which was contained a pipe (126 gallons) of wine in bottles. He refers to 'many other vaults running parallel to this'. In the claret vaults, there were about 294 bottles in each bin – 'about 618 bins in all, and Mr French said that frequently there was £100,000 of wine in those cellars'. He observed an 'infinite' number of empty bottles and was informed that the company often spent £200 a month on bottles. He was impressed with how different wines were kept, 'the Madeira cellar is kept warm and with a flue round them: white wines are in cool cellars', and he notes that corks had to be aired to get rid of the 'new' smell, and that 'French corks were the best'.[86]

Nathaniel Sneyd, who was governor of the Bank of Ireland 1818–20, suffered a violent death in 1833 – he was shot in the head while making his way to his office in Upper Sackville Street, by a deranged man, who had an unspecified grudge against the three business partners of Sneyd, French & Barton, and he was reported as saying that it did not matter to him which partner he killed.

Caesar Colclough of Tintern Abbey in Wexford wrote to Thomas Dillon & Sons of Dublin: 'I'm informed that you have the best Burgundy and Champain in town if you will send me a dousin [dozen] of each and let me know the lowest price you will oblidg …'[87] The firm of Newman & Gamble supplied Trinity College Dublin with wine to celebrate the installation of the duke of Bedford as chancellor of the university on 17 September 1768, which cost £57 6s. 1d. The previous year £62 10s. 10d was paid for wine when Trinity entertained the lord lieutenant to dinner.[88] The college spread its patronage for wine in the first half of the nineteenth century: the Dublin firms of Kinahan's, and Sneyd, French & Barton were the main suppliers, the latter being paid £211 4s. 8d. in 1821 for supplying wine for a royal dinner on campus for the visit of George IV; another main supplier was called Litton & Hewson.[89]

A letter dated 1765 from Walter Woulfe, wine merchant of Carrick-on-Suir (probably related to Thomas Woulfe of Cadiz), to Patrick Ronayne to whom he had sent a hogshead of claret and two gallons of brandy, 'which is very good', continues: 'I will not say much in the Claret's praise as Mr Mathew Woulfe tried it in the Cellar and drank a Decanter of it after Dinner wch he allowed to be as good as any ever he tasted' and, continuing the sales pitch, Mathew himself added a personal note: 'I took care to chuse you a very good hhd [hogshead] Claret it has a good boddy and well flavoured 'twill always be a great pleasure to me to serve you'.[90]

In the cellar book of Charles O'Hara of Annaghmore, Co. Sligo, is a note from his wine merchant in Dublin, Bartholomew Molière Tabuteau, on how the wines that he is sending should be treated upon their arrival:

> please have them packed on their sides with dry Saw dust (or if that cannot be procured, dry turf mould in a <u>dry</u> cellar free from any draught or current of air – All <u>White </u>French & Rhenish[91] wines are better in a cool place & packed on their sides with laths instead of saw dust.[92]

Tabuteau, trading at 123 Abbey Street Upper, and at 11 Jermyn Street, London, was supplying wines from 1840 to Edward Donough O'Brien, fourteenth Baron Inchiquin, at Dromoland Castle, Co. Clare, and Hereford House, Park Lane, London.[93] Much later, in 1878, the company informed Inchiquin that they were sending the consignment ordered by rail to 'Ardsollas & Quin station' and that the claret was packed in two cases – 'No. 1 contains 4 doz claret @18s per doz; No. 2 contains 3 doz claret @ 30s per dozen this latter one labelled B 30/- … '. From their London shop in April 1880 they sent '4 doz Light Claret and samples … with reference to the samples we would beg to mention that the after dinner Clarets are both very superior & fine wines. The one "Leoville", the other "Margeaux". The champagnes are both Superior and Dry wines and we think that labelled "A" will claim your preference'. They advise that these should be put down in his cellar to be drunk in two to three years 'of whichever of the fine Clarets you select as it makes such a difference to a wine coming straight on the table from the cellar'.[94]

Ralph Sampson, whose family were originally Scottish, but who was born in Dublin, became consul in Bordeaux and La Rochelle in 1714; by the 1730s he was importing wine to Dublin, and selling it to, among others, his wife Jane's aunt, Katherine Conolly of Castletown, 'a connection which brought him valuable custom among the Irish elite'.[95] The wealthy Mrs Conolly sent an occasional hogshead of French wine to her sister, Jane Bonnell, in London: the wine was of high quality, as she told her sister 'I buy none under 16 or 18 pounds a hogshead' and 'I pay a great prise and I desired it might be the best he [Sampson] had'.[96] On the death of her husband, Jane Sampson and their daughter Angel took over the business, and among their clients was St Patrick's Cathedral, Dublin.[97]

In 1759 Christopher Harrison, a Dublin wine merchant, sent to his client, Thomas Mahon of Strokestown House, Co. Roscommon, a hogshead of 'Murgou' [Margeaux] which he claimed was the best claret of the second growth. In 1763, Mahon rebuilt and re-stocked his cellar at Strokestown, and his November wine bill for the previous six months came to over £700 (*c*.£145,000 today) – a staggering amount. Harrison also supplied Mahon's son, a student at Trinity College Dublin, with two dozen bottles of claret and half a dozen of hock.[98] Richard Edgeworth's son, another student at Trinity College, regularly had a local innkeeper bring food and wine to his college chamber.[99] Members of the Huguenot community in Portarlington, Co. Laois, who were natives of Bordeaux, were able to continue imbibing their native wine in the 1720s through a M. Pennetes, a French wine merchant in Dublin from whom they could purchase claret costing £11 for a hogshead. Samuel Beauchamp, a wine merchant resident in Portarlington, was said to have 'well furnished' vaults, and later in the 1750s, another merchant, Joshua Pilot, imported large quantities of wine to the town direct from the house of Barton & Co. of Bordeaux.[100] Huguenots established themselves in cities and towns in Ireland, and in Waterford they had a considerable share of the wine trade.

Merchants supplying the Honorable Society of the King's Inns with wines are named only from 1899: Thompson & D'Olier at 22 Eustace Street; John Morgan & Sons, 36 Dawson Street; Findlater & Co.; Mitchell & Son, 21 Kildare Street, and J. Kelly, all in Dublin. However, prices charged to members of the society for wine are given from as early as the 1600s when a quart of white wine cost 6*d.*, and a quart of sack, 1*s*. By 1794 the prices charged to members were port at 1*s*. 1*d*. per bottle, of which 1,138 bottles were drunk, and claret at 3*s*. 3*d*. each, of which 608 bottles were drunk.[101] Individual barristers signed for the wine consumed at Commons (a meal at which practitioners and students of law meet, eat and drink): from 1833 to 1835, bottles of port and claret were most in demand by the members, followed by sherry.[102] An undated list of wines, possibly from the second half of the nineteenth century, shows that wine was priced per bottle, and some, including champagne, port and sherry, per pint.[103] A meeting of the wine committee in 1861 recommended that two hogsheads of 1854 claret be ordered, in addition to the two of 1858 already ordered, and that one hogshead of 'a lighter kind of claret be furnished for the Bench and Hall for general use'.[104] A rule at the Inns, laid down in the 1790s and later rescinded, was that 'it was usual to send a gallon of wine as a present from the Bench table to the senior Barrister and senior Attorney's mess' on the last day of the Commons during the law terms.[105] It is interesting to note that Donough, earl of Thomond, soliciting an admission to the King's Inns in 1610, presented the institution with a hogshead of wine, and on the same day, Lord Butler of Tullowphelim, Co. Carlow, on becoming a member of the Inns, made a presentation of two hogsheads.

The prices paid for wine are not often specific, but the accounts of Thomas Taylour, first earl of Bective, whose seat was Headfort House in Co. Meath, give an idea of the cost. To take 1784 as an example, Taylour paid almost £400 for wines from a number of suppliers over the year: one transaction was a tun of claret (252 gallons) plus 2 dozen [bottles] of claret which cost just over £111; a pipe (126 gallons) of Lisbon and a hogshead (63 gallons) of Hermitage together cost just under £63. A pipe of port was £36 and a hogshead of Madeira £30.[106] At Borris House, Co. Carlow, a valuation of Walter Kavanagh's personal possessions in 1818 valued his wines and spirits at just over £962, which amounted to 16.9 per cent of his total possessions.[107] Obviously the wine purchased was not just for the entertainment of guests, but for the consumption of the family. James Kelly cites the examples of two families: in the 1710s the household of the 'abstemious' Pole Cosby of Stradbally Hall, Co. Laois, consumed two hogsheads per annum (the equivalent of *c*.1.6 litres per day). The de Vesci family of Abbeyleix, Co. Laois, spent £260 on wine over a twelve-month period in the 1750s, an amount that would have purchased fifteen hogsheads of 'choice' claret, allowing them twelve litres per day.[108]

AUCTIONS

Wine was also purchased at auctions, after the owner had moved away or died. A sale of the contents of Lord Conway of Lisburn's cellar following his death in 1731 included 48 hogsheads of claret of 'the great growth of Lafitte'; 12 hogsheads of Margeaux [*sic*]; 7 hogsheads of choice Graves claret, and 8 hogsheads of French white wine – 'the best Priniaque'.[109] The auction of the contents of William Houghton's Dublin house at 9 North Frederick Street in 1838 included a fairly good selection of 'Hock, Claret, Madeira, Port, Sherry, Sauterne, Cote Rotie Red and White Hermitage, White and Pink Champagne, Bucellas, Chably [*sic*], and other Wines'.[110] A sale of sherry from the vaults of the late Sir W. Stamer, 37 Dawson Street, Dublin, was advertised in 1841 where prices were £125 per butt; £65 per hogshead and £35 per quarter cask.[111] The late Godfrey Greene's cellar was valued by William Forbes in 1768: six hogsheads of claret were valued at £741, a hogshead of claret lees (the dregs or sediment that settles at the bottom of a container during the making and ageing of wine)[112] at £8. 8s. 0d., 218 dozen and seven bottles of claret at £147. 10s. Together with red port, Malaga and Lisbon wine, Frontignac, Madeira and hock, the entire cellar was valued at £1,195. 10s. 8d.[113]

The departed owners were often bishops who tended to have excellent cellars and who had entertained accordingly. In 1807 the marquis of Abercorn's agent wrote to tell him of the death of the bishop of Raphoe: 'I understand there will be a quantity of good wines of his sold, and beg to know if [you] would wish any purchased and what kind?'.[114] Frederick Hervey, the bishop of Derry (1730–1803), was also the fourth earl of Bristol. During the last of his frequent tours in Italy, Hervey, a man who enjoyed intrigue, and loathed the French, was arrested and accused of passing on unsolicited observations of troop and naval movements to Sir William Hamilton at Naples and Queen Maria Carolina of the Two Sicilies. He was imprisoned in a castle at Milan for nine months in 1798. Hamilton's reaction to the news was low-key: 'We all know that his Lordship's freedom in conversation, particularly after dinner, is such as to make him liable to accidents of this nature'.[115] The same year, Bishop Barnard of Limerick wrote to his niece Isabella to thank her for informing him of the 'Disposal of Lord Bristol's precious Wines'; but

> the Distance from Down Hill to Limerick is so immense that the carriage would run away with the Profits, even if I were sure that the wines were really of *prime* quality, which I rather Doubt, because the wines I tasted when I was at his House Ten years ago, were far otherwise … and they are not likely to be Improved by so long keeping, which always injures claret.[116]

It was said of the Earl-Bishop that his last wish as he lay dying in Italy in 1803 was that his body be shipped back to England in a cask of sherry. A visitor in the 1790s remarked that 'The bishopric of Derry is one of the best of Ireland. They say it is worth £12,000 per annum. Oh, what a lovely thing it is to be an Anglican bishop or minister! These are the spoiled children of fortune, rich as bankers, enjoying good wine, good cheer, and pretty women, and all that for their benediction.'[117] Among Nathaniel Johnston's clients was an Irish archdeacon who ordered 'sixty dozen of the best Claret in bottles of the first growth of Lafitte [*sic*] and twenty dozen Chateau Margaux'.[118] There was a considerable amount of wine in Lord Charlemont's cellar in 1726 after his death, much of which was later sold to retailers, and the balance 'disposed to Gentlemen' as gifts.[119]

On a rather poignant note, in an accounts ledger kept by Lady Louisa Conolly, she writes in 1805, 'From the sale of about 5 Hogsd of Claret, Doubt, whether it was my property, or not, but as I did not intent to use it, I thought it might spoil, I consider'd it to be the best Article to part with, for the Discharge of the Servants

Legacies, and it remains with the Trustees to decide on whose Property it is For I do not know.' She made £374 1*s*. 7*d*. on this sale. This was two years after the death of her husband Tom Conolly, when she was left dealing with the huge debts he had run up, and was forced to let go many of their servants.[120] As might be expected, the cellar at Powerscourt House, Co. Wicklow, kept a substantial amount of wine. After the death of his father in 1853, the mother of eight-year-old Mervyn Wingfield (now the 7th Viscount Powerscourt) retained a Belfast merchant, Mr Gordon (possibly from Robert & Alexander Gordon), to assess the state of the wine in the cellar. He wrote that there was

> a very large quantity of Claret, almost all is of the Vintages of 1825 and 1834 – two of the best vintages on record – of the former there are about 27 dozens and 3 bottles, and of the 1834 about 65 dozens and 3 bottles – there are also about 8 dozens and 2 bottles of Claret supposed to be of the famous vintage of 1815 – the wines of that year may be considered extinct – a few bottles perhaps being still in some private Cellars.

He states that there was no port in the cellar; but that there was a considerable quantity of sherry – about 96 dozen and three bottles 'of different kinds, but all good', together with '6 bottles of good dinner sherry and 16 dozen for housekeeper's [kitchen's] use'. Of the 69 dozen bottles of Madeira, 'none of it is good' while the 2 dozen champagne were fit only for use in the kitchen.[121]

The marquis of Abercorn's agent alerted him in 1816 to the sale of wine at Sir Henry Montgomery's '… circa 200 dozen of wine, among which is … excellent madeira … and his port, claret and sherry are very good'.[122] An account of wines in the Dublin cellar of Lord Castlereagh, chief secretary (1798–1801), taken in March 1801, includes four hogsheads each of port and claret, and one of Madeira, all supplied by Blackwood, as well as 206 bottles of claret from Sneyd.[123] According to the second earl of Shannon, 'the Late Chancellor's [Lord Clare] wine in town [he lived in 6 Ely Place, Dublin] is valued by Blackwood at £2,100.' Shannon had been horrified at the damage caused by events in Co. Kildare during the 1798 Rebellion; in a letter to a family member, he wrote about the devastation of wine cellars there:

> Gangs of freebooters all over [the county] – they have rob'd the poor Bog [?] of 11 doz[en] of Richards' fine madeira and a quantity of old Hock that the D[uke] of Rutland gave him, took away his books, broke his looking Glasses, and Cabinet work with hammers, took 25 doz[e]n of old port from Ho[r]t's house, and 60 doz[e]n of wine from a Mrs Burdett. … Whilst a person was giving the above account of the robbery of cellars, Dillon did not fail to tell the circle in an audible voice that he had 37 h[ogs] h[eads] of claret alone at his house in Mayo …[124]

For the most part, claret in Irish cellars went by the name of the wine merchant, e.g. 'Sneyd's claret' or 'Stewart's claret', up to the mid-eighteenth century, after which the name of the chateau was sometimes used, e.g. Château Lafite, Château Latour, Château Margaux and Château Haut-Brion. In the 1855 classification of Bordeaux wines, requested by Napoleon III to showcase French wines at the Exposition Universelle de Paris of that year, these four wines were classified as *Premiers Crus* or First Growths. This was based purely on price – not, as Penning-Rowsell emphasizes, 'on the reputation of the estate or owner, the size or style of the château which counted, but the hard commercial facts as they existed on the Bordeaux market. By grouping the vineyards in classes it was easier to establish a price-structure for the roughly fifty to sixty best growths of the Médoc'.[125] Though from Graves rather than the Médoc, Haut-Brion had to be included because of its reputation and for the fact that it sold for as much if not more than the other First Growths. It is interesting to find that Thomas Jefferson, having toured Bordeaux vineyards as US ambassador to Paris in May 1787, came up with his own classification in the travel notes of his tour, which coincide with the much later 1855 classification, describing these four vineyards 'of first quality':

1 Chateau Margau[x], belong to the Marquis d'Agricourt, who makes about 150 tonneaux of 1000 bottles each. He has engaged to Jernon [Gernon] a merchant.

2 [Chateau] La Tour de Segur, en Saint Lambert, belonging to Monsieur Mirosmenil, who makes 150 tonneaux.

3 Hautbrion, belonging 2/3 to M. le comte de Fumelle who has engaged to Barton [Irish] a merchant the other third to the Comte de Toulouse. The whole is 75 tonneaux.

4 Chateau de la Fite, belonging to the President Pichard at Bordeaux, who makes 175 tonneaux. The wines of the first three are not in perfection till 4 years old. Those (of) de la Fite being somewhat lighter, are good at 3 years, that is the crop of 1786 is good in the spring of 1789. These growths of the year 1783 sell now at 2000 l. the tonneau, those of 1784, on account of the superior quality of that vintage, sell at 2400 l.[126]

ADVERTISEMENTS

The earliest-known advertisement for Haut-Brion wine was, apparently, in the *London Gazette* in May 1705, when '200 Hogsheads of neat choice new red Obrian' wine were 'exposed to Sale by the Candle, at Lloyd's Coffee-house in Lombard-street'.[127] Years later, advertisers were still having difficulty with its spelling. Prospective purchasers of wine from retail merchants were spoilt for choice if looking at newspaper advertisements, an aspect that James Kelly has dealt with comprehensively, so it is not necessary to do so here.[128] It is probably sufficient to say that, just like today, advertisements in newspapers all over Ireland tried to out-do each other with special offers. In 1752, Christopher Quin informed his customers that he had 'removed' to the house 'next door to the Sign of the Brazen Head in Bridge-street, being determined to continue the Wine Trade' and having fitted out the house and its 'commodious cellars', he advises them that he has a 'Parcel of choice old neat Clarets of different Growths, the Vintage 1747 and 1748'. Prices for the 'Neat Claret of the first Growth of Obreone [Haut Brion]' were £18 per hogshead; 18s. per dozen; 6s. per gallon and 18 pence per quart.[129] It is interesting to look at another advertisement of a century later when, in 1852, Kinahan, Sons & Smith notified prospective buyers that they were 'about to Bottle a large quantity of Wines … with a view to encourage Orders for Ten Dozen and Upwards … all of superior quality' and invited those interested to come to 'our extensive Wine Vaults situate at the rere of No. 11 Merrion-square North where they can be tasted or … Samples will be sent to those who desire them'.[130] The market catered not just for the upper but also for the middle classes. It was possible to purchase wine by the bottle, by the dozen, by the gallon, by the pipe or the hogshead. Prices of claret varied: for example, in the *Freeman's Journal* in December 1828 one Dublin merchant offered 'choice' claret at 42s. per dozen or 3s. 6d. per bottle; while in the same newspaper in 1831 another offered 'excellent' claret at 3s. per bottle, or 36s. per dozen.

Thomas Conroy from his premises in Capel Street sold 'wines for ready money only', offered fourteen bottles for every dozen purchased; and for those who did not relish bottling their wine themselves, John Wilson offered to do it for them 'in his vaults' and they would 'be accommodated with clean new bottles at glass-house price'.

In another advertisement, N. Carolan, a Dundalk merchant, states that he 'is honoured with the sale of Clicquot's Champagne: Widow Clicquot's Champagnes are of the highest character, being hitherto used in the continental courts and are now offered for sale in Ireland for the first time … [it] is admittedly the most superb Wine in the world'.[131] In 1829, Robert Edwards, 'at the Corner of Castle Lane, under the Shakespear's Head, in Dames-Street', advertised his sale 'every Day, the Sabbath excepted: Right-good Bordeaux-Claret, at 10s. per Dozen or 10s. per Quart, also fine Margoos-Claret, bottled, at 12s. per Dozen or 1s. per Bottle (Returning the Bottles)'. A further development among many traders was to stock in their premises a range of grocery products, including coffee, tea, etc. thereby widening their appeal to families, housekeepers, etc.

One of James Malton's images of Dublin in the 1790s, that of *St Catherine's, Dublin*, shows, beside the church, a shop selling alcohol, bearing the rather unlikely

2.12 James Malton (*c.*1764–1803), *St Catherine's, Dublin.* Ink and watercolour on paper. Courtesy of the National Gallery of Ireland.

name of Patrick O'Murphy with an emblem over the door showing prince of Wales feathers over a harp. A large sign on the first floor shows a punchbowl under which reads 'Rum, Brandy, Arrack, Mead, Whiskey – Wholesale and Retail by Licence'. The customers are on horseback, one holding what looks like a wine glass, the other (who has a woman behind him on the horse) is being served a tankard of beer (plate 2.12).[132]

It is not easy to calculate prices of claret as the quality of growths can and do differ year on year, and the prices react to that. Not many cellars mentioned list the prices paid, but a few comparisons might be in order at this point. First, Sir Robert Walpole made his purchases of claret in 1732/3 in England, paying £36 per hogshead for 'ordinary' claret, and £45 per hogshead for Margaux. This was the most expensive end of the market and, as stated previously, it was the very wealthy (usually titled) English buyers who purchased the top Bordeaux wines. In Ireland, on the other hand, Katherine Conolly, as has been seen, boasted in the 1730s that she never paid less than £18 per hogshead for her and her sister's claret while Lady Louisa Conolly's hogsheads were valued at *c.*£75 each in 1805. The huge gap between Christopher Quin in 1752 advertising his 'Haut Brion 1st growth' at £18 per hogshead which, if his claim was true, seemed like good value, and Godfrey Greene's claret valued in 1768 at just over £123 per hogshead, seems somewhat strange. Lord Clonbrock, who kept a meticulously well-detailed cellar-book (1814), ordered his wine already bottled, at the rate of twenty-three dozen per order (276 bottles: there are *c.*300 bottles in a hogshead), for which he paid 95 guineas for the 1811 Château Margaux – an exceptional vintage, called the 'comet vintage', as it coincided with the appearance of the Great Comet of that year – and he paid £100 for the same amount of another excellent vintage claret of 1807.

SMUGGLING WINE

Another method of acquiring wine was through smuggling though this was not done on as major a scale as might be expected. Wine was shipped in hogsheads that were heavy and bulky to handle, and movement did not improve wine. It was not so with brandy which came in more manageable casks and a lucrative business was carried on with cargoes of tea, tobacco and spirits. One or two hogsheads or smaller casks, destined for the personal use of a wealthy family, would be the most to be smuggled. The O'Connell family of Derrynane, Co. Kerry, were known to engage in smuggling up to the 1780s: it was said of them, 'Their faith, their education, their wine, and their clothing were equally contraband' (plate 2.13).[133] But that may not have been the case by 1828 when Prince Pückler-Muskau was entertained at Derrynane, later commenting on O'Connell's 'old and capital wine'.[134] The tower house, built by the Mahony family on the Dromore estate in Kerry, overlooking the Kenmare River, was reputedly used as a lookout post to protect the family's wine smuggling.[135] They were not the only families in rural Ireland involved in this trade, as Cullen has pointed out. Through their contacts or agents in Nantes, among them the Galweys, the O'Connells regularly supplied tea to the merchants of Cork.[136] Nantes, a noted centre for smuggling, particularly tea and wine to Ireland in return for Irish wool, had a settled Irish merchant community from the seventeenth century. In Galway in 1737,

> Thomas Blake of Menelaugh and Jonuck Bodkin and Leo Bodkin merchants in this town, loaded a ship with wool at Round Stone Bay in the beginning of October last, which Richard Morrish was master of said ship; the said Blake and Bodkins loaded another ship with wool at Round Stone Bay in the month of October last which Januck Lynch was master of said ship … and the said

2.13 Derrynane House, Co. Kerry, home of the O'Connell family, seen from the beach. Courtesy of the OPW, Derrynane House.

> Bodkins runned many hogsheads and ankers of brandy in the said Round Stone Bay and brought it safe to Jonuck Bodkin's and Leo Bodkin's farm to Oranmore…[137]

The smuggling of wool was a result of the 1699 Woollen Act that prevented Irish wool production, manufacture or export to any country except England: in fact Irish wool was produced at such a low cost that it harmed some English woollen mills. In the early 1720s Jonathan Swift remarked that 'our beneficial traffic of wool with France has been our only support for several years, furnishing us with all the little money we have to pay our rents' and, in a pamphlet attributed to the dean, relating to the smuggling of wool for wine and brandy, 'though England has constrained us to be poor, they have given us leave to be merry'.[138] And with a usual supply of seven or more hogsheads of wine in his cellar, the dean could afford to be quite merry. However, when he discovered that, as the result of a bad harvest in France in 1734, and the subsequent price rise of twenty per cent, he wrote to a friend that he 'will make Mr Hall, an honest Catholick merchant' in Dublin 'who deals in Spanish wine, to bring me over as large a cargo as I can afford, of wines as like French claret as he can get'.[139]

Shipwrecks off the coast of Ireland attracted locals in the hope of salvage. In 1549 a row erupted between the towns of Limerick and Wexford: the mayor and corporation of Limerick complained to Lord Deputy Bellingham that a Limerick boat 'laden with wines' had been wrecked off the coast of Wexford and the goods plundered by the inhabitants, who were, apparently, very reluctant to make reparation.[140] Also in the sixteenth century, in Cork, Donal MacCarthy Reagh, whose Irish title was the twelfth prince of Carbery (1505–31), was also known as 'Donal-of-the pipes' [of wine] due to his adroitness at 'finding' cargoes of wines from shipwrecks off the west Cork coast, and in Kinsale the story goes that Anne Boleyn's family (known then as Bullen), who had a house on the Old Head of the town, made their fortune as 'wreckers'.[141] In 1728 the *Mary* was wrecked near Castlehaven, Co. Cork: a hogshead of wine had been seized by the surveyor and held as excisable goods. The delay in dealing with the case resulted in the wine being forcibly removed and 'carried away by the people of the country'; and an example of what could happen to an informer occurred in Boyle, Co. Roscommon, where, in a riot in 1744, the informer's ears were cut off by the mob.[142] Smuggled brandy accounted for at least one-third of the total consumption of spirits in Ireland from the 1730s to the early 1770s.[143] The municipal records of the town of Galway describe how it and wine were conveyed into it:

> A large breach in the town wall, by Dominick Bodkin's house;
> A door in the town wall, into Peter Lynch's house;
> A door near the mayor's house;
> A passage through Martin's-mill into Kirwan's-land;
> By the marsh, a hole broke through at Val Browne's house, shut up and opened as often as he has occasion to bring ankers of brandy into town;
> A large conduit into Simon Lynch's yard, much frequented in the running trade;
> A hole through the town wall into Jonathan Bodkin's yard shut up now, but opened as often as he has occasion.[144]

Whenever a shipwreck occurred, the authorities were at pains to salvage the cargo before the locals did. Such cargo would be bought by wine merchants and sold on. In 1749, part of the cargo of the *Jason*, a French East India Prize ship, was advertised to be auctioned in the cellars of a Mr Bradshaw of Cork. This included 150 hogsheads of claret, eighty pipes of Malaga, fifty pipes of old cognac, one of Bordeaux brandy and a large quantity of wine in bottles. Being a customs officer could be a dangerous occupation, as David Richardson's experience in Limerick shows. He told of many attempts to bribe him, and one attempt to poison him, and that he had been assaulted with drawn swords in the cabin of his sloop by unknown persons until three pipes of Madeira were forcibly taken and 'run' on shore.[145] Smugglers operated around the coasts of Ireland and Britain. Many ordinary people approved of smuggling and even took part in it; men could make more money in one night's work than they could in a month's labour in the fields. In Britain, particularly in the south, which was only a night's sail from France, large gangs formed that were prepared to use violence, and the few customs officials would be outnumbered. At Portsmouth in 1748, customs officials went to the home of a naval officer who was suspected of smuggling a cache of wines and spirits. There the officials found brandy, rum, hogsheads of claret, Spanish and Portugese wines, but their efforts to remove these was prevented by a crowd including the naval officer, and 'as fast as the Officers endeavoured to bring the said Liquors away, the same was taken from them by the Country People ... [the officers' efforts] proving ineffectual, they were obliged to leave behind them the Said Liquors'.[146] In Scotland, smuggling was rife: Ludington quotes a letter from Alexander Oliphant, a wine merchant from Ayr, to a Thomas Barry at Guernsey in 1767, which gives an idea of methods used:

> Please ship on board [Captain McGown's] vessel for our account 10 tuns of claret, the best you can afford at about 700 livres per tun and one tun of good malaga white wine. You'll please get the claret rack'd into Spanish casks – one half in pipes and the other in hogsheads and clear it out and ship under the denomination of Spanish Galicia; we must request you'll keep this to yourself, you need not even let the captain into the secret.[147]

Like Scotland, Ireland was ideal for smuggling with small coves around the country too numerous to be well-guarded. According to F.G. James, even horses were said to have been smuggled into Ireland from Scotland, and it was commonly known that this illicit trade was carried on with the knowledge, and even the connivance, of customs officials.[148] The French tourist De Latocnaye was well aware of this:

> The safe and deep bays into which this coast [he was in Connemara] is cut, as well as the freedom from fear of customs officials, accounts for the presence of a number of people who are for what is called quite openly the 'smuggling business', as if it were an ordinary trade. I have gone into different cabins and asked, straight away, for brandy or claret without finding any surprise to be expressed. One good woman, like many others, said to me, 'There is nothing at present in the house but my husband is at sea, and if you come back in a month you can have all you want'.[149]

This underlines the dramatist John O'Keeffe's comment that good claret could be had at 'every thatched ale-house in Ireland'.[150] In Kerry, trading connections with

France were maintained. Sir Maurice Crosbie purchased his wine directly from the catholic Curé William O'Scanlon who wrote to him in July 1750 to say that he was glad that the wines had arrived safely, and would Sir Maurice let him know the price he intended 'to give for ye two hogsheads of old wine'. Finola O'Kane suggests that 'Crosbie may have acted as wine wholesaler for the Kerry families': the two hogsheads sent to William Crosbie cost £353; and the other item was three and a quarter tuns of wine (plus charges) sent to Sir Maurice which amounted to £1,598.[151] In Co. Mayo, a sportsman and his guests sat by the fire in a lodge enjoying the 'excellent claret that had never paid the revenue a farthing, or brewed toddy from the more potent spirit which was at once the produce and scourge of the district'.[152] Anne Crosbie thanked her Dingle friend 'for ye Brandy and Teas' while asking her to 'procure [further] pounds of green tea'. Dingle, with its 'good harbour', was probably where these consignments arrived.[153] In 1824 James, another member of the Crosbie family, wrote from the family seat, Ballyheigue Castle, Co. Kerry, to Dublin Castle complaining about a report in the *Dublin Journal* regarding the discovery of a cave on his father's property, and denies the allegation of any involvement by his family with smuggling. He protests that the allegation 'is a vile attempt to injure me & my family'.[154] A letter from the chief police magistrate for Co. Clare to the chief secretary at Dublin Castle that warned of the likelihood of trouble in Co. Kerry, noted that 'many of the better classes are concerned in smuggling', and are therefore reluctant to have police established in the county.[155] According to a legend set in Killarney, the entrance to the 'wine cellars of O'Donoghue Mór' was to be found between some rocks at the edge of 'Loch Lane' inside which was 'a doorway like one of the ould arches in Mucruss Abbey' where 'a great cellar full of barrels, on golden stillons' was alleged to have been found.[156] 'Wrecking' was an extension of smuggling and was practised in the Ballyheigue area: lanterns were attached to the tails of grazing cattle to simulate the bobbing lights of vessels at sea, and lure unsuspecting ships onto the rocks of Tralee Bay.[157] Sir Lucius O'Brien of Dromoland wrote to a friend in 1749 to inform him that a small vessel, with a Mr Russell on board, had just arrived from France:

> In a tide or two, she will come to anchor or run ground *by chance* near Nick McInerhinys – she has choice old claret, some burgundy and champagne on board and Mr Russell will sell it to you or me cheaper than to the merchants in Limerick; or than we can buy it from any Irish merchant (but this is entre nous).[158]

A member of Jonah Barrington's dinner club, Counsellor Townley Filgate, had a pleasure boat in the 'harbour of Dublin', and used it to smuggle claret for the club from the Isle of Man, so 'we consequently had the very best wines on the cheapest possible terms'.[159] Louis Cullen refers to the Isle of Man, the Channel Islands and the French coast from Dunkirk to Boulogne as entrepôt centres, i.e., distribution centres for smugglers. Goods were delivered by the producers to the entrepôts in large commercial vessels usually using false documentation, from where smaller and faster crafts smuggled them to their markets. The Isle of Man was ideally located between Ireland and England for such an operation.[160]

Henry Sandford (1719–96) of Castlerea, Co. Roscommon, was MP for Roscommon and later for Kildare and Carrick, but his main claim to fame is that he was the first resident of No. 1 Royal Crescent in Bath where he lived for twenty years until his death in 1796. His 'commonplace book' – an item similar to a scrapbook in which the owner compiled facts and figures that were of interest to him or her, including newspaper cuttings – was discovered in recent years in the National Library of Ireland. An entry in this document (undated, but between 1780 and 1783) is headed 'Hogshd. Of Claret from Dublin to Bath', on which are details of the costs incurred. The hogshead, purchased in Dublin, cost £26 5s., but of interest here is 'Freight from Do. to Bristol *smugling included*' cost £11 11s. 0d'.[161]

Charles Smith, writing in 1749, remarked that there was a considerable trade between the town of Timoleague, Co. Cork, and Spain, 'being much resorted to by Spaniards, who imported large quantities of wine here' and that the town at that time had 'no less than fourteen taverns that sold sack'. Another writer remarked on 'how splendid the building [Franciscan Friary] must have been … in the days when ships came up the harbour, as far as Timoleague, laden with wine from Spain …'.[162] An account of the burning of Timoleague in 1642 describes how 'we burnt all the towne, and their great Abbey, in which was some thousand barrels of wine'. It could be suggested that this wine, that probably kept the taverns well stocked, was illicit. The space in the Abbey that would normally be the chapter room was, according to Cochrane, used for cellarage (with the actual chapter room above it), as it was adjacent to the river allowing cargo to be delivered directly to the friary, and it was common practice for Franciscan houses to be established at trading ports 'where the friars would have the greatest opportunity of coming into contact with all sorts of men'.[163]

A lucrative market regarding the movement of wines was re-exportation from Ireland to Britain or elsewhere as the duties on wine in Ireland were a lot lower than those in England, and it is significant that the tax was levied on quantity, not quality nor, interestingly, on alcohol content. For example, at the end of the seventeenth century the tax on wholesale imported wine levied by England was £55 per tun: in Ireland in 1700 it was £24 per tun. Between 1700 and 1760 the tax levied in Ireland was £20 per tun, raised during 'war years' to between £24 and £30 per tun, a significant difference.[164] The Methuen Treaty of 1703 between Britain and Portugal meant that, in return for a Portuguese promise to admit British woollen goods, the British agreed that duty on French wines should never be less than 50 per cent higher than those on Portuguese wines. The market for Bordeaux wines declined greatly in Britain – officially. English imports of wine for 1700 were 13,649 tuns from Spain, 7,757 from Portugal, 1,430 Rhenish [hock] and only 664 from France. However, the English aristocracy continued to show a preference for claret: between 1720 and 1739 half of the wines in the earl of Bristol's cellar were French and the duke of Chandos was describing claret in quite lyrical terms, 'the Clarets that suit my Taste are the Margaux ... the fuller & richer they are in the Mouth the better I like them'.[165] It was no wonder that Sir Robert Walpole, when an Admiralty official, took advantage of his position to smuggle wine and champagne into Britain in the holds of Admiralty barges. His wine bills for 1732 and 1733 show his preference for clarets for which he paid £36 per hogshead for ordinary claret and £45 for Margaux, which was his favourite.[166] The earl of Bristol remarked that 'when you were entertained at Houghton Hall (Walpole's seat), you were likely to be up to your chin in meat and over your chin in Claret'.[167] Walpole was by no means alone in smuggling. One way of getting around it was to smuggle French wines in Spanish or Portuguese casks, as mentioned earlier.[168] In this way large amounts of claret was imported fraudulently into England through Portugal. As Jancis Robinson has pointed out, judging by 'the prevalence of Bordeaux in the household sales conducted by Christie's after their foundation in 1766', it is evident that smuggling was rife.[169] In contrast to the English, the Dutch, by the early eighteenth century, preferred cheaper white wines, which they purchased, then re-exported to other northern European countries: it was reckoned that they drank one-third of what they bought annually, and re-exported the rest.[170]

STEALING WINE

A report in the *Limerick Chronicle* of 27 October 1785 gave details of a robbery that took place the week before in the home of the amateur architect, William Leeson, in Co. Tipperary. Having tied up the steward, bundled three women of the house into a room where they were 'guarded', taken silver, jewellery, clothes, house deeds, and, interestingly, a crock of butter from the dairy, they settled themselves in the kitchen. There for the next two-and-a-half hours they ate, and drank four bottles of claret. They left taking two dozen bottles of wine with them.[171] Those who robbed Gilbert Mellefont's home in Co. Cork in 1777 may have been more discerning: they came away with twenty-two dozen bottles of claret.[172]

On 6 August 1798, the French General Humbert's 1,000-strong army landed at Killala Bay, Co. Mayo, in support of the Irish Rebellion, took the town of Killala having defeated the British garrison, and requisitioned Killala Castle, the residence of the protestant bishop, Joseph Stock, as their temporary headquarters, holding the bishop captive, and installing almost 300 soldiers with their baggage in the castle. During Stock's period in captivity, when supplies ran out for those occupying the residence, the French requisitioned wine and food from the cellars and larders of the bishop's neighbours. Stock, in his account of the invasion, refers to this:

> At times, the company at the castle even felt a disposition to be merry on the arrival of one of these felonious cargoes. Some bottles of excellent hock, drawn from the cellars of the Right Hon. Colonel King, at Ballina, came as a present from the French officer there to M. Charost. The wine on trial was found so good, that conscience began to mutter at the sin of assisting in the robbery of so hospitable a gentleman as the owner must have been, unless he might be proved guilty of some crime.[173]

Selecting, purchasing, and caring for wine were not easy tasks in the eighteenth century. But it was a time when great progress was made in its production, for example, the development of standardized glass bottles, corks that prevented contamination, both of which led to the successful binning of wine. For the few, being in a position to employ a butler with a knowledge of wine, was a definite advantage. In most cases, however, the purchaser – for example, the bishop of Elphin, a man who was acutely aware of the care required – expected to spend an amount of time organising and planning his cellar, particularly when he purchased wine from different merchants. Cellar books needed to be kept and updated regularly. Wine – its purchase, its quality, its price – and its uses (as will be seen later) was a subject of discussion among men, just as they discussed other matters relative to their estates.

CHAPTER 3

Dining and wining

Pass the bottle and d---n the expense,
I've seen it observed by a writer of sense,
That the labouring classes could scarce live a day,
If people like us didn't eat, drink and pay.
So useful it is to have money, heigh-ho!
So useful it is to have money.
from *Spectator ab Extra*, Arthur Hugh Clough (1819–61)

THE OFT-MENTIONED HOSPITALITY in Ireland dates back to medieval times when there were legal obligations to it that included 'the right of a traveller to food and lodging, the right of a lord to be entertained by his vassals and the right of a king to billet his servants on the inhabitants of his kingdom'; Richard Stanihurst commented in the sixteenth century that Gaelic Irish chieftains were 'the most hospitable of men, nor could you please them more in anything than by frequently visiting their houses willingly of your own accord, or claiming an invitation from them'.[1] So too was Patrick Sarsfield, mayor of Dublin 1554–5, of whom it was said 'his house [in High Street] was so open as commonly from five of the clock in the mornings to ten at night his buttery and cellars were with one crew or another frequented …', and twenty tuns of wine were consumed during his mayoralty.[2] The Irish poet, Aodhagán Ó Rathaille (1670–1726), describes the hospitality of Donal O'Callaghan of Co. Clare:

Wines, newly opened, being drunk, and jollity,
Viands on spits, and usquebaugh on tables …
Every moment fresh casks being opened for the multitude,
With no ebb in the liquid coming to that drinking feast.[3]

While the eighteenth-century Anglo-Irish ascendancy adopted the tradition in part, an Englishman's comment that 'the Irish Gentry are an expensive People; they live in the most open hospitable manner, continually feasting with one another', might indicate that by this time conspicuous consumption in food and wines now played its part in the hospitality stakes of the elite. Perhaps the inscribed stone on the road close to Clodagh Castle, Co. Cork, belonging to the MacSweeney family, that directed all travellers to repair to Mr Edmund MacSweeney's house for hospitality, might be more in line with the ancient practice.[4] While hospitality was acknowledged, up to the latter decades of the eighteenth century there was criticism, rightly or wrongly, that Ireland's elite were living beyond their means. Charles Smith observed, 'Claret is often drunk, rather for vanity, than health or pleasure. In England, there are many gentlemen of £1,000 per annum who never drink wine in their houses, which can scarce be said of any in Ireland who have even £100 per annum'.[5] Mrs Mary Delany wrote in a similar vein, 'you are not invited to dinner to any private gentleman of a thousand a year or less that does not give you seven dishes at one course, and Burgundy and Champagne: and these dinners they give once or twice a week'.[6] As lord lieutenant, Lord Chesterfield railed against the large amount of claret that was consumed in Ireland per annum, expressing the hope that 'God by His thunder' would 'turn all the wines in Ireland sour'.[7] Judge Day, visiting Tralee, Co. Kerry, during the Munster circuit, noted 'I have visited Tralee for a fortnight and have never dined twice at the same table … I condemn the vice and extravagance that plies friends with heavy dinners followed by an immoderate overflow of the grape'.[8] And a Persian traveller to Ireland, Abu Taleb, tells of a dinner to which he was invited: as soon as guests were seated at six o'clock,

> The master of the house immediately commenced asking us to drink wine, and under various pretences replenished our glasses; but perceiving that I was backward in emptying mine, he called for two water glasses, and having filled them with claret, insisted upon my taking one of them. After the cloth was removed, he first drunk the health of the king, then of the queen; after which he toasted a number of beautiful young ladies … none of which I dared to refuse. Thus the time passed till 2 o'clock in the morning; and we had been sitting for 8 hours; he then called to the servants to bring a fresh supply of wine. Although I was so much intoxicated that I could scarcely walk, yet on hearing this order I was so frightened that I arose and requested permission to retire …[9]

Excessive wine-drinking was not new: in the sixteenth century, Shane O'Neill was described as 'sociable, hospitable, but frequently intemperate at table … a persevering votary of Bacchus'. His cellar at Dundrum Castle in Co. Down was said to contain usually 200 tuns of wine. When he became intoxicated and aggressive, 'his attendants placed him chin-deep in a pit, then cast earth around him. In this clay bath he remained until the velocity of his blood had abated'.[10] Obviously there was no need for such drama regarding Lord Kenmare in 1767 of whom it was reported 'his table was elegantly spread, his venison excellent, his wines genuine; and he gives them … like the son of an Irish king'.[11] Samuel Johnson observed that 'few people had intellectual resources sufficient to forego the pleasures of wine. They could not otherwise contrive how to fill the interval between lunch and dinner'.[12] Arthur Dawson, appointed baron of the exchequer in 1741, composed a song about claret, hospitality, and Thomas Morris Jones from Muine Glas, Co. Antrim, in which is the following stanza:

> Ye good fellows all
> Who love to be told where there's claret good store,
> Attend to the call of one who's ne'er frighted,
> But greatly delighted with six bottles more:
> Be sure you don't pass the good house Money Glas,
> Which the jolly red god so peculiarly owns;
> 'Twill well suit your humour, for pray what wou'd you more,
> Than mirth with good claret, and bumper Squire Jones.[13]

Nor was there anything new about excessive eating. At his home, Quilca, Co. Cavan, Thomas Sheridan was said to have entertained lavishly 'in the manner of the ancient Irish' when he had his dining room strewn with rushes, then enjoyed the effect on his guests by producing what he called 'swilled mutton' – a sheep roasted whole, stuffed with geese, turkeys and chicken packed in with vegetables – after which it was all swept away 'and the best of modern dinners served up with plenty of claret and champagne to wash away unsavoury memories'.[14] Just as in other countries, food and drink played a symbolic role in country houses in both Ireland and England: the provision of it suggested power, wealth and hospitality. In both countries, offering more food for a guest than he or she could actually consume was a marker of status for that guest.

In 1737, it all became too much for the fastidious John Boyle, fifth earl of Cork and fifth earl of Orrery, a friend and biographer of Jonathan Swift and Alexander Pope, who described a dinner that he attended in Co. Cork in a letter:

> I have been at a Feast. Paper Mills, Thunder and the King's Kitchen are soft Music to the Noises I have heard. Nonsense and Wine have flowed in plenty, gigantic Saddles of Mutton and Brobdingnagian Rumps of Beef weigh down the Table. Bumpers of Claret and Bowls of White-Wine were perpetually under my Nose, till at last, unable to bear the Torture, I took Advantage of a Health at which We were all oblig'd to rise: and slipt away leaving a Hat and Sword to be my Representatives. I would have left a Leg or an Arm behind Me rather than not have made my Escape. This short Sketch may give You some faint Idea of our Entertainments in this part of the World. They are esteemed according to Quantity, not to the Quality of the Victuals, be the Meat good or be it bad, so that there is as much as would feed an Army.[15]

Apart from the 'nonsense' spoken, and bumpers and bowls of wine drunk, Orrery stresses the excessive sizes of the mutton and the 'Brobdingnagian' rumps of beef that 'weigh down' the table. One wonders if he was ever a dinner guest at the Dublin town house, on St Stephen's Green, of Robert Jocelyn, lord chancellor of Ireland (1739–56), where he would have tasted something entirely different, not just in choice of food, but in size. Jocelyn's 'Dinner book', in which he drew diagrams of the table layout on which was the menu, together with the names of the guests, was the subject of an article by Alison FitzGerald.[16] Twelve peers were invited to dine in July 1747, presumably to celebrate William III's victory on the anniversary of the Battle of the Boyne. The choice of food was interesting, consisting of over forty dishes that included lambs' ears ragout, fricassée of frogs and badger flambé served with cauliflower. Not all of Jocelyn's meals had so many dishes, and the guests were not expected to sample them all, usually just those closest to them. It appears that badger flambé made a regular appearance on the Jocelyn menus, and can be found in some eighteenth-century recipe books, in one of which, Charles Carter's *The complete practical cook* (1730), were guidelines for preparing potted badger, potted otter and even potted bear. According to FitzGerald, Jocelyn's dinners were frequently men-only affairs, with the object of cementing the confessional and political bonds among the elite, a subject that will be looked at in Chapter 5.

On a visit with her husband to their Irish estates in 1769, the countess of Shelburne was surprised at the variety of alcohol stocked at a Kildare inn, where they stopped to dine with their friends, Dean Coote and his son. The Cootes brought tench and venison for their meal, but the innkeeper supplied them with champagne, burgundy, claret and Madeira, 'none of which', the countess observed, 'were to have been expected in such an inn, he had none of the more salutary and simple liquors of beer, ale, or cider, and it is too common among all ranks of people in this country to find luxury and show than convenience or comfort'.[17] It is possible, if not probable, that the Cootes had, prior to the visit, stocked the inn with what they considered were the most suitable beverages for their guests.

A 'breakfast' – presumably a charity affair as these were popular at the time – was given to the 'friends of the marquis of Kildare' at the Rotunda in the New Gardens, in Dublin in the 1760s and, though the number attending is not given, obviously a large attendance was expected. The following was the bill of fare:

> 100 Rounds of beef; 100 Neats tongues; 100 Sheeps ditto; 100 Baked pies; 100 Sirloins of beef; 100 Geese roasted; 100 Turkies ditto; 100 Ducks ditto; 100 Pullets ditto; 100 Wild fowls; 1000 French loaves; 2000 Large prints of butter; 100 Weight of Gloucester cheese; Tea, coffee, and chocolate, in abundance; 2000 Saffron cakes; 4000 Plain ditto …

In addition, 2,500 bottles of wine were provided and there was 'a most splendid and large pyramid of sweetmeats in the middle of the dessert in the centre of the room; likewise a great number of stands of jelly, and a curious fountain playing, handsomely ornamented with ivy, &c.'.[18]

3.1 Illustration by the amateur architect Frederick Trench (1746–1836), taken from a table plan for a dinner held in the Supper Rooms of the Rotunda, in Ian Campbell Ross (ed.), *Public virtue, public love* (Dublin, 1986). Photograph courtesy of the Irish Achitectural Archive.

Functions were held regularly at the Rotunda Assembly Rooms during the season. The ballroom usually opened at 9 p.m., tea, coffee, lemonade, ices were served 'in the Tea Room and Recesses', and the Card Room was 'lighted and prepared'. Concerts were held in the Rotunda, 'the Rotunda supplied with a separate Band for Quadrilles, &c.'. Supper was served at midnight 'on 25 Tables, 16 Persons each; covered alike, to prevent Crowds and avoid Questions of Preference; with plain Meats and Wines'.[19] An interesting decorative device, said to be designed by the architect Frederick Trench (1746–1836), for what was probably one of these assemblies, indicates the type of fare that the subscribers would hope to be served.

Within what looks like a fringed cape (*un mantelet*), a garland of sausages links at one end, a leg of Westphalian ham, with at the other a leg of pork, interspersed with crossed wine glasses, mallet-shaped bottles of Lisbon, port, sherry, Madeira, claret, hock, a mug for porter and a jug for punch; mustard and pepper pots hang from curling smoked tongues, around the central medallion which reads: 'Plan of Supper Apartments Distributed in 25 Tables equally covered For Sixteen Persons each affording Sufficient accommodation for 400 Guests' (plate 3.1).[20]

A smaller gathering took place at Shane's Castle, Co. Antrim, the seat of Lord O'Neill, in 1809 to celebrate the golden jubilee of King George III. A 'sumptuous dinner', according to the *Dublin Journal*, was provided for the local gentry and 'his Lordship's principal Tenants', that comprised turtle, fish and game, 'while Champaigne, Burgundy, Hock, and powerful libations of Claret proclaimed in bumpers to his Majesty's health and earnest wishes for the prolongation of his valuable life … the Castle was brilliantly illuminated from top to bottom with wax candles, and the reflection of the blaze from Loughnea … was beautiful beyond description'.[21] For more casual dining, Jonathan Swift often stayed with a clergyman friend of his in Baldoyle, Co. Dublin. He would bring his own provisions; according to his custom, the supply for a stay of five days being eight bottles of wine, and bread and meat for three days.[22] When Swift stayed at an inn, his servant knew exactly what his duties were: having ensured that the horse was comfortably stabled and fed, he was, according to his employer's instructions, 'to step yourself now and then into the kitchen to hasten [the meal] and observe whether they be cleanly …'. If his master wanted wine, he was to 'chuse a bottle well filled and stopped; if the wine be in hogsheads desire to taste it' to see if it was sour. Further, the servant was to ensure that the salt was 'dry and powdered, the Bread new and clean, and the Knives sharp'.[23] An amusing story was told about Oliver Goldsmith who, as a young man riding to his home in Co. Westmeath from a long school term, found that he was tired and had lost his way, but had a guinea in his pocket. At Ardagh, he asked for directions to 'the best house in the place', meaning an inn, but the joker of whom he inquired, directed him instead to the residence of the town's landlord, Sir Ralph Fetherstone, and Goldsmith was shown into the parlour where the master of the house was sitting by the fire. Recognizing both the young man and the mistake, Fetherstone played along. The poet 'ordered supper, invited his host and the family to partake of it, treated them with a bottle or two of wine, and at going to bed ordered a hot cake to be prepared for his breakfast'. After he called for his bill the following morning, he discovered his mistake.[24] The experience formed the basis for the plot of Goldsmith's play, *She Stoops to Conquer* (1773).

The dining room of Georgian houses in Ireland and England was considered the most important room in the house. It was different in France where it was a room in which one simply ate. The architect Robert Adam was of the opinion that

3.2 James Gillray (1756–1815), 'A decent story' (published 1795). Courtesy of the Art Institute of Chicago.

the French 'trust to the display of the table for show and magnificence', not to the décor, and that, as soon as they have eaten, they retire to the 'rooms of company'. He goes on,

> It is not so with us. Accustomed by habit … we indulge more largely in the enjoyment of the bottle. Every person of rank here is either a member of the legislation [*sic*], or entitled by his condition to take part in the political arrangements of his country … these circumstances lead men to live more with one another and more detached from the society of the ladies. The eating rooms are considered as the apartments of conversation, in which we are to pass a great part of our time.[25]

3.3 Thomastown House/Thomastown Castle, Co. Tipperary, engraved view by J.P. Neale, 1819. The house was enlarged in the castle style by the architect Richard Morrison from 1812. Courtesy of the Irish Architectural Archive.

It is no surprise, then, to find that the dining room was considered a male domain, while the drawing room was a female space, to which the women were accustomed to retire, 'for their tea and gossip', as the playwright William Congreve put it, after dessert had been served. For the men, this was often the signal for 'serious' drinking to begin, after which they would re-join the ladies (plate 3.2). Richard L. Edgeworth described how, at midnight, the carriages would come to the door 'to carry off the bodies of the dead, or till just sense enough being left, to find their way straight to the tea-table, the gentlemen could only swallow a hasty cup of cold coffee or stewed tea, and be carried off by their sleepy wives, happy if the power of reproach were lost in fatigue'.[26] It brings to mind Mr Snodgrass in Charles Dickens' *Pickwick Papers*, 'It wasn't the wine' he murmured, in a broken voice, 'It was the salmon'. This separation of the sexes, however, was virtually unknown in continental Europe, and much remarked upon by visitors.

The size of the dining room increased from an average of *c.*28 x 21 feet in the eighteenth century to *c.*36 x 23 feet between 1800 and 1842. However, at Thomastown House, Co. Tipperary (built in 1670 by George Mathew, a half-brother to the duke of Ormond and agent for the Ormond estates) (plate 3.3), improvements to the building from 1711 under his grandson, 'Grand' George Mathew, included the provision of a large dining room that measured 50 feet long and 20 feet wide. There, 'Grand' George, as he was known, entertained lavishly, encouraging guests

3.4 *Aesop* ceiling, rococo stucco work executed by Bartholomew Cramillion in the 1750s, now in Áras an Uachtaráin, Phoenix Park, Dublin. Courtesy of Dublin City Council, photograph Paul Tierney.

(who included Jonathan Swift) to stay as long as they wanted. The house contained forty 'commodious apartments' for guests, together with accommodation for their servants. On arrival, Mathew showed the guest to his apartment, saying, 'this is your Castle, here you are to command as absolutely in your own house'. Also to be found at Thomastown house was 'a detached room in one of the extremities of the house', described as the 'Tavern', where those who enjoyed drinking could celebrate 'the midnight orgies of Bacchus'.[27] It is ironic that this was the birthplace in 1790, and childhood home, of the Capuchin priest and temperance reformer, Father Theobald Mathew.

The growth in the size of dining rooms in the nineteenth century is not surprising as it coincides with a time when people travelled more, in better-sprung carriages and on improved roads, stopping to eat or to stay with friends en route.[28] As much time was spent eating and drinking in that room, so a great deal of money, time and thought was spent on fitting it out and furnishing it. Robert Adam warned against the walls being hung with fabric such as tapestry or damask, but rather finished with stucco and hung with paintings 'that they may not retain the smell of the victuals'.[29] In dining rooms, stucco ceilings, such as that at Belvedere, Co. Westmeath, were decorated with bunches of grapes and vine leaves, and chimneypieces were similarly decorated, indicating the function of the room. The ceiling of Dr Edward Barry's (see Chapter 2) ground-floor study/dining room in his Dublin home, Mespil House (built *c.*1751), has numerous bunches of grapes included in its decoration: attributed to the stuccodor Bartholomew Cramillion (*fl.* 1755–1772), the ceiling is aptly called *Medicine with Arts and Sciences*, referring to Barry's interests (plate 3.4).[30]

From the 'big' houses such as Carton, Russborough, Co. Wicklow, Castle Coole, Co. Fermanagh, and Headfort, Co. Meath, to the more modest houses of the gentry, the best furniture and furnishings they could afford (or often could not afford) were invested in the decoration of the room and the acquisition of accoutrements for dining. At Castle Coole, a 'sideboard suite' was designed by the architect James Wyatt for the dining room: the plain mahogany sideboard was flanked by urns on pedestals. Beneath it was a fluted sarcophagus wine cooler with a lion mask: when filled with crushed ice, it kept wine cold, or it could be filled with water for washing glasses. Silver would be proudly displayed on the sideboard (especially if, like the case of the Orrerys at Charleville in Cork, it was engraved with the family's arms) and up to the mid-century, the glasses to be used at dinner were placed on a side table or sideboard until called for. Only from the mid-eighteenth century were wine glasses and tumblers placed to the right of the diner on the table. The wine cooler was often on wheels, so that it could be moved from under the sideboard for convenience, for example after the departure of the ladies. The large dining table was covered with a white linen tablecloth which extended to the floor. This protected the wood, and hid any joins in the table. Diners used the tablecloth as a napkin, to wipe their mouths, much to the horror of foreigners. The tablecloth's removal at the end of the main course was a signal of a change in the nature of the dinner: before, the business was eating; after, it was drinking.[31] Drinking wine during dinner occurred only when a toast was given. Small wine glasses, sufficient for one draught, were kept on side tables, together with the wine and would be served by the footman/servant, and re-charged for the next toast and, if a different wine was being used, the glass was rinsed before being refilled. Incidentally, in the early eighteenth century, tall, slim 'toasting glasses' were made to be broken after a single use by snapping off the stems; it was considered that, after toasting the health of a fair lady present, it devalued the toast to use it to drink to another lady. As glass was expensive, this was not a common occurrence (plate 3.5).

The butler was responsible for the wine at dinner and his job of decanting began before any guests arrived. There was advice available in books regarding all aspects of domestic economy, including the duties of servants. One was *The footman's directory and butler's remembrancer* (1823) where the butler could find instructions on decanting wine:

a)   it is important not to shake or disturb it so place the bottle on the floor between your feet and hold it there with one hand, using the other to draw the cork.

b)   If decanting Port, keep the same side uppermost as it lay in the cellar and be careful not to drain it too much as there are generally two-thirds of a wine-glass of dregs in each bottle. Regarding white wine there is little sediment, but when decanting, pour it slowly and raise the bottle up gradually.

c)   Wine should never be decanted in a hurry.

d)   If there are guests for dinner and several types of wine are required, be careful not to confuse them, rather use silver labels on each bottle and, if you run out of silver, use written labels.[32]

A wine funnel, used from the middle of the eighteenth century, solves the problem of decanting. Because wine was decanted in the cellar, silver funnels can reflect whatever light there is to ensure no sediment gets through. The job is generally done by holding the neck of the bottle over a candle or other light source so that as soon as any sediment is discerned, the decanting can be stopped.[33] Incidentally, regarding the cleaning of decanters, while the following have been used – sand, cinders, coals, eggshells, wood ashes etc. (some of which could scratch the glass) – the *Footman's directory* recommends thick brown paper, 'cut into very small bits, so as to go with ease into the decanters, then cut a few pieces of soap very small, and put some water *milk-warm*' on top, and 'work this about'.[34]

Formal dinners in the eighteenth century were served *à la française*, which meant that the table was already laid with the first course, comprising various dishes, sweet and savoury, before the guests entered the dining room. It was recommended that the hostess tell her guests that they should 'see the dinner' and inform them what wine or other drink was on the side table.[35] Servants handed heated plates to each of the guests who then served themselves from the dishes nearest to them. Among the papers of the Maunsell family from Limerick are plans, possibly drawn by the hostess, of the layout of the dining table that included the names of the guests and where they were to be seated, the food and wines to be served, and where each of the dishes and the table decorations should be located (plate 3.6), rather similar to Chancellor Jocelyn's custom (noted above).[36] Cookery and housekeeping books had helpful illustrations of neatly balanced arrangements of dishes on a table for the prospective hostess. Usually the first course consisted of soups, stews, vegetables, fish and meat, all arranged around an attractive centrepiece. Just before the guests had finished the first course, the servants brought in one or sometimes more 'removes', which meant the removal of one or two dishes, replaced with one or two more. Together, this comprised the first course. As already mentioned, guests would help themselves from the one or two dishes in front of them, then offer them

3.5 Gawen Hamilton, *Group portrait, probably of the Raikes family* (*c.*1730), oil on canvas.
Courtesy of the Yale Center for British Art, Paul Mellon Collection.

to their neighbour; in order to get a dish further away, it was imperative to catch the eye of the footman or, as Paston-Williams puts it, 'a seasoned diner would make sure the footman was suitably bribed beforehand'.[37] And, as wine was not placed on the table, guests were again dependent on the footman when they wanted a drink. However, service *à la française* was replaced in the second half of the eighteenth century by service *à la russe*, which dispensed with the 'removes', and it became the role of the servants to serve each guest in turn with vegetables and other dishes, an arrangement that is familiar to us today. This new way of dining heralded the various ranks of cutlery placed on each side of the plate, and the assortment of drinking glasses for different wines at each place setting, laid in advance of the guests being seated. Another innovation on the table after 1800 was the decanter

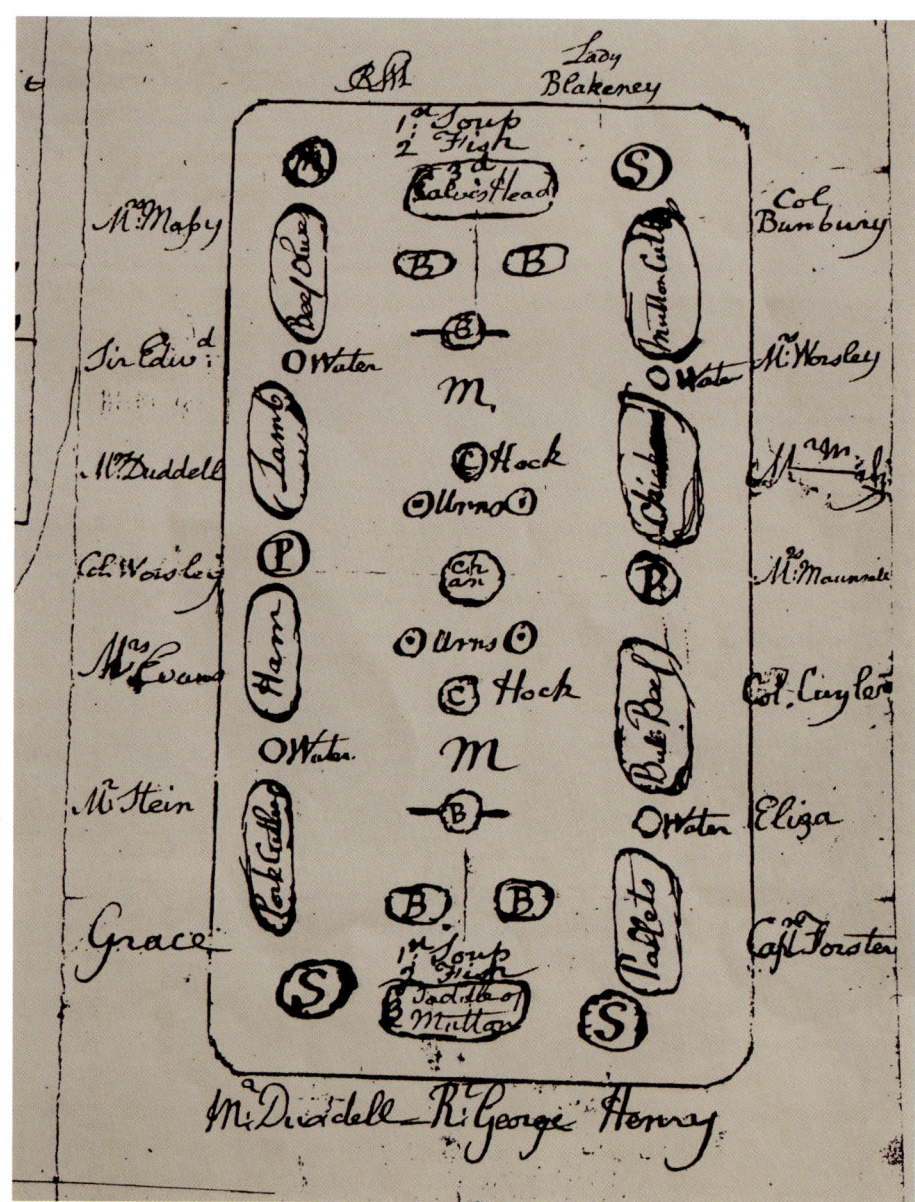

3.6 Table place setting from the Maunsell Papers. Courtesy of the late Knight of Glin.

carriage or trolley on which one or two decanters could be wheeled around the table for the convenience of the guests (see Chapter 4).

If the supply of wine was drying up, having the cellar directly under the dining room to which the butler or the host could descend by way of a trapdoor must

3.7 Philippe Mercier, *The sense of taste* (*c*.1745), oil on canvas. Courtesy of the Yale Center for British Art, Paul Mellon Collection.

have been convenient, though somewhat alarming for the guests. This was an architectural innovation at Barbavilla in Co. Westmeath, enjoyed by the Smythe family.[38] However, in the dining room at Monticello, President Thomas Jefferson's home in Virginia, was a device designed by the president and built into each side of his chimneypiece: a dumbwaiter – a box into which a servant in the wine cellar below would insert a bottle which would then be pulled up to the dining room and removed by Jefferson or a servant. When not in use, the apparatus was concealed by doors.

Desserts included numerous candied fruits and dainty dishes of nuts and olives: a show-stopper like a 'pyramid' could be created if you had a 'confectioner's room' as the FitzGerald family had in the basement of Leinster House. Unfortunately, there appear to be no accounts extant regarding the desserts and confections that came from that room. However, the dessert table at a formal dinner at London's Norfolk House in the 1750s gives an idea of the artistry involved. A guest described '… a Beautiful Park, round the edge was a Plantation of Flowering Shrubs, and in the middle a Fine piece of water, with Dolphins spouting out water, & Dear [*sic*] disbursed Irregularly over the Lawn, on the Edge of the Table was all the Iced Creams & wet & dried Sweetmeats, it was such a piece of work it was all left on the Table till we went to coffee'. In an advertisement in the *Dublin Journal* in October 1749, Elizabeth O'Brien, 'flower maker from London', informed readers that at her shop in Capel Street she 'makes and sells all kinds of artificial Flowers, Trees, Hedges and Arches for Deserts [*sic*]'.[39] Failing that, then sets of two to six glass salvers on top of each other in diminishing size, laden with ice creams, creams and all kinds of decorative delicacies, with perhaps a syllabub in a glass on the top (and smallest) salver, was quite acceptable (plate 3.7). Horace Walpole described these as 'puerile puppet-shows'.[40] Apart from the 'puppet-shows', the dessert course was an opportunity for some, like Thomas Cobbe at Newbridge House, to display his 'magnificent' china dessert service for thirty-six people.[41]

When the tablecloth was removed, the ladies would take a glass or two of wine, and retire to the drawing room. At this point, the men shunned the small glasses preferring the larger goblets.[42] The painter and poet Caroline Hamilton (1777–1861) described in a poem 'A Country Dinner' what seemed to be the correct moment for the ladies to retire:

> … No, No Sir my Dicky [his son] shall write a good hand
> And learn from myself the true value of land.
> For Gentlemen tell me what man is the worse
> For knowing the secret of filling his purse?
> A wink makes the parlour with laughter resound
> And the Hock and the Claret go briskly around:
> So Madam conceives it high time to retire,
> And the ladies encircle the Drawingroom fire …[43]

From this point, drinking among the gentlemen required the availability of a chamber pot, often to be found within the sideboard or behind the shutters or a screen, to the horror of a Frenchman who wrote that 'it is a common practice to relieve oneself while the rest are drinking; one has no kind of concealment and the practice strikes me as most indecent'. At Strokestown House a chamber pot was kept in a 'secret' place outside the dining room door, to be brought in by a servant as required. Apparently it was not uncommon in England: Prince Pückler-Muskau (who also visited Ireland) wrote to his wife of 'an old admiral who, clad in his dress uniform … made much use of this facility for a good ten minutes, during which period we felt as if we were listening to the last drops from a roof gutter after a long past thunderstorm'.[44]

Invitations to dine were excuses not only for those who wanted to show off their houses and possessions, but for those who wanted to see both. The very act of the 'parade' from the drawing room or library, where the guests assembled before dinner, to the dining room, was choreographed so that guests could admire the furniture, paintings, and the décor as they made their way to dine. Robert Smith, at an auction at Dawson Grove, may have felt that his guests would be impressed at his purchase of much of the silver cutlery on which Viscount Cremorne's coronet was engraved or, was he planning to have it melted down and recreated, a practice that was not unusual? As for the amount of food and wine enthusiastically served at dinners, it was undoubtedly excessive though those hosting firmly believed that they were being hospitable and taking care of their guests' needs. It was similar in England. There, a French visitor wrote in 1784, 'You are compelled to extend your stomach to the full in order to please your host. He asks you all the time whether you like the food, and presses you to eat more'. Apparently nothing had changed greatly since John Loveday's remark in 1732, that the Irish 'always praise the dishes at their own tables' and expected the same from their guests.[45]

CHAPTER 4

The paraphernalia of wine-drinking

'The principal point of ambition is to outdo his neighbours in hospitable profusion'.[1]

Displaying their wealth was of prime importance for the ascendancy in Ireland, and from the second half of the eighteenth century the dining room provided the ideal setting, a place where hosts and guests would sit for hours enjoying the room itself, its décor, furniture and furnishings, as well as the vast amount of food and wine served in various items of silverware, glassware and china. Many dining rooms announced their function by the appearance of bunches of grapes in plasterwork on the ceilings and/or walls, and often in the decoration on the marble chimneypieces, as has been mentioned earlier. Silver accoutrements came into their own at this time, enhancing the pleasures of drinking wine – small items such as labels or tickets, funnels, strainers, nutmeg graters, tasters, waiters for serving, coasters, as well as, for those who could afford them, punchbowls and monteiths; there were also larger (and more expensive) items such as cisterns and fountains, ice buckets, wine coolers and, possibly, a candelabra as a centrepiece on the table. As one writer puts it, 'Silver for serving wine had … probably the longest pedigree of any silverware'.[2] But silver was only part of the wine equipage. This chapter will look at some of these items as they appeared in inventories of the period, or that were to be found among collections that were often disposed of by sale or by auction.

WINE COOLERS AND CELLARETS

The wine cooler was not just for showing off the abundance or the quality of one's wine, nor purely to keep the wine cool or at room temperature: it became an object of desire for its own sake, as its design and decoration adapted to current fashions. There were basically two forms of wine coolers: those that held one or two bottles that were placed on a side table or sideboard and could be brought to the dining table after the departure of the ladies and the servants, and those that held a number of bottles standing in iced water on the floor. It is probable that the '4 gilt fluted vine and grape wine coolers (1814) 596 oz' in the Powerscourt plate inventory were not for the floor.[3] Those for the table usually had baize bases that allowed the wine to be moved around without damaging the mahogany tabletop.

Cellarets[4] could also stand on the floor: they are designed to keep the wine at room temperature. Wine coolers are lined with metal to allow for ice, cellarets have

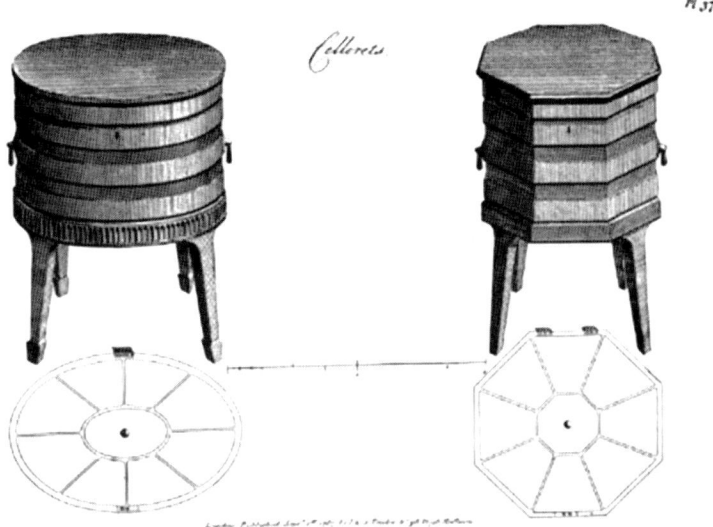

4.1 Drawing of cellarets from George Hepplewhite, *The cabinet maker and upholsterer's guide* (1794, 1897 ed.), plate 37.

interior divisions to separate the bottles (plate 4.1). An advertisement in the *Dublin Evening Post* in March 1793 lists furniture belonging to the bishop of Down at his Dublin house on the corner of Clare Street and Merrion Square, that included an 'elegant side board with pedestals, vases, wine cooler, and two pier tables to match'. This set of dining furniture may have been similar to James Wyatt's suite, already mentioned, designed for Castle Coole, Co. Fermanagh, and executed by John Stewart of Dublin, where, shaped like a sarcophagus, the large wine cooler was fluted and had a lion mask and painted *tôle* medallion.[5]

An unusual nineteenth-century Irish mahogany wine cooler, auctioned in Adam's in 2007, was described as 'of tapering tub shape', with corners wrapped by bands of acanthus; on each side was a laurel wreath, one filled with the crest of the Mathew family (see Chapter 3), the other with the initials 'F.M.' for Francis Mathew who had commissioned the architect Richard Morrison to extend and rebuild Thomastown House in Co. Tipperary in the early nineteenth century, after which it became known as Thomastown Castle (plate 4.2). Wine coolers were made in a variety of shapes and materials – from the early oval or round, to the later square, octagonal, hexagonal, even kidney shapes and, in the late eighteenth and early nineteenth centuries, the classical sarcophagus shape became popular. Most of those to be found in Irish inventories were made of mahogany, many produced by Irish cabinetmakers who were probably working from the same pattern books as their English counterparts. Size varied from small, which could be placed on

4.2 Nineteenth-century mahogany wine cooler, Irish, of a tapering tub shape, measuring 93cm long, 64cm wide, 68cm high. Reputedly from Thomastown Castle. Courtesy of Adam's, Dublin.

the table or the sideboard, to a large piece of furniture that was left on the floor, often beneath the sideboard or side table. Lined with tin, lead, zinc or brass to hold the iced water, many were on legs that terminated with castors, to be rolled out when required, and some (after the 1770s) had hinged lids. At Borris House, Co. Carlow, a large circular mahogany wine cooler with a deeply gadrooned lower section, after a design by Gillows, the English furniture-makers, is typical of earlier European marble versions. Here too is a pair of sarcophagus style wine coolers.[6] Wine coolers were also made of gold, silver, porcelain, glass and marble. According to Alison FitzGerald, the workshop of Thomas Sutton was the most productive in Dublin during the 1720s, where a silver wine cooler (1727) was made for Robert FitzGerald, nineteenth earl of Kildare.[7] These were highly valued items of display in the dining room and much featured in paintings, drawings and caricatures of the time. According to Philippa Glanville, author of *Silver in England* (1987), the idea of a wine cooler for a single bottle was a French refinement: she cites the earliest and most valuable as the pair of gold buckets, formerly at Althorp, the Spencer seat at Northampton, but apparently originally made for the first duke of Marlborough. They appear in the Marlborough plate inventories of 1712 as 'two very large gold ewers'.[8]

Most large houses had a supply of ice all year-round from the specially constructed icehouses in the grounds. The most common construction of these consists of a large egg-shaped space usually of brick, entered through a brick or stone-vaulted tunnel, the floor level of which strikes at its mid-point. The lower portion was packed with snow and ice, crushed to form a solid mass, and a layer of straw applied for insulation. The earliest example of an icehouse in Ireland is thought to be that at Tristernagh Abbey, Co. Westmeath, and they were often built close to a river or pond to facilitate the workers who filled it. That at Castletown, Co. Kildare, is on the banks of the River Liffey, and among the eighteenth-century accounts, is the cost of the whiskey provided to warm the men who were filling it.[9]

DECANTER STANDS

Decanter stands were usually made of mahogany, square or rectangular in shape, with six or eight compartments and a handle. Some were on castors for ease of movement. Called 'gardevins' or 'wine coopers' in furniture inventories, where a substantial number are to be found, including three at Clogrenan Lodge, Co. Carlow: 'an oval cooper', a '4-bottle cooper' and '1 box cooper with lock and key'.[10] Another item, called a decanter carriage, or trolley, became available from about 1800 as a vehicle that could be transported easily around the table on small castors or rollers: the early versions were made of wood, boat-shaped with a bow each end, two coasters inside for the decanters, a baize base, and the castors tucked in underneath. Later the boat became a trolley, made in silver or silver-gilt and the wheels were larger and highly visible.[11] A description of a pair of these carriages is contained in a bill from Edward Thomason, a goldsmith, to King George IV: 'Two Carriages with complete Axled to move and turn Conveniently upon the Dinner Table – each capable of holding 2 decanters made of Silver stamp'd at H.M. Assay Office ... surrounded with all the Battles of the Late War [Napoleonic], beautifully worked in Alto Relievo'. The price for both, and a 'Canteen with Lock and lined with Crimson' in 1826 was £99.[12] Apparently the king had been concerned that his guests who sat on either side of him had to rise from their chairs to pass the wine, and so had someone enquire of Thomason if he could invent something to solve this inconvenience.

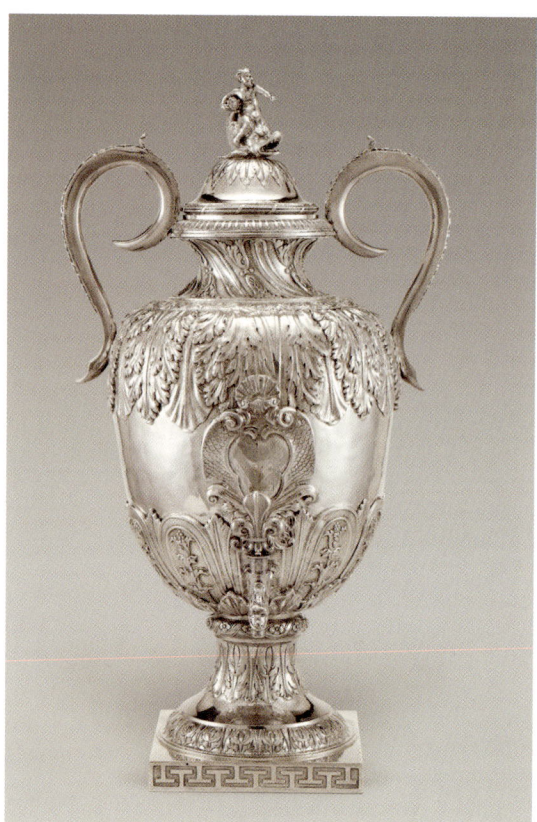

4.3 a&b Two views of a silver fountain, made in Paris (1661–3), possibly by Jean Leroy (French master, 1625). Courtesy of the J. Paul Getty Museum, California.

CISTERNS AND FOUNTAINS

Cisterns were used with fountains in the service of wine. They were convenient for washing glasses between toasts (plates 4.3 a&b). Glasses, filled at the sideboard, were served to guests on a salver or waiter, and returned for rinsing at the fountain. The cistern below the fountain served to catch the water. These large items of silver proclaimed the status of the owner and were prominently displayed – often in an alcove – in the dining room. They were luxury items, often the most expensive of the owner's possessions. To illustrate this, according to information on the Parker wine fountain in the Victoria and Albert Museum, in the eighteenth century 'a coach could cost between £60 and £120, and a Kneller full-length portrait about £35; the cost of a silver wine fountain could be £1,220'. According to the same source, these items were issued to ambassadors for state dinners, and to the speaker of the House of Commons.[13]

'One large silver cisterne' is listed among the possessions of the duke and duchess of Ormond at Kilkenny Castle and Dunmore House, Clonmel in 1675.[14] Another appears in the inventory of Nathaniel Clements at his Henrietta Street home, listed one hundred years later in 1775; a cistern and fountain, marked by the London silversmith David Willaume, believed to have been supplied to Chambre Brabazon, fifth earl of Meath, in 1707, was later bought by the future King George II in 1727. Joseph Leeson in 1742 ordered a substantial amount of silver from the English silversmith George Wickes that included a cistern.[15] Wickes had provided the famous Leinster dinner service for the nineteenth earl of Kildare in the 1740s, which cost over £4,000 at the time. Said to be the most complete surviving aristocratic service, it was sold at auction in Christie's of London in 2012 for £1,721,250. In 1727, Thomas Sutton, the Dublin goldsmith, provided the earl with a silver cistern and his son, the twentieth earl (later first duke of Leinster), completed the set in 1754 with a wall fountain for washing glasses, by Robert Calderwood. The cistern was used as a table centerpiece in the 1730s and later when the fashion for cisterns had long passed.[16] More unusual is the 'French China' (annotated '*Rouen Faience*') cistern and fountain listed at Dromoland House, Co. Clare in 1753.[17]

GLASSES AND DECANTERS

Mention is made in *Wild sports of the West* (published in 1832) of an 'eggshell' drinking bout in a poteen house in rural Ireland, and a note explains that, as glass was not plentiful, eggshells were substituted as drinking vessels.[18] Indeed two shells are illustrated among a collection of glassware in a book called *Popular songs of Ireland* (1839) (plate 4.4). How successful this was as the drinking session progressed is not recorded. According to Westropp, a Venetian glassmaker, Giacomo Verzelini,

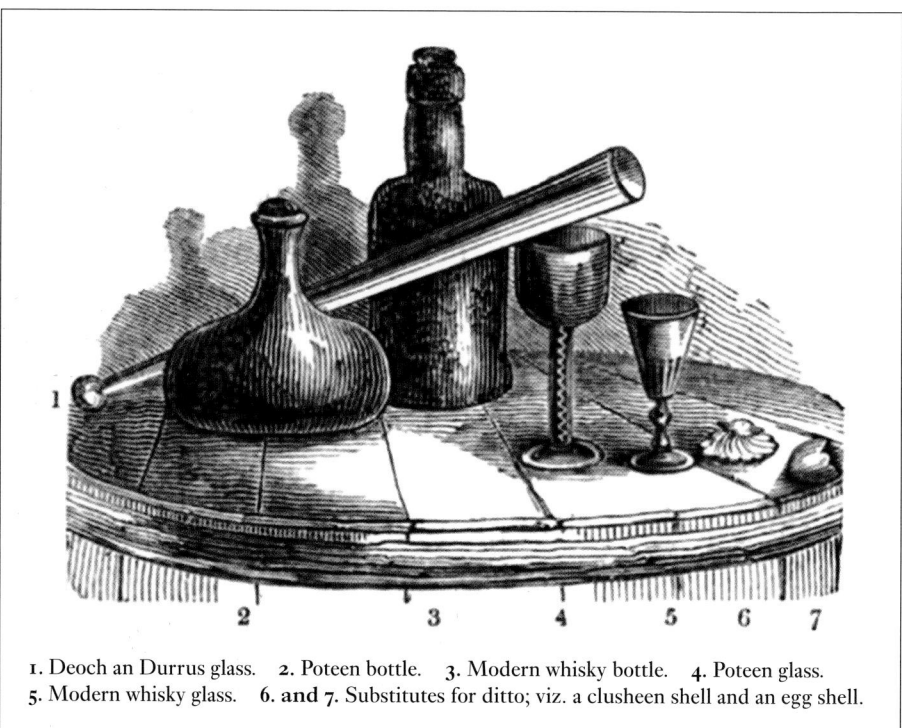

1. Deoch an Durrus glass.   2. Poteen bottle.   3. Modern whisky bottle.   4. Poteen glass.
5. Modern whisky glass.   6. and 7. Substitutes for ditto; viz. a clusheen shell and an egg shell.

4.4 Irish drinking vessels, including eggshells, illustrated in Thomas Crofton Croker (ed.),
Popular songs of Ireland (1839).

in 1575 obtained a patent from Elizabeth I to make Murano-style glass in England
and Ireland for twenty-one years and, in a 1628 inventory for Geashill, Co. Offaly,
residence of Lettice Digby, Baroness Ophaly, 'ten Venis [*sic*] glasses' are listed.[19]
In 1674 an English businessman, George Ravenscroft, impressed with the clarity
and transparency of the Venetian *cristallo* glass that allowed the colour of wine to be
fully appreciated, developed a new formula for glass using lead oxide and applied to
Charles II for a patent giving him the right to be the sole manufacturer in England.
The glass was strong, durable, clear and suitable for cutting and it revolutionized
glassmaking in that country. By the eighteenth century, the style of glass in Ireland
was dominated by English taste, according to Mary Boydell, and advertisements in
Dublin papers, such as the following from *Lloyd's News Letter* in 1713, acknowledges
the challenge:

> At the Round Glass House in St Mary's Lane, Dublin … is made and sold
> the newest fashion drinking glasses and all other sorts of flint glasses as good
> as any made in England at very reasonable rates.[20]

4.5 The Cobbe Goblet or, Williamite Loving Cup, *c.*1745, 32.5cm high. Image taken from Mary Boydell, *Irish glass* (Dublin, 1976).

Boydell is of the opinion that the Cobbe Goblet (plate 4.5), apparently also known as the Williamite Loving Cup, was made at the Round Glass House, dating it to around 1745, and the detailed engraving of King William on his horse was probably executed by a craftsman from England or the Continent.[21] The goblet, which is 32.5cm high, was the property of Archbishop Cobbe of Newbridge House, Donabate, Co. Dublin, sold by his descendant Thomas Leuric Cobbe at Christie's auction house in 1936, and is now in the Ulster Museum. It is described in the auction catalogue as

A Large Williamite Goblet, the bowl engraved with an equestrian figure of William III riding in a landscape with soldiers in the distance, and round the rim with a border of running scroll foliage; inscribed 'The Glorious and immortal memory of King William and his Queen Mary and perpetual disappointment to the Pope, the Pretender and all the enemies of the Protestant Religion'.[22]

Possibly thousands of wine glasses were engraved in the eighteenth and early nineteenth centuries to commemorate the Battle of the Boyne (see Chapter 5) but, as Boydell states, 'only a few are so magnificently engraved [as this] which is considered by some to be the most important surviving example of eighteenth-century engraved Irish glass'.[23] Also in the Ulster Museum is a set of six Williamite commemorative toasting glasses dated between 1770 and 1800; they are small (*c.*11cm), engraved on one side with a classical bust which may or may not be George III which is surrounded by the words THE IMMORTAL MEMORY, and on the other with a crowned harp flanked with fruiting vine. In an auction document among the Townley Hall Papers dated 1741, a glass engraved to THE GLORIOUS MEMORY was sold to Sir Laurence Parsons for nine shillings.[24] André Simon refers to such glasses as 'Jacobite', in which 'rare wine' was drunk 'in these beautiful glasses, the possession of which was at the time a treasonable offence'.[25]

An interesting aspect of some of these glasses was recognized later: a Bohemian glass-engraver, Franz Tieze (*c.*1842–1932), came to Ireland in 1865, and was employed by a number of glassworks in Dublin, where his engravings on glass, exhibited at the 1882 Irish Art and Manufacturers' Exhibition, were highly praised. It was later revealed that Tieze, and a Cork historian called Robert Day, collaborated from about 1900 to supply a ready market of collectors with fake Williamite glassware and Jacobite toasting glasses, often using eighteenth-century glassware with designs provided by Day, and engraved by Tieze. Research published by Peter Francis in the *Burlington Magazine* (23 October 1994) revealed that almost every glass item supposedly engraved in support of the Irish Volunteers of the late eighteenth century was by Tieze.

In his book on Irish glass, Westropp illustrates a goblet used on the occasion of King George IV's state visit to Ireland in 1821 which, he suggests, was probably made in Dublin. The engraved message on the glass reads 'Caed Mille Failte' which might indicate that it was not engraved by a true-born Irishman. The important archaeological find at Rathfarnham Castle in Dublin in 2014 produced a large cache of lead-crystal stemmed wine glasses, most of which were probably manufactured in Ireland or England between 1685 and 1710, and glass bottles between the sixteenth and eighteenth century. Eleven of these bottles are complete, and among the shards found at the site were five glass seals, or discs impressed with the owners' marks, as has been noted in Chapter 2.[26]

A visitor to Ireland in the 1760s remarked that 'One very favourable circumstance for the drinker, custom has here established, their glasses are very small; the largest of these in common use will not hold more, I believe, than about one third of a gill' (1 gill = 5 fl.oz).[27] As already mentioned, drinking wine during dinner in the early eighteenth century was restricted to when a toast was given, but once the ladies departed, the larger wine glasses or goblets were brought into use. The smaller glasses had gone out of fashion by the beginning of the nineteenth century, when 'rummers'– glasses with a large bowl and short stem, often made with thicker glass that made them ideal for use in taverns – became popular.[28] Images of men sitting or sometimes falling around tables in paintings, drawings and caricatures in the eighteenth and nineteenth centuries show rather small glasses. These would appear to be for toasting as they hold less than the average wine glass, and it was expected that the wine be drunk in one go.

Decanters, too, could show off the clarity and colour of wine that had been hidden by the dark green and black of the original wine bottle. It was more elegant to transport the wine from barrel to table by decanter rather than by the contemporary stoneware jars, or by bottles. Decanting enhances the drinking qualities of the wine itself, it separates the sediment from the wine, and it allows the wine to oxygenate. The decanter came into its own with the advent of the corkscrew and the laying-down of wines to mature. Early versions were similar to the 'shaft and globe' shape of wine bottles, but like the bottles themselves, by mid-eighteenth-century, they had become more cylindrical. The late eighteenth century saw the introduction of decanters with broad bases making them stable for shipboard use. Some of these, with more curved sides, were known as 'Rodney' decanters, named after the victorious British Admiral Lord Rodney. Like glasses, the decoration was in the cutting and engraving, such as bands of diamond shapes, stylized leaves and berries, and festoons of roses, thistles and shamrocks, the latter decoration appearing on numerous decanters after the Act of Union in 1800. The decoration and cutting on the lead glass would have been greatly enhanced by candlelight. At Newbridge House, '10 glass decanters with silver tops' appear on an inventory in 1839.

WINE JUGS, CLARET JUGS AND EWERS

Claret jugs or ewers were items that could be proudly displayed on a sideboard. There can be some confusion with the usage of these terms, but 'wine jugs' covers them all. 'Claret jugs' were known as such after about 1830 but the term does not mean that only Bordeaux wine should be served from them (plate 4.6).[29] Those made of silver can look like coffee pots, except that the latter had handles of wood, or of metal which was covered with wicker for insulation. At Newbridge House, the Cobbes had two claret jugs listed in their 1821 inventory. In *c*.1740 the Dublin

4.6 Pair of Irish wine jugs or ewers, with handles modelled as vine branches, by James Fray, Dublin *c*.1840. Courtesy of Adam's, Dublin.

Huguenot silversmith, David Bomes, made a pair of wine ewers, decorated with bunches of grapes, and with pinecone finials from the thyrsus, or staff, of Bacchus. In his inventory of silver, Lord Powerscourt lists '2 Pompeiian claret jugs'.[30] Apart from decorating the sideboard, these jugs frequently became presentation pieces by the mid-nineteenth century. The fashion for silver and glass wine jugs did not last long and they were replaced with the handled glass decanter that had a lip and a stopper, and which also became known as a 'claret jug'. Quite common in

4.7 Monteith bowl, silver gilt, 1715–16, English, made by Benjamin Pyne (active 1693–1727). Courtesy of the Cleveland Museum of Art, gift of Mr and Mrs Warren H. Corning, 1965.

Ireland were those made of a tough durable glass, suitable, as Boydell puts it, 'for the rumbustious entertainments of the time'.[31]

PUNCHBOWLS AND MONTEITHS

Punch, as has been discussed, was a popular drink in Ireland from the second half of the seventeenth century, usually made with wine or spirits, water, lemons, sugar, and spice. It was served from a large bowl, usually of silver. Monteiths, large circular or oval bowls with scalloped rims, often detachable, had a dual purpose: to keep wine glasses chilled[32] – the notched brim allowing glasses to hang from the foot into iced water – and, with the rim detached, it served as a punchbowl (plate 4.7). They could be made of glass, porcelain or silver. By 1730 the monteith was no longer fashionable, and while punch was continuing to be imbibed, punchbowls of porcelain imported from China (which could be personalized) became more popular.[33] In a list of plate, marked 'Weight of Plate by Mr Thomas Walker', dated 1741, among the Townley Hall Papers, a silver monteith (97 wt) was sold for £32 14s. 9d.[34]

SALVERS OR WAITERS, AND FUNNELS

Frequently mentioned in household inventories, salvers or waiters are like small trays and used for serving food or wine – in the case of the latter, they also help to save clothes from accidental spillage. The Ashmolean Museum has an example of one dating to 1734–5 made by John Hamilton of Dublin engraved with the coat-of-arms of Loftus impaling Hume, for Nicholas Loftus, first earl of Ely, who married Mary, daughter of Sir Gustavus Hume, in 1736. It is an early example of Irish rococo silver with an asymmetrical cartouche and shell decoration.[35] 'Four Square Waiters' are included in a list of Bishop Cobbe's plate in 1730.[36]

It is perhaps not surprising to find that Robin Butler, in his book on wine accessories, is an advocate for wine funnels (and decanted wine), and he lists the potential dangers of not using one:

> First, wine can easily be spilt between two narrow-necked glass vessels (i.e. bottle and decanter). Second, when one piece of glass touches another either or both can chip or crack. Third, when a corkscrew penetrates a cork, a piece of cork is sometimes dislodged into the bottle. Finally, old wine and port can throw a sediment, and this should be disturbed as little as possible.

He also mentions that any examples of silver funnels prior to 1750, while rare, are usually Irish.[37] Another writer, Michael Clayton, noted that the ribs on the outside of the funnel's stem allow air to escape from the decanter as it is being filled, and that the bend at the tip of the stem to one side prevents excessive aeration of the wine while being decanted.[38]

CORKS, CORKSCREWS AND NUTMEG GRATERS

Without cork as a wine bottle stopper, bottle ageing and the appreciation of fine wines might never have occurred. Before its arrival, wine was drunk, while still new, straight from the barrels in which they were shipped, using bottles and jugs to bring wine from cellar to table. Air could leak in and out of the barrels, turning the wine to vinegar before it could age, in a time when the ageing of wine was unknown. As mentioned in Chapter 2, the bottles were stoppered with tapered wooden bungs, wrapped in cloth that had been soaked in wax or oil, that projected from the bottle. Cork was found in ancient Egyptian tombs, and the Romans used it for many purposes: for example, they made beehives because of its low heat conduction, they used planks of cork in the construction of their houses, and it was useful for floating fishing nets. The use of cork in the seventeenth century was found to prolong the life of the wine by retarding the oxidation process, and thereby improving its flavour. Early corks were long and conical, with the smaller end driven into the neck of the bottle and extending, like the wooden bungs, from the bottle neck, so that it was easy to remove them with fingers.[39] But when bottles became standardized in the eighteenth century, a cylindrical cork of a standard size was required.

Cork oak trees, called *Quercus suber*, grow in the Mediterranean Basin.[40] According to Jancis Robinson, the tree is 'unusual in that its bark is so thick and resistant that it can be stripped from the trunk and large branches without hurting the tree', and 'the bark is sufficiently thick to yield commercially useful cork in its twentyfifth year'.[41] A report from two representatives of Gilbey, wine merchants, who travelled to the Spanish province of Gerona in 1876 to source a supplier of cork for the company, describes 'the mountains covered with [cork] trees in all directions … it is customary to strip a tree every seven or ten years … one proprietor of a cork forest sold £3,000 worth of cork wood annually, and his only expense was £60 a year for "stripping"'.[42]

Once the cork was fully inserted in the bottle, it required a tool with which to extract it. The earliest use of a corkscrew found by Robin Butler is in the minutes of the Wardens of the Goldsmith's Company in August 1648, where a 'scourer and worme' (or helix) is mentioned, but in 1605, the Star Chamber Accounts of the Vintners' Company mention 2*s*. 6*d*. paid for 'Corks to stop bottles'.[43] It seems that corkscrews derive from a gun worm, a tool from the 1600s with a single or double spiral end fitting used to clean musket barrels and to remove unspent charges from them. Ted Murphy, however, reveals that a Belfast academic, Helen Waddell, in her translation of the Latin lyrics of Sedulius Scottus of Liège, a ninth-century Irish scholar (and a lover of wine), found the earliest known reference to a corkscrew: 'Doth not the cork redolent of Balsam/Suffer the piercing of the iron corkscrew/Whence from the fissure floweth out,/A precious drop of liquor'.[44]

The arrival of the corkscrew meant that shorter, cylindrical corks could be driven in flush with the neck of the bottle, and the bottle could be laid on its side and left to mature. As André Simon points out, 'Vintage port and all vintage wines had been impossible before the invention of the corkscrew … wine merchants, … who locked up in their vaults wines of the finest vintages for future generations to enjoy, replaced mere importers of wine …'.[45]

4.8 Miniature silver nutmeg grater, H.V., London, 1698–9, possibly made by
Alexander Hudson. Height: 7cm. The Joseph M. and Aimee Loeb Collection,
1963, Metropolitan Museum, New York.

A popular design for Irish corkscrews in silver in the eighteenth century is
called a folding harp, but there were many examples of others made with bone, wood
and mother-of-pearl. A rare example was by Thomas Read whose business was at
4 Parliament Street, Dublin in the late eighteenth century. According to Butler,
'It is quite possible that Read's corkscrews, which employed the same principles
as Henshall's (Revd Samuel Henshall, who took out the first patent in August
1795), were produced earlier, but as he did not patent them, Henshall received all
the glory'.[46] Jonathan Swift, in an inventory of his household goods dated 1742,
mentions '2 Cork screws, one gold, other silver'.[47] Swift liked to make a display of
his gold and silver, taking at one stage an inventory of his 'plate and prices' which
showed £365 of purchases, a large amount at that time. He prized at least one of

the corkscrews, when he paid £6 6*s.* 5*d.* in 1703 to 'goldsmith for screw case'.[48] Laetitia Pilkington tells of Swift accusing her of stealing his gold corkscrew; he said very sternly to her that 'he was sure I had stolen it: I affirmed, very seriously, "I had not", upon which he looked for it and found it where he himself had laid it; "tis well for you", says he, "that I have got it, or I would have charged you with theft": "why, pray, sir, should I be suspected more than any other person in the company?" "For a very good reason", says he, "because you are the poorest".'[49] In 1735 Archbishop Bolton wrote to Swift to recommend that he call to a thatched cabin 'on the road between Kilkenny and Dublin', the home of a parson 'who is not poor', who possesses 'a little cellar of his own … where he always has a hogshead of the best wine that can be got, in bottles well corked upon their side, and he cleans and pulls the cork better, I think, than Robin': the latter was the Reverend Robin Grattan who kept 'a vast wine cellar in Belcamp, north of Dublin'.[50]

A corkscrew was often part of a gentleman's travelling cutlery set or canteen, such as that to be seen in the National Museum of Ireland, dated 1894. Another is part of the silver-gilt canteen set of Prince Charles Edward Stuart ('Bonnie Prince Charlie') in the National Museums of Scotland, that was possibly a twenty-first birthday present, and lost by the prince at the Battle of Culloden on 16 April 1746. It was made by Ebenezer Oliphant, Edinburgh, in 1740–1, and among the thirty-one pieces are two wine beakers, a wine taster and a combined mace-shaped nutmeg grater and corkscrew. The container of this set measures 18cm by 11cm, and is chased and embossed in the rococo style with thistles, flowers and leaves, representing the collar of the Order of the Thistle. The use of ground nutmeg and other spices, including mustard, to flavour wine, spirits and punch was common particularly among the Scots in the eighteenth century, and it was known that the prince enjoyed both (plate 4.8).[51] Apparently the poet John Keats (1795–1821) liked to cover his tongue with red pepper to intensify the coolness of his claret.[52]

SILVER BOTTLE AND DECANTER LABELS

One of the results of the binning of wine bottles was the introduction of wine labels: while the bin label indicated the contents in a particular bin, the wine label (known as a bottle ticket up to the twentieth century), identified the wine taken from the cellar and decanted. It should be noted that this wine label was quite separate from the printed paper labels that we are familiar with, that were introduced only from about 1860 when glue, strong enough to stick to glass, was available.[53] The eighteenth-century wine label was made of silver, and suspended from a chain around the neck of the decanter (plate 4.9). They became fashionable about the same time that decanters were appearing, the earliest dating to the mid-1730s. Jonathan Swift, in his will dated 1740, writes, 'I bequeath to the Earl of Orrery the enamelled Silver

a.

b.

c.

4.9 Silver bottle and decanter labels, *from top left*,
a. 'Claret' – an Edwardian Irish silver neck ring label by
M. Harris, Dublin, 1906; **b.** 'Claret'– George III label
with winged eagle by Hester Bateman, London, *c.*1780;
c. 'Sherry' – a George IV cast silver label by Edward
Farrell, London, 1827; **d.** 'Port' – a George III silver
label, modelled as an anchor, *c.*1800. Images courtesy
Woolley & Wallis Salisbury Salerooms.

d.

Plates to distinguish Bottles of Wine by, given to me by his Excellent Lady …'. The description was obviously an aid to his executors to identify the objects, as it appears to be the earliest-known reference to wine labels in an Irish context.[54] They were also used to identify spirits, sauces, toilet waters or cordials. In advice for the decanting of wines, the butler (or whoever was doing the job) was warned to be careful about confusing different wines: 'you will not be able to distinguish wine by colour, therefore have a number of written labels if you have not enough of silver ones to put on all the bottles'.[55]

The London goldsmith George Wickes included fifteen silver tickets with a dinner service ordered by the prince of Wales in 1740.[56] The quality of silver wine labels produced in Ireland in the last quarter of the eighteenth century was particularly high. One of the leading specialists in Dublin in the 1780s was John Sherwin Jr, who submitted over 300 labels for assaying in that year.[57] Benjamin Taitt, John Teare Sr, John Teare Jr, and Samuel Teare were also prolific in that area, and examples of their work can be seen in the National Museum of Ireland. Here too is a label, probably one of a set, that depicts the achievement of Richard Crosbie, an Irish aeronaut, ascending in an air balloon from the lawn of Leinster House in July 1785 in a failed attempt to cross the Irish Sea.[58] The design on early labels took the form of a putto or putti reclining among scrolls and bunches of grapes, with the name of the wine on a banner or scroll across the centre. These early examples were called escutcheons. Labels are much sought-after by collectors (particularly those where the name of the wine has been misspelt) and are greatly varied in their design. A fashionable shape in the 1780s was a crescent, and a neo-classical example of this, on which is engraved 'CLARET', complete with vase (on which were the owner's initials), swags and ribbons, was created by the Dublin silversmith Benjamin Taitt in about 1785. An alternative from about 1830 was the initial label. According to Butler, these were mainly for fortified wines and spirits: P, S and M for port, sherry and Madeira (or Marsala or Mountain), and W, G, R and B for whiskey, gin, rum and brandy. Sometimes a C is to be found, probably for claret, and H for Hollands (gin) or hock.[59] Included in an auction in 1778 at Hugh Henry Mitchell's house at 28 Dominick Street, Dublin, were 2000 ounces of plate, among which were four wine labels, described as 'highly chased and in the present taste'.[60] Nine silver bottle labels are listed in an inventory of Newbridge House, Co. Dublin.

METHERS, TWO-HANDLED CUPS AND OTHER DRINKING VESSELS

Methers were traditional drinking cups carved from wood, used from the medieval period to the nineteenth century.[61] They were round at the bottom and quadrangular at the top, with two or four handles, making it convenient to be passed from one guest to another for communal and ceremonial drinking.[62] A rare example of a

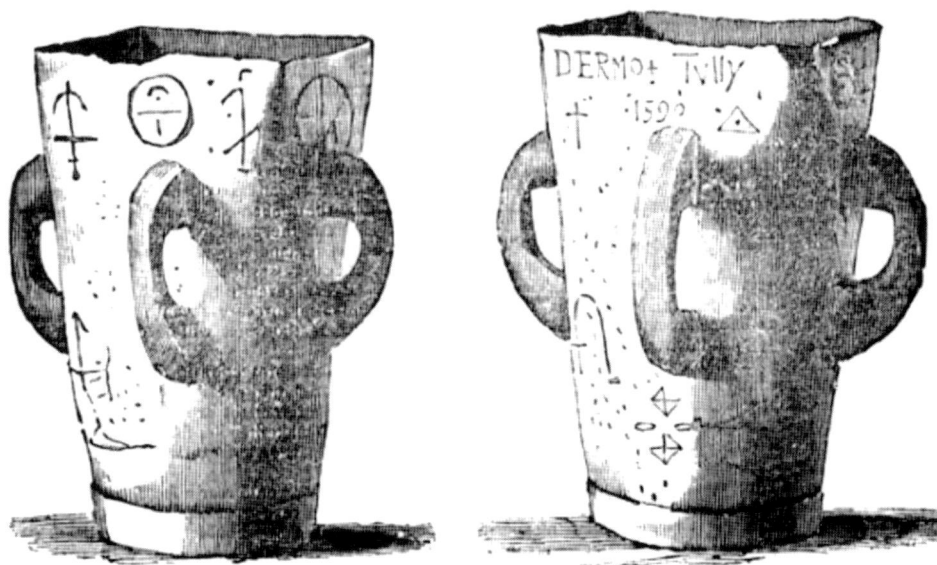

4.10 Drawing of 'The Irish Mether' from *Dublin Penny Journal*, 8 February 1834.

mether is that in silver-gilt by John Sherwin (1811) in the collection of the National Museum of Ireland, which has a band of vine leaves and bunches of grapes around the rim. Its use in whiskey-drinking in Co. Cavan (and, presumably elsewhere in Ireland) both before and with meals in the 1740s is interesting: according to Isaac Butler, 'To make it more agreeable they fill an Iron pot with ye spirit, putting Sugar, mint & butter & when it hath seeth'd for some time, they fill their square Cans which they call Meathers & thus drink out ym to each other'. What surprised him greatly was that while they drank it 'to intoxication', they were never sick after it.[63]

In a letter to the *Dublin Penny Journal* in 1834, a gentleman, who signs himself 'W. A---n.' at an address in Henry Street, writes that he is in possession of a mether, and sends the editor two drawings of it (plate 4.10). He describes it as eight-and-three-quarters inches high, the circumference of the top is eighteen inches, and its contents exceed two quarts. It is made of 'solid crabtree … with an inscription "Dermot Tully 1590" on one side. The upper part is square, while the bottom forms a circle'. He believes that methers were intended, not for whiskey-drinking, but 'for the rich wines, foaming ales and other generous drinks which were used in Ireland long before whiskey had been known to its natives'. He cautions anyone drinking from a mether, 'you must apply one of the four corners, and not the side to your mouth', and mentions that when Lord Lieutenant Townshend left Ireland, he had two massive silver methers made in London, where they were regularly introduced at his dinner parties; the guests usually applied the side of the vessel to the mouth, and seldom escaped with a dry neck-cloth vest, or doublet; Lord Townshend, however, after enjoying the mistake, usually called on his friend, the late Colonel O'Reilly, to teach the drill, and 'handle the mether in true Irish style'.[64]

Also for communal drinking, especially by societies and clubs, were two-handled cups, vast quantities of which were made in Ireland in the eighteenth and nineteenth centuries: in 1787–8 the goldsmith Matthew West made nearly 500 cups and had them assayed in Dublin.[65] They were used on occasions for toasting, such as christenings and weddings, and as presents, as well as prizes at the Curragh races and elsewhere. A number of these are listed in the Powerscourt inventory of plate (1885), which include the following:

1. Large plain two-handled cup 7 & three quarters [inches] by 6 & one qtr [inches], Irish, T.P. Baronets Arms one side, Boars head crest on reverse, dated 1743, 36 oz;
2. A large do., harp handle 6 & three qtrs. [inches] by 6 [inches], coat of arms, Crest & Motto Fidelis et Constans (dated 1726, w. 30 oz)[66]

Other drinking vessels of silver and plate are found in furniture inventories, such as a 'silver tanckard, double gilt, and one aquavitae cup', property of Robert Fitzsymons, a Dublin merchant, in the sixteenth century; and a 'Large Cup and Cover wt. 55 oz' in the Cobbe inventory.[67]

THE CLARET, SOCIAL OR HUNTING TABLE

In addition to the 'botle tray' in the dining parlour at Howth Castle was a round mahogany 'drinking table'. This may have incorporated a mechanism that enabled the bottle-tray to be moved about the table in relative safety (plate 4.11). A similar type of table was encountered by an army officer, staying near Limerick, in 1810, who described how, after the ladies had departed the table, 'a horse-shoe table, of curious workmanship, was placed before the spacious dining-room fire, and the master of the house sat in the centre of his friends' with a large cooper of claret at his feet. The host looked around at his guests in turn and, 'having passed them all in review, lifted up a panel from the table, discovering a figure of William III on horseback'. A bumper was filled, and the officer, curious about such deference, asked his host what the toast might be, to which he replied, 'The glorious, pious, and immortal memory!'.[68] The writer Evelyn Waugh was impressed when he encountered such

4.11 Claret or drinking table, attributed to Gillow's of Lancaster and London. The demi-lune leaf is removable and the hinged flaps can be folded down as in the image. Courtesy of Ronald Phillips Ltd.

'an excessively rare eighteenth-century piece' that had 'brass tramlines and a little wheeled carriage to carry the decanters'. He was convinced that any man who possessed such a piece of furniture, 'must confine himself strictly to male company, for no body of men once established there can be persuaded to leave for the chintz and chatter of the drawing room'.[69] An inventory of 1801 lists a claret table in the back parlour at Antrim House, Dublin, and at a furniture sale at Dawson Grove, Co. Monaghan in 1827, Sir Charles Coote of Ballyfin purchased one for £23 2s.[70] These became available towards the end of the eighteenth century for after-dinner drinking round the fire, but were fairly uncommon. To protect the drinkers from the heat of the fire, some had folding screens or a rail on which a curtain could hang, 'while coasters attached to a metal rod, or sliding in a well, were provided to hold the bottles' or decanters, protected from the heat by the shield back of the double coaster.[71] One appears in the furniture-makers Gillow's costbooks in 1801, described as a 'social table', fitted with japanned ice pails.[72] James Dowling Herbert, in his book published in 1836, described how, when the tablecloth was removed after a dinner at Kilkenny Castle, 'the table changed to a horse shoe form near the fire, [where] the flow of soul succeeded the feast of reason'.[73]

DUMB WAITER

On a tripod base with two or three tiers of revolving circular trays (usually of mahogany), dumb waiters were used when the servants had been dispensed with. More than one could be used on occasion, laden with wine, glasses and perhaps biscuits or sweetmeats, positioned next to the host at the table. Thomas Jefferson, who had five of these (though rectangular in shape), used them at dinner in his private dining room at the White House; he disliked having servants in attendance there, 'believing that much of the domestic and even public discord is produced by the mutilated and misconstructed [*sic*] repetition of free conversation at dinner tables, by these mute but not inattentive listeners' (plate 4.12). He brought back from France the idea of such a piece of furniture on which were arranged the entire meal, and placed between the guests who helped themselves. Another dumb waiter of Jefferson's was the pulley kind in his home at Monticello, mentioned in Chapter 3, where wine and other items were conveyed from the cellar to the dining room.[74] First made in the 1730s or 1740s, Irish versions often have turned or built-in coasters incorporated. A study of eighteenth- and nineteenth-century furniture inventories shows few dumb waiters in Irish houses: this might indicate that families living in Ireland were not bothered by the presence of servants (who probably knew all of their business anyway) or, as with colonial societies such as those in the West Indies and later in India, that they simply enjoyed being waited upon.

Another item in Jefferson's private dining room was a painted canvas cloth that covered the floor to protect it.[75] This material was frequently used in Irish dining rooms, halls and stairs. In 1785 at Caledon, Co. Tyrone, the hall was covered with canvas painted to resemble the marble pavement beneath it, and in many Irish dining rooms it was also used around sideboards to protect the floor from food and wine stains.[76]

There can be no doubt about the fact that entertaining – dining and wining – was of great importance in eighteenth-century Ireland. While the drawing room is usually associated with women, where comfortable seating, fashionable furniture, and beautiful fabrics (often lining the walls) were to be seen, the dining room is one room into which men put lots of thought, money and time. It was used mainly when the family had company and it was from this room that the women removed

4.12 Mahogony two tier drink waiter with revolving top on three elegant cabriole supports with brass castors. Courtesy of Adam's, Dublin.

themselves to the drawing room after the meal had been served. Men frequently chose the dinner service, the silverware – often, picked up at auctions, which could, if necessary, be melted down and re-designed to their taste – and all the accoutrements as outlined above. Added to all of that came the choice of wines. They were aware that on this display they would be judged.

CHAPTER 5

Male bonding and toasting

The old habit at dinner parties of men settling themselves down to serious drinking sessions after the women had departed to tea and coffee in the drawing room, which was carried on well into the twentieth century, has finally died out. The custom was as strong in Ireland as in England. There, a visitor described the departure of the ladies as 'the signal for alarming drinking … there is not an Englishman who is not supremely happy at this … moment'. In Ireland in 1825 Lord Blayney of Castle Blayney, Co. Monaghan, was described as trotting off 'with all his merry men to a little adjoining room, which was called his own glory hole, and there we had such fun, such jolly stories, that it was difficult to leave our seats'.[1] The Scottish statesman and philosopher, Sir Gilbert Elliot, succeeded in remaining sober at a dinner in London with colleagues because he was the only one drinking port and 'had not the circulation of my bottle to draw me on'. He wondered how men of business and of politics managed to reconcile drinking to excess with their public lives: 'Fox drinks what I should call a great deal, though he is not reckoned to do so by his companions, Sheridan excessively, and Grey more than any of them … Pitt, I am told, drinks … generally more than any of his company…'.[2] An anecdote recounted in *Bottlescrew days* tells of another Scotsman, the author Henry Mackenzie, at a drinking party:

> He was keeping as free from the usual excesses as he was able, and as he marked companions around him falling victims to the power of drink, he himself dropped off under the table, among the slain as a measure of precaution, and lying there his attention was called to a small pair of hands working at his throat. On asking what it was a voice replied: 'Sir, I'm the lad that's to loosen the neckclothes'. Here, then, was a family, where on drinking occasions it was the appointed duty of one of the household to attend, and, when the guests were becoming helpless, to untie the cravate in fear of apoplexy or suffocation.[3]

Looking back in her autobiography, Frances Power Cobbe (1822–1904) of Newbridge House, Co. Dublin, suggests that drinking among men 'must have prevailed to a disgusting extent upstairs and downstairs'. She goes on,

> A fuddled condition after dinner was accepted as the normal one of a gentleman, and entailed no sort of disgrace. On the contrary, my father has

told me that in his youth his own extreme sobriety gave constant offence to his grandfather, and to his comrades in the army; and only by showing the latter that he would sooner fight than be bullied to drink to excess could he obtain peace.[4]

The second part of her remarks brings up the subject of 'manliness' and the expectations that came with it. For young men in this society, it was about getting the balance right. From early on in their youth they were possibly exposed to the use (and abuse) of alcohol in their own homes, by their families and family friends. But they were also made aware that, while social ritual usually involved the consumption of alcohol, it was the mark of a 'gentlemen' to exercise self-control in this regard, to handle liquor, and to keep himself at a distance from bad behaviour. In *Castle Rackrent*, Sir Patrick remembers how, 'when I was a little boy, the first bumper of claret he [his father] gave me after dinner, how he praised me for carrying it so steady to my mouth – here's my thanks to him – a bumper toast'. Indeed it was said of the same that 'not a man could stand after supper but Sir Patrick himself, who could sit out the best man in Ireland, let alone the three kingdoms itself'.[5] Often it was a case of 'Don't do as I do, but do as I say'. On the other hand drinking to excess was almost a rite of passage for young men: the bottle was handed around in turn at male gatherings, each man keeping pace with the others, forming a type of fraternal bond, an unspoken challenge felt by each one, and nobody would risk losing face by opting out.[6] William Conolly, heir to his uncle's Castletown estate, who came to Ireland in the 1730s, was aware of the social obligation to drink: his wife, Lady Anne, remarked that 'his head had not been enough settled to do anything for drinking you know does not agree with him 'tho he must practise it a little at his first coming into the country or he wou'd not please'.[7] Frequently drinking got out of hand as is evident from not only fiction of the period, but from the dramatist John O'Keeffe's *Recollections* in which he describes what some of the 'young bucks' of the period were up to. One was a wealthy young Limerick man known as 'the Child' who attended a performance in the theatre where he appropriated two rows in the gallery, one for himself and his friends, the other for their bottles of wine, and from where they shouted and verbally abused prominent members of the audience, before being ejected from the theatre.[8]

In spite of Lord Orrery's account of the dinner he attended in Co. Cork (see Chapter 3), such excess was not always the rule, according to some. In 1731, Viscount Perceval's agent advised him that though Ireland possessed a deserved reputation for 'hard drinking' this was no longer justified; it was, he explained, 'reckoned churlishness to withhold liquor from a person who likes to drink, yet it is accounted ill manners to press it upon those who show a dislike to it'. And in 1759, another visitor 'noted that even when the bottle circulated freely, individuals were not required to charge their glass other than at their own pace'.[9] Comments like these, however, separated by almost thirty years, cannot be taken as general trends. While, towards the end of the century, figures show that less wine was being imported into Ireland, the accounts of wine being 'pressed' or even forced upon guests simply varied from one host to another throughout the century.

Having the capacity to hold one's drink was considered the mark of a 'real' man. In medieval England, round-bottomed drinking glasses, which had to be emptied before they could be set down (upside-down), were in use, and the Prince Regent, in the eighteenth century, instituted the practice of snapping off the stems of wine glasses at parties 'to ensure that his guests always drank the whole thing'.[10] A visitor to Derry, the actor John Bernard, was invited to join a group of 'six-bottle men', as they were proud to be called, where 'bumpers were drunk for the evening out of half-pint goblets which were without a stand, in order to compel the bibber to empty their contents at a draught'. They were a group of 'old fox-hunters and country squires who, like certain plants, seemed to be kept alive by perpetual soaking'. Apparently it was surprising if one of the 'initiated' was unable 'after making a cellarage of his stomach, and stowing away his half-dozen' to stand 'with the most mathematical precision'. The same visitor found that, in more refined company, 'it was the custom to put a bottle of wine at each person's elbow, and let him fill as he pleased'.[11] William Hickey (a relative of the artist Thomas), son of an Irish lawyer in England, led a fairly wild life in the late eighteenth century dominated by drinking, mostly claret. In his memoir, he said of his own dinner parties, 'I always was ambitious of sitting out every man at the table where I presided' (i.e., drinking more than others while keeping sober); this, he claimed, made him 'a capital host', and confirmed his manly strength to himself and to his guests. He did not enjoy fox hunting, which would have appeared decidedly 'unmanly' to others at this time, but he managed, in his own mind at least, to maintain the reputation of a 'real man' due to his ability to consume vast quantities of wine. At dinner during a weekend in the country 'the men often remarked that although I shunned the chase, over the bottle I was as keen a sportsman as the best of them'.[12] Lord Orrery, as early as 1736, clearly saw what was happening and was, as always, forthright:

> Drunkenness is the touchstone by which they try every man, and he that cannot or will not drink, has a mark set upon him. He is abus'd behind his back, he is hurt in his property and he is persecuted as far as the power of malice and intemperance can go. A right jolly glorious-memory Hibernian never rolls into bed without having taken a sober gallon of claret to his own share. You wonder perhaps who this animal is? It is a Yahoo that toasts the glorious and immortal memory of King William in a bumper without any other joy in the Revolution than that it has given him a pretence to drink so many more daily quarts of wine.[13]

5.1 George Cruikshank (1792–1878), Mr Lambkin enjoying some wine in the company of friends. George Cruikshank, *The bachelor's own book* (1845). Courtesy of the Wellcome Collection.

Another writer described the pressure that was put upon men: 'You will think it rather of the marvelous, but it is no less true, that a middling drinker here will carry off his four bottles without being in the least apparently disordered. A man is looked upon, indeed, as nothing with his bottle here, that can't take off his gallon coolly.'[14] And in an English tract, *The tricks of the town*, sports, like hunting, hawking, fishing and fowling, are commended as 'noble, manly and generous'.[15]

The well-known rake, Thomas 'Buck' Whaley (1766–1800), who famously made a wager to travel from Ireland to Jerusalem and back within a year – and won it – admitted he 'should have been kicked out of the ballroom' in Brighton for his 'familiarity' and rudeness to the duchess of Cumberland, to whom he had just been introduced by the prince of Wales. Whaley blamed the wine he had drunk and the fact that he was Irish, 'But she good-naturedly imputed my conduct to the effects of wine – the only excuse our poor countrymen can make for their various absurdities and errors in all parts of the world'.[16]

Even in fiction 'manliness' and drinking go hand in glove: in Maria Edgeworth's *Ormond* (1817), Sir Ulick O'Shane entered his drawing room, accompanied by what he called his 'rear-guard, veterans of the old school of good fellows, who at those times in Ireland, times long since past, deemed it essential to health, happiness, and manly character, to swallow and show themselves able to stand after swallowing, a certain number of bottles of claret per day or night'.[17] However, in the same book, the eponymous Ormond, pressured into gambling rather than drink, had a way of dealing with it: he decided in advance to lose a certain sum and, upon reaching it, would promptly stop; 'by this means I have acquired all the advantages of yielding to the fashionable madness, without risking my future happiness'.[18]

The dramatist Robert Jephson was a friend to Edmund Burke and Oliver Goldsmith and an intimate friend to the Irish Shakespearean scholar Edmond Malone. Jephson secured a government appointment in Ireland where he remained for the rest of his life. Malone wrote of Jephson in his *Memoirs:* 'In the society of the "Castle" and its chief – amid the wit, talents and hospitality which then shone pre-eminent in Dublin, he found the position fitted above all others for that species of enjoyment, where the "flow of soul" was aided by liberal streams of claret and whisky punch'.[19] Tom Conolly of Castletown enjoyed Jephson's company and they wrote to each other occasionally in verse (plate 5.1). The following is an invitation from Conolly to Jephson in Blackrock, Dublin, dated 16 November 1802:

> Come here My Dr Jephson, come soon from The Black Rock …
> I'll give you some Good Wine, & some that will pass
> Upon those that don't know, A good Horse from An Ass
> But if you & I drink the good wine to ourselves
> It may last out some time between us drunken[?] --- [word unclear]
> For if once you let go, the key of the Wine Vault

> Give the good wine to all, it soon will be worth nought.
> As the wine we now get, between Taxes & Mixture
> Will lighten our Pockets, not mending our Fixture[?]
> To Mumm, when we have Company, Drink when we've done [?]
> The better our Beverage, The Better our Fun.

To which Jephson replied the following day:

> In verses so various your mind is enclos'd
> That I'm sometimes obliged to wish them transpos'd
> But thus much with pleasure I plainly make out,
> That you're witty, and funny, and merry and stout.
> As to wine I'm not nice, and all I require
> Is some Claret, some Wit and a good winter's fire.
> If you'll send me a Carriage next Tuesday by times
> I'll be with you by four, and explain all my rhymes.[20]

Another example of male bonding took place in Mayo in August 1798, during the occupation of Bishop Stock's residence, Killala Castle, by the French, mentioned in Chapter 2. Their enforced intimacy with the French officers over the period was helped by the bishop's fluency in their language, and evenings were spent in conversation, playing cards, 'enjoying the fine food and excellent wine that the French had requisitioned from the cellars and larders' of the bishop's loyal neighbours.[21]

TOASTS AND FRATERNITIES

In the early years of the seventeenth century the English military engineer, Sir Josias Bodley, was invited to the house of a Mr Morrison in Downpatrick, where he and others enjoyed a supper in the midst of which, Morrison lifted a glass goblet filled with claret 'which measured ten or eleven inches roundabout, and drank to the health of all and to our happy arrival'. Then, taking the glass from their host, each guest in turn thanked him and drank from the cup 'as much as he drank before us'. He then drank 'four or five healths of the chief men and of our absent friends'.[22]

    The origin of the term 'toast' – as in drinking to somebody's health – is linked to wine. It comes from, literally, a piece of spiced or charred toast that was dropped into a cup or bowl of wine either as a type of hors d'oeuvre or to improve the taste: when Falstaff calls for a quart of spiced wine in Shakespeare's *The Merry Wives of Windsor*, he asks for 'a toast in it'.[23] Unlikely as it may seem, toasting among men was yet another test of manliness. Perhaps this originated in Greece – offering a libation to the gods is not too far from proposing a toast to honour one's friends. Toasting was not as random as it is today: in formal settings there was a hierarchy attached to it – who could toast whom and when, and the king or queen was invariably the recipient of the first toast. Among Protestants, King William and the 'glorious revolution' were favourites and, according to Orrery, 'The person who refuses a goblet to this prevailing toast is deemed a Jacobite, a Papist, a knave'.[24] But supporters of the Jacobites 'would covertly toast "the king over the water" by picking up their wine glasses and passing them over the water jug'![25] They also developed other ways of toasting, for example, 'To Sorrell' – the horse that threw William III to his death; 'To £3 14*s*. 5*d*.' (James III, Louis XIV and Philip V), and 'To the three Bs' ('The Best Born Briton James III').[26] The toasts became so popular that they frequently appeared in newspapers throughout the country, which further fuelled the competition for the cleverest and the wittiest. They could, however, be sufficiently extreme to incite the masses. Toasts at Thomas Sheridan's Beefsteake Club during the Money Bill dispute were said to have played a part in rousing the Dublin crowd against him that ultimately resulted in his Dublin theatre, Smock Alley, being badly damaged.[27] As Powell puts it, ' … eighteenth-century toasting created an additional degree of unity and purpose, a collective bonhomie, an awareness of a shared past and a common set of goals in the present, and allowed the identification of friends and enemies in public'.[28]

Toasting, and the consumption of alcohol among groups of men, led to the forming of all-male clubs, fraternities, and associations throughout Ireland where they could meet, eat and drink (plate 5.2). According to Kelly, 'it was integral to the forging and maintenance of personal relationships that were necessary for the conduct of civil and political activity'.[29] Many coffee houses and taverns had established themselves in the cities and towns in Ireland and encouraged the custom of these associations. There were clubs dedicated to particular events like the Aughrim and the Culloden Societies. The Protestant Society of Dublin, which had been established by 1740, celebrated the first of July (the anniversary of the Battle of the Boyne) with a sermon at St Catherine's Church, Dublin, followed by dinner, with numerous toasts to King William, then paraded through the city 'wearing Orange cockades in their hats and carrying banners, to the accompaniment of drums and trumpets, cheering and pistol shots fired into the air'.[30]

Meanwhile, at the Royal Hospital, Kilmainham (*c*.1712), on an occasion celebrating the birthday of Queen Anne (1665–1714), over thirty-seven 'healths' (or toasts) were drunk, according to a document in the British Library, in which they are listed.[31] Next to the first three of these: 'Our Glorious Queen Anne', 'The Church as by Law Establish'd' and 'The Succession of the illustrious House of Hanover', it was noted that 'Guns [were] to be fired at Each of these Healths'. It is a most interesting list and, while too long to note here, the following gives a taste of what it contains:

Prosperity to Ireland under his Grace the Lord Lieut.,
His Grace the Duke of Shrewsbury, Lord Lieut of Ireland,
Prosperity to Great Brittaine,
To all Lovers of our Constitution in Church & State,
That her Majesty's Reigne may be longer as it has been more Glorious than
    any of her Predecessors;
May the interest of the Established Church always prosper & Increase
    against all Papists, Dissenters, & Friends of ye Pretender;
Prosperity to the University of Dublin & may it never want Encouragemt
    and Resolution to teach loyall & Orthodox Principles …

And the final two:

All other Lords & Members of her Majesty's Privy Councill present were
drank singly, Vizt (there follows a list of 20 people, concluding with 'The
Eight Stewds who tooke care of ye Company');
That we many never Want such a Number of Loyall & Honest Gentlemen to
Celebrate this Happy Day.

That these toasts were recorded and kept in the Southwell Papers is a measure of
how political the toasts were.

Non-political toasting, for those who simply wanted to enjoy themselves, but
did not feel up to the wit expected, there was help at hand in the form of *The royal
toast master containing many thousands of the best toasts old and new to give brilliancy
to mirth …*, published in 1791. Perhaps some members of the legal fraternity made
use of such a publication. They met in Dublin at the Bilton Arms in Sackville
Street where it was said that the wine consumed each term 'would have floated a
battleship'. The owner kept a coach for conveying his patrons to their chambers.[32]
They also frequented the Black Lion in Queen Street and the Rose Tavern in
Dame Street. Members of the Belfast Whig Club were described by Alexander
Haliday (a member of same) as 'our northern guzzlers', while the Dublin Whig
Club was described by Lord Chancellor Fitzgibbon as nothing but a 'porter club'
(plate 5.2).[33] In 1771, on Tuesday evenings, the Constitutional Society, opposed to
the government of Lord Townshend, met in the great room of the Phoenix Tavern,
to discuss politics: the admission charge was one shilling, purchased at the bar from
where wine was 'moderately distributed'. The society, which awarded medals to
the best speakers, became so popular that they had to transfer the meetings to the
Music Hall in Fishamble Street.[34]

The notorious Dublin Hellfire Club (plate 5.3), founded by Richard Parsons,
the first earl of Rosse, and the painter, James Worsdale (whose group portrait of
the club is in the National Gallery of Ireland), met in 1735 at the Eagle Tavern on

5.2 Thomas Rowlandson (1757–1827), *The brilliants* (1801). Courtesy of the Elisha Whittelsey Collection, The Elisha Whittelsey Fund, 1959, Metropolitan Museum of Art.

Cork Hill, Dublin and occasionally at a former hunting lodge built in the mid-1720s by Speaker William Conolly (1669–1729) in the Dublin mountains at Montpelier, where they reputedly drank copious amounts of punch and claret, were rumoured to play cards with the devil, and to indulge in blasphemous oaths and orgies.[35] Lord Rosse, as president of the club, apparently dressed as Satan with horns, wings and cloven hooves, and was called the 'King of Hell'. It seems a like-minded group met in 'a crumbling folly tower' overlooking the River Shannon at Doonass, Co. Clare.[36] Limerick had its own Hellfire Club, also immortalized in oils by Worsdale, commissioned by Edward Croker of Ballynagarde, which met at Askeaton Castle. The portrait includes, among the Limerick squires, the alleged only female member

5.3 Hellfire Club, Dublin. Photograph courtesy of Neil Jackman, Abarta Heritage.

of the club, Mrs Blennerhasset. The following poem by Daniel Hayes illustrates their activities:

> But if in endless Drinking you delight
> Croker will ply you till you sink outright,
> Croker for swilling Floods of Wine renowned
> Whose matchless Board with various plenty crowned
> Eternal scenes of Riot, Mirth and Noise
> With all the thunder of the Nenagh boys
> We laugh, we roar, the ceaseless Bumpers fly
> Till the sun purple's o'er the Morning sky
> And if unruly Passions chance to rise
> A willing Wench the Firgrove still supplies.[37]

Local folklore in Limerick tells of a test by which admission was gained to the club: '[They] had to show their prowess by drinking a bottle of wine, bottle of brandy, bottle of whiskey and a bottle of rum. Then he should walk along a straight line

5.4 Worsdale goblet, English, *c.*1745 (with later engraving?). Courtesy of the George H. Lorimer Collection, 1953, Philadelphia Museum of Art. The goblet is engraved with a scene of nine men at a table, with punchbowl, decanter and goblets, and the words The Hell Fire Club. Engraved on the back: 'James Worsdale Master of the Revels'.

some twenty yards in length'. If he didn't succeed in this trial, he was thrown from the window into the River Deel.[38]

A set of wine glasses, bearing the names and honorary titles used, were commissioned by members of the Dublin Hellfire Club; one, belonging to Worsdale, has survived. Engraved on it are 'The Hell Fire Club' and 'James Worsdale Master of the Revels', and an illustration similar to that of the portrait by Worsdale in the National Gallery of Ireland (plate 5.4).[39] A drink that was popular in Ireland and said to be imbibed by members of the Hellfire Club was called *scaltheen*, described as strong enough 'to make a corpse walk'. It was made from half a pint of whiskey, half a pound of butter and six eggs, carefully heated to avoid burning (which would spoil the taste) and to be 'taken red hot'.[40]

In 1792, the *Hibernian Magazine*, in a satirical exposé of the Cherokee Club of Dublin, a group of wealthy indolent young men who were terrorizing the citizens of Dublin in the late eighteenth century, set out a list of the ten reputed qualifications for membership, five of which are:

> In order to become a member … it is first necessary that the candidate should have carried off and debauched a MAID, a WIFE, and a WIDOW, or an indefinite number of each. Secondly, that he should have fought three duels; in one of which, at least, he must either have wounded, or have been wounded, by his antagonist. Thirdly, he must at some one time of his life have drank six bottles of Claret after dinner, in half pint bumpers, and given a new Cyprian[41] toast with each bumper. Fourthly, to arrive at the honour of the President's chair, it is absolutely necessary that the member should have killed, at least; one man in a duel, or a waiter in a violent passion. Fifthly, that no religious distinctions should disturb the tranquillity of the several meetings, it is absolutely necessary that the members in general should disavow every theological knowledge.

Despite the satire, the publication fairly accurately reflected the club's behaviour and, apparently, any member found sober after dinner was subject to a fine of thirty pounds for a first offence, fifty for a second, and expulsion from the club for a third. They wore a uniform of scarlet lined with yellow and edged with black and, having consumed their claret and dinner, they discussed 'what places of public amusement are open for the evening', and that being determined, whether their attack should commence with cat-calls or whistles, by direct assault or surprise and, having made their decisions, they would 'sally forth for action'. At places of entertainment, for example at the Rotunda or the theatre, they would enter with loud cat-calls, extinguish the candles, and terrify the crowds in the dark.[42]

Not many clubs were as extreme as the those described above. However, drunkenness frequently led to duelling, an activity about which it was said that

5.5 Thomas Rowlandson, *Sportsman's Hall, or Fox-Hunters Relaxing* (1806). Courtesy of the Elisha Whittelsey Collection, Metropolitan Museum of Art.

one was not a real man until he had 'smelt powder'. Beauchamp Bagenal from Dunleckney House, Co. Carlow, kept a couple of pistols on his dinner table. After the meal, the claret was produced in an unbroached cask, 'he would tap the cask with a bullet from one of his pistols, while he kept the other for any of those present who failed to do justice to his wine'.[43] Men with sporting interests in common established clubs that bound them together; members of the Sportsman's Club met at the Rose Tavern – they organized prizes for races run at the Curragh in Co. Kildare (plate 5.5).[44] There was the Jockey Club at the Curragh (called the Coffee House) and the various hunting societies, many of which were formed as subscription clubs, where every member paid towards the upkeep of the hounds and other fairly substantial expenses. To encourage conviviality rather than drunkenness, a Limerick hunt restricted the intake of wine at their gatherings to a bottle per man. When the president of the Duhallow Hunt failed to take his place at the head of their gathering he was levied a bottle of claret as a fine, while a bottle of champagne was levied at another hunt to anyone appearing without their uniform. Hunting songs that celebrated a good day's sport were fairly common – one was 'The Kilruddery Hunt', commemorating that event in 1744 in Co. Wicklow with the hounds of the earl of Meath, after which

> We return'd to Killruddery's plentiful board
> Where dwells hospitality, truth, and my lord ...
> Thus we finish'd the rest of the day and the night
> In gay flowing bumpers and social delight.[45]

Another club, The Ouzel Galley Society, had a rather fanciful story attached to it about the disappearance and much later reappearance of a merchant ship of that name from Dublin, which will not be gone into here (plate 5.6).[46] The society, made up of Dublin merchants, proudly and, perhaps with some exaggeration, claimed for itself 'the two outstanding achievements of Galley influence', namely, in the building of the Royal Exchange (now the City Hall, built 1769–79) and 'the formation in 1783 of the Chamber of Commerce through their power in the Guild of Merchants'. In 1763 Thomas Allen (described in their story as 'that inhuman monster') was appointed to the sinecure of Taster of Wines in Dublin and proceeded to propose a tax of two shillings per tun on all wines. This was opposed by the city merchants who formed a committee to block it, collecting subscriptions to help their case, which they won. The funds left over from the collection, they claimed, went towards the building of the Exchange ('that Temple of Trade on Cork Hill'). Part of the inauguration ceremony for the incoming 'captain', as he was appropriately called, was that a bumper glass engraved with the ship, *The Ouzel*, on one side and the figure of *Equity* on the other was filled to the brim, presented to the captain, who was obliged by the rules of the society to 'drain it at one swallow'. Like other societies they met in different taverns, e.g., the Rose and Bottle in Dame Street and the Phoenix Tavern in Werburgh Street in the eighteenth century, and in the Shelbourne Hotel, and the Royal Marine, Kingstown, in the nineteenth century. Albert Gladstanes, a Dublin wine merchant who supplied Dublin Castle in the 1740s, was admitted as a member of the society in 1756.[47] On the subject of things maritime, it is said that Admiral Nelson's body was shipped home in a cask of rum which was, allegedly, drained on the voyage from Trafalgar to London, hence the toast 'a drop of Nelson's blood' among members of a drinking club that was probably associated with the Royal Navy.[48]

Probably the most famous clubhouse in eighteenth-century Ireland was Daly's, originally a chocolate house when it opened at 2–3 Dame Street in the 1760s,

5.6 The common seal of the city of Dublin dates from the thirteenth century, the back of which indicates Dublin at peace with a merchant ship under sail. On this side to the right is a sailor holding a goblet, possibly indicating that the cargo is wine. Courtesy of Dublin City Library and Archive.

where it occupied a large building with a 'sumptuously-furnished' interior that comprised, according to one visitor, 'a coffee room, reading room, writing room, hazard room & private dining rooms'.[49] It was quite discreet, famous for gambling where, it was said, 'half the land of Ireland has changed hands'. However, from about the 1780s, many gentlemen's clubs no longer met in taverns, preferring the privacy of their own premises, like the Kildare Street Club, founded in 1782, the

Stephen's Green Club (1840) and the University Club (1849).[50] It should be said that there were numerous societies that met for purposes other than sociability and drinking, for example the Dublin Society (now Royal Dublin Society), the Dublin Chamber of Commerce, and the Turf Club, whose motives were the promotion of an 'improving' agenda in the country. The same motives drove the establishment of what John Gilbert refers to as the 'Friendly Florist Society', to encourage the cultivation of flowers in Ireland: prizes were awarded 'to the person who shall raise the best polyanthus from seed … and the second best ditto etc.'.[51] However, this appears to be, or was also known as, the Dublin Florists' Club, a dining club begun by Huguenots, whose membership comprised many 'prominent Noblemen and Gentlemen, both here and in England'.[52] Women were not admitted. One of the rules of the club stipulated that every member should 'bring a nosegay on the day of meeting or forfeit a bottle of wine'. From 1749, dissatisfied with the quality of food and wine in their (un-named) meeting place, they met in the Phoenix Tavern where they drank toasts in bumpers, not only to flowers, including carnations and auriculas, but to 'The King', 'Princes, Princess & all the Royal Family', 'The Glorious Memory', 'This society and all Florists', 'Absent members', and 'Health of all members present'.[53]

The success of a club can mean that the ideals and aims of the original members can get submerged beneath a burgeoning membership. This happened in London at *The* Club (with the emphasis on the first word, later renamed the London Literary Society). Founded in 1764 by Dr Johnson and Sir Joshua Reynolds, the membership comprised a group of intellectual luminaries that included Edmund Burke, Oliver Goldsmith and James Boswell. Weekly meetings were held on Fridays in the Turk's Head Tavern in Soho, where they dined and gossiped. But by the 1780s its membership had swelled so much that it had lost its original intimacy, at which point Boswell decided that he had little relish for it but that he had 'enjoyed the wine'.[54] Thomas Jefferson regretted that he was unable to accept an invitation to be initiated into the Philadelphia Irish Society or its official title, the Sons of Saint Patrick, as he had departed Philadelphia before the invitation arrived. Or perhaps he had heard of George Washington's initiation to the society, part of which involved emptying a full bottle of claret over the general's head?[55]

Apart from all-male gatherings, toasts were proposed in domestic settings when men and women dined together though it became less fashionable later in the century. On these occasions, glasses would be raised to the king, to each guest and to absent friends. One young woman at a dinner in Kildare was dismayed to find she had 'to take Wine with every gentleman present, and after the cloth was withdrawn, the son [of the host] began Miss Ham, your health and so on to each individual. This was followed by all the company in the same rotation. The solemnity of the rite was quite ludicrous'.[56] To 'take wine' is, according to the *Oxford English dictionary*, 'to drink wine with another in a ceremonial way, i.e. a token of friendship'. However, it was apparently considered 'undecorous to touch a glass to your lips' before being 'challenged'. This meant that each lady 'must be solicited to drink wine by a gentleman, who first drinks to her, then to the hostess, and the master of the house, and so on, until he has gone through the whole company'.[57] The system did not quite work for the vicar in Trollope's *Framley Parsonage* when, during a lull at a dinner party where the service was proving slow, he 'ventured to ask [a lady] to drink wine with me. But when I bowed my head at her, she looked at me with all her eyes, struck with amazement. Had I suggested that she should join me in a wild Indian war-dance, with nothing on but paint, her face could not have shown greater astonishment'.[58] On the other hand, Samuel Johnson succeeded diplomatically when, dining at Lord Newhaven's, a relative of his host, described as the 'beautiful Miss Graham', asked Johnson, as Boswell puts it, 'to hob or nob with her'. Flattered by the attention, Johnson politely informed her that he never drank wine, 'but if she would drink a glass of water, he was much at her service' and she accepted. When two glasses were brought, he smiled at the young lady and said, 'Madam, let us reciprocate'.[59] A Frenchman visiting England in 1698 observed that 'to have drunk at table without making it the occasion of a toast would have been considered an act of gross discourtesy'. He further stated that the person whose health was drunk must remain perfectly still from the moment his name was uttered until the conclusion of the health: 'Nothing appears so droll as to see a man who is in the act of chewing a morsel which he has in his mouth … who suddenly takes a serious air, when a person of some respectability drinks to his health, looks fixedly at his person, and becomes as motionless as if a universal paralysis had seized him'.[60] It would appear that the French were the experts at this activity. At 'the Rhenish wine-house' in London, Samuel Pepys was instructed by Mr Moore who 'showed us the French manner, when a health is drunk to bow to him that drunk to you, and then apply yourself to him, whose lady's health is drunk, and then to the person that you drink to, which I never knew before; but it seems it is now the fashion'.[61]

But Lord Chesterfield was critical of the habit of toasting in a letter to his son in the mid-eighteenth century: '[it] is deemed impolite in good company … What can be more rude or ridiculous than to interrupt persons at their meals with an unnecessary compliment?'[62] However, the same lord was renowned for his witty toasts and for being a lover of champagne with which he chose to toast his fair friends:

> Give me Champaign, and fill it to the brim,
> I'll toast in bumpers e'ry lovely limb …
> Why then averse to love? Ah, leave distain,
> And pledge thy lover in the brisk Champaign.[63]

A traveller in Ireland in 1779 was relieved to find that 'the practice of drinking healths at dinner was entirely laid aside'.[64] In the United States however, in 1778,

5.7 William Hogarth, *A midnight modern conversation*, 1733. Metropolitan Museum of Art.

a gentleman's club known as the Anacreon Society, dedicated to 'wit, harmony and the god of wine', adopted a musical composition called 'To Anacreon in Heaven', and opened each meeting with a rendition of the song as a musical toast. Also in the United States, the French General Jean de Chastellux (1734–88) of the expeditionary force sent to North America during the War of Independence, who became a close friend of General Washington, remarked of the 'absurd and truly barbarous' custom of endless toasts when dining in the 1780s:

> The actor in this ridiculous comedy is sometimes ready to die of thirst, while he is obliged to inquire the names, or catch the eyes of, twenty-five or thirty persons, and the unhappy persons to whom he addresses himself are dying of impatience, for it is certainly not possible for them to bestow much attention on what they are eating and on what is said to them, being incessantly appealed to from right and left.

He further remarks that 'the Americans themselves feel the ridiculousness of these customs borrowed from Old England, and since laid aside by her'.[65]

No such scruples were held by the Barrington brothers. Sir Jonah's elder brother, in 1778, fearing that the snow might put an end to his usual week-long hunting fest held every Christmas, decided on a course of action to entertain his friends for that period; a hogshead of 'superior claret' was delivered to the hunting lodge as the beverage for the group – to be taken 'cold, mulled or buttered'; a fat cow, skinned, was hung up by its heels, and some chickens, bacon and bread were also admitted. Two pipers and a 'blind but famous fiddler' were employed to enliven the banquet, which it was determined that the party should continue 'till the cow became a skeleton and the claret should be on its stoop'. On St Stephen's Day, a few neighbours were invited to the opening banquet of what they called their 'shut-up pilgrimage'. Numerous toasts intervened –

> every man shouted forth his fair favourite, or convivial pledge; and each voluntarily surrendered a portion of his own reason in bumpers to the beauty of his neighbour's toast. A week later, the cow was a mere skeleton, the claret was upon its stoop – the last gallon, 'mulled with a pound of spices, was drunk in tumblers to the next merry meeting!'.[66]

WOMEN AND ALCOHOL

As has been seen, the therapeutic value of alcohol, that included wine, 'sanctioned the daily consumption by women of three to four glasses, and by men of a bottle of wine per day'.[67] In Ancient Rome there were laws to discourage drinking among women due to the fear that in a drunken state, they might commit adultery, thereby casting doubt on the legitimacy of heirs. Fynes Moryson, who travelled in Ireland from 1599 to 1603, wrote about 'usquebagh' [whiskey] which he says is 'held the best in the world of that kind', that 'the English-Irish drink largely, and in many families (especially at feasts) both men and women use excess therein … I have in part seen and often heard … that some gentlewomen are so free in this excess', that they would 'pledge health after health with men; not to speak of the wives of Irish lords … who often drink till they be drunken, or, at least till they void urine in full assemblies of men'.[68] William Palmer, in his discussion of the criticism levied by English writers at the drunkenness of Irish women in the early seventeenth century, argues that they 'believed that women posed a particular danger to the establishment of order and stability', that like promiscuity, it was viewed as 'the inability to control one's desires', with the result that they were perceived as an obstacle to civil government.[69] A visitor to Limerick observed that 'Limerick people are more given to drink than the inhabitants of Cork. The use of whiskey is general and extends even to the women'.[70]

It was not unknown for some eighteenth-century aristocratic women in Ireland to enjoy the pastimes pursued generally by men. One was Lady Gertrude Seymour Conway, wife of the second Earl Grandison of Dromana, who was addicted to the gaming table. Known as the 'toast of the town' in Dublin, she gambled all night until dawn, when she regularly pelted the crowd, who had gathered under the windows, with (empty) wine bottles that she and her friends had consumed. It was also 'whispered' that she disguised herself as a 'gentleman of fashion' in which garb she appeared at various taverns and gaming houses.[71] Another was the unfortunate Limerick heiress, Frances Ingoldsby, who thought nothing of quaffing a pint of wine before dinner, 'thought a bad habit for ladies', and who was observed to have 'rendered herself quite stupid' by drinking strong white wine to excess; two years after her 'covert' marriage in 1741, she was seen drinking and singing 'in her cups in her old uncouth manner'.[72] In an inventory after the death of Miss Annritta Cust in Armagh in 1797, a large number of empty bottles were found in a bedroom closet together with wine glasses, and 'an old chest and therein 14 bottles of claret wine'.[73]

Undoubtedly many women in the upper echelons of society drank alcohol in the privacy of their homes, either with or without the knowledge of their husbands. Lady Kildare drank a bottle of wine before going to a ball, with the knowledge and sanction of her husband, as will be seen in Chapter 8. It was apparently quite acceptable for women to drink wine in spas, if not elsewhere, in the 1740s when Isaac Butler wrote his journal. He mentions one in Swanlinbar, Co. Cavan, where, at 'Mr Castle's' accommodation, dinner cost sevenpence, 'lady's wine 6*d*., the gentlemen pay the remainder of the wine bill'.[74] Mention has already been made of Katherine Conolly and her sister Jane Bonnell who, between them, within their respective homes, got through a fair amount of wine per year. But they would be aware that there was no place in society for a woman who was seen to drink to excess. In this connection, consider the comments made by Lord Chief Baron Willes in 1760 about 'Irish ladies':

> 'tis very uncommon to hear any scandal upon their reputations. Both single and married ladies in general behave with great virtue and I do attribute to virtue rather than prudence and caution in concealing intrigue because Dublin is like a large market town in England where everyone knows and is known by everybody and there is scarce anything done by anybody but it is publicly known.[75]

Interestingly, it was the custom among Quaker women to remain at the dinner table after the meal, something that was frowned upon in England (if not in Ireland) for not facilitating the men and their drinking session, a habit that was described as 'barbarous and odious' by those supporters of equality. The women could enjoy the conversation as they had before the meal was served, but the decision whether or not to remain was left entirely up to them. Sometimes they did choose to retire, particularly if they were mixing with people of other confessions but one writer felt that if women did remain, 'chastity of expression and decorum of behaviour … would be insured and their presence … a check upon drunkenness'. However, in Quaker society, if the men remain at the table, they spend their time conversing rather than drinking and, there were no toasts obliging them to drink perhaps more than they would desire.[76]

For young men, the drinking of alcohol tended to be a double-edged sword: on the one hand, they were introduced to it at a very young age in the course of social rituals while, on the other hand, they were exhorted and expected to behave like gentlemen at all times, keeping themselves at a distance from bad behaviour, and generally having the ability to control their passions, including the imbibing of alcohol. Lord Orrery's comment about the non-drinker being a marked man was probably true. While drinking might be considered what 'real men' did, gentlemen had to learn how to balance that while retaining their authority and honour. The example given by the older generation was not always a positive one. Toasting had the potential for men 'to get drunk soberly' in all-male company – each taking a drink in turn, keeping pace with the others, unable to withdraw without being noticed or losing face.[77] That seemed reasonable and civilized, and most likely it worked well in some cases. And to avoid losing face, we have seen how one Scotsman pretended to be drunk by sliding under the table; and how William Conolly had to 'practice' drinking more wine than he would normally take so that he would be considered more 'acceptable' at Dublin Castle.

CHAPTER 6

Nothing but the best at Dublin Castle

DUBLIN CASTLE WAS THE CENTRE OF social activity in the capital and never more so than in the eighteenth century. There, the representative of the British sovereign, the lord lieutenant (or viceroy), who up to 1767 was a member of the British cabinet, attended the Irish parliament when in session, which was about six months every two years. In his absence Ireland was ruled by lords justices who presided over the government of the country. After 1767, the lord lieutenant resided in Ireland for his term of office, and as the position was no longer of cabinet rank, it did not encourage politically ambitious peers to seek the post.[1] His job was to maintain British interests in Ireland, not always an easy task. It came with a reasonable salary of £12,000 at the start of the eighteenth century, rising to £20,000 at its end, plus allowances but, by the last quarter of the eighteenth century, it was falling well short of what was required for the lavish lifestyle and entertaining that was expected at the Castle, and many had to dip into their own resources to subsidize their role. Lord Chesterfield reckoned he would be about £5,000 out of pocket. Swift remarked that lords lieutenant wooed gentlemen with 'Dinners', 'good Words, Burgundy' and 'Closeting'.[2] The standard of hospitality set by the minority Protestant ruling class in Ireland ensured that any incoming lord lieutenant would have been made aware of what was expected.[3] The fact was that the quality of the Castle's cellars and the regularity of balls and dinners undoubtedly played a major part in the popularity of the lord lieutenant. Some, like Townshend (1767–72) and Rutland (1784–7), took to it with enthusiasm; for others, like Harcourt (1772–6) and Buckingham (1787–9), it was a daily grind (plate 6.1).

As early as the 1580s, a great deal of alcohol was being consumed at the Castle. Lord Deputy Sir Arthur Grey's household expenses mention 'Clarret wyne 6 Tonnes per ann., at £18, le Tonne' which would be about 1,500 gallons.[4] Between May 1682 and September 1683, during the term of office of the earl of Arran (fourth son of James Butler, first duke of Ormond), 6,000 gallons of French, Canary and Rhenish wines and large quantities of other alcohol were consumed by the earl's household and guests.[5] Lord Chesterfield (1745–7) was shocked by the amount of claret consumed, as he put it, by 'those of superior rank'. He may have included in this one of his predecessors, the duke of Wharton (1708–10), who was often found wandering around Dublin streets at night like 'a drunken madman'.[6] According to Nathaniel Clements in 1747, the lord lieutenant was allowed to bring into Ireland twenty tuns of wine duty-free.[7] Wine could be used as a bribe: in 1748 Sir Richard

6.1 Engraving by Edward Goodall (1795–1870) after drawing by George Petrie, RHA, *Great Courtyard at Dublin Castle*, 1832. Photograph courtesy of the Irish Architectural Archive.

Wolseley from Mount Wolseley near Carlow, failing to obtain a commission for his nephew through the previous lord lieutenant, asked Robert Wilmot, secretary to the lord lieutenant, in a rather cloying letter, to intercede for him with the duke of Devonshire, and offered '… a present … of fifty pounds, to please yourself in a hogshead of French claret'.[8]

There was no shortage of wine with the Butlers of Ormond. They came to Ireland originally in the retinue of Prince John, son of Henry II and his wife Eleanor of Aquitaine, who was granted the lordship of Ireland. At the end of the twelfth century, Theobald Walter, a knight, was granted the hereditary office of chief butler of Ireland, from which his descendants took their surname.[9] This came with the honour whereby he and his senior male descendants were to attend the kings of England at their coronation, and on that day present them with the first cup of wine. The word 'butler' came from the French 'bouteillier' or cup-bearer. Theobald was also granted the prisage of wines – which meant that he and his heirs were entitled to two tuns of wine out of every ship that entered any Irish trading port that was loaded with 20 tuns of wine, and one tun from every ship that had nine

6.2 Coat of arms of the Butlers, earls of Ormond[e]. Courtesy of University of Delawere Library, public domain via Wikimedia Commons.

to twenty tuns. The grant ensured that the family was enabled financially to uphold the dignity of the office, and they became not only the earls and dukes of Ormond, but the greatest landowners in Ireland. The three covered cups in the family coat-of-arms acknowledge the honour (plate 6.2). The Butlers enjoyed this privilege for 500 years up to 1811 when the Crown paid the eighteenth earl of Ormond the huge sum of £216,000 to buy it back.

It was no surprise therefore when James Butler, first duke of Ormond (who served a number of terms as lord lieutenant of Ireland in the seventeenth century), brought with him rich furniture and carpets for the Castle, together with an entourage of over one hundred officials and servants. As previously mentioned, during the period from May 1682 to September 1683, according to records, six thousand gallons of French, Canary and Rhenish wines were consumed by his household and guests, in addition to large quantities of other forms of alcohol.[10] His grandson, another James, second duke of Ormonde (lord lieutenant 1710–13), invited, on one occasion, the sitting members of parliament (who were on the side of the current administration) to select wine from any hogshead in the Castle's cellar and drink as much as they desired. However, no chairs were allowed in the cellar, as he 'could not encourage any gentleman's drinking longer than he could stand'. Another custom was associated with the annual banquet given by the lord lieutenant to the lord mayor of Dublin, whereby after the lord lieutenant had toasted 'the King', 'the Prince of Wales and all the Royal Family', 'the Glorious Memory of King William', and 'the first of July 1690', he then drank bumper toasts to 'Prosperity to the City of Dublin', 'Prosperity to the Linen Manufactory of Ireland' and 'Prosperity to Ireland and the Trade thereof'. After this he withdrew, recommending his guests to the care of the steward, comptroller, and gentleman usher, and the lord mayor with his entourage of aldermen and officials were conducted to the cellars 'where a table is placed with glasses'. A large glass of wine was given to the mayor into which he placed a piece of gold and drank to the health of the lord lieutenant. The glass was passed around, constantly replenished, while each man toasted the lord lieutenant and each man present placed a piece of gold in it. Unfortunately, the recipient of this bounty is not divulged. The practice continued through the eighteenth century but when in 1762 the incumbent lord mayor asked the then lord lieutenant, George Montagu Dunk, second earl of Halifax (1761–3), to be excused the demands of the wine cellar, consent was given.[11] Incidentally, a later lord lieutenant, the fourth duke of Richmond, wrote admiringly of one of Dublin's mayors that he had 'a very pretty method of getting drunk. He is so well used to it that he knows his way back in the dark and is always sober when he gets up in the morning'.[12] In 1762, Halifax himself wrote to a friend from Dublin Castle that 'from claret and business' he was 'almost dead'.[13] Among the Ormond Papers, possibly relating to Kilkenny Castle rather than Dublin Castle, is a 'House Book with Accounts of stores and Provisions' in which, in June 1703, French 'Clarrett' appears and below it, 'Hous' Clarret. Here too, 'Obryon' [Haut Brion] appears on the lists from November 1701.[14]

In 1755 there was 'a very prodigious great Castle drinking bout from dinner till past eleven': the following day one of the participants, Lord Kildare, admitted to his wife, 'I don't think I ever drank so hard and fast in my life: every one of the company complain today'.[15] It should be noted that dinner could be served as early as 3 p.m. Also in the 1750s, Charles O'Hara from Annaghmore, Co. Sligo, was quite shocked at the amount of drinking he found at Dublin Castle: the lord lieutenant, the duke of Bedford (1757–61), and his entourage, including 'even his first chaplain', were all quite drunk. Again, at a party at Nathaniel Clements' new house in the Phoenix Park, Bedford turned up, 'drunk from Annesley's, where they had been settling the plan for future power'.[16] In July 1757, it was arranged that a Major MacCulloch was to secure a stock of claret for Bedford's consumption at the Castle; 'eight to ten hogsheads will do to begin with', and the following month Bedford's secretary wrote that 'The Irish are going to be pleased with their Lord Lieutenant for he has ten times more patience with the Major's arrangement of claret, than he has with all our nonsense of politics, etc.'[17]

Whatever about the volume of wine, the quality was something else, as the earl of Charlemont observed of Simon Harcourt, first earl of Harcourt (1772–6), that 'he knew the importance of a table, especially in this country, and distributed

6.3 William Dickinson (engraver), after Joshua Reynolds, Portrait of Charles Manners, fourth duke of Rutland (1754–87), lord lieutenant of Ireland (1784–7), mezzotint (1791), image courtesy of the National Gallery of Ireland.

his best Margoux with a very becoming profusion'.[18] George Boyd, the Dublin wine merchant, was contacted by the Castle regarding the supply of wines for the incoming lord lieutenant, the second earl of Bristol (1766–7): in response he assures the Castle that 'no person at present is better prepared for that purpose than I am ... I daily expect of the best kind to be got in France having had the honour of supplying Lord Halifax & Lord Northumberland & Lord Hertford …'.[19] A summary of the bills for 'Wine, Arrack &c.' laid into the cellars of the Castle for the use of the duke of Bedford in October 1757 amounted to the large sum of just over £1,128, and a list of the wines consumed there in the period September 1757 to April 1758 shows that every night in the Green Room where, in the eighteenth century, officers and possibly upper servants employed at Dublin Castle took their meals, fifteen to twenty bottles were drunk, mostly of port, but also of champagne and burgundy.[20] In spite of this, the Bedford lord lieutenancy was criticized for its parsimony.

Described as an 'exacting epicure', Charles Manners, the fourth duke of Rutland (plate 6.3), as lord lieutenant (1784–7), dispatched his chief cook to France to expand his culinary repertoire by spending time in some of the great kitchens there such as the royal kitchen at Fountainebleau, and those of the duc d'Orleans and the Franco-Irish archbishop of Narbonne, Arthur Richard Dillon (whose life, incidentally, was described as 'more gay than episcopal'). In addition, a member of his military staff, George Kendall, was also sent there to source the finest food and, importantly, wines for the Castle cellars.[21] The latter resulted in a consignment that included '500 bottles of the very best Sillery champagne' as well as '300 bottles of Hautevillers champagne, the growth preferred in Paris to any other'; Kendall adds of the latter 'I had it directly from the prior of that convent by the archbishop of Narbonne's intercession'.[22] It should be mentioned here that these champagnes were introduced in the second half of the seventeenth century to Versailles by the marquis de Sillery. It was the only wine to be exported in bottles, specially made in Britain of stronger, thicker glass, as the release of carbon dioxide could shatter the flimsier bottles used at the time. This made it expensive for the consumer, but obviously attractive to those in Dublin Castle, especially the duke of Rutland. One writer said of the duke,

> Never was viceroy more formed to conciliate affection throughout that convivial kingdom! Splendid in his establishment, his table presented every delicacy which luxury could accumulate or display. Vessels laden with fruit and other expensive productions of England, came over by his direction weekly to Dublin, during the whole period of his viceroyalty.[23]

Apart from the enjoyment of food and wine, Rutland complained to Lord Chatham in 1785: 'I would rather be at Belvoir [his castle in Leicestershire] breaking my neck all morning, and Bottles & Glasses all ye Evening than Disposing of Bishopricks Peerages &c However Pleasant Power & Patronage most certainly is'.[24] Rutland (and his duchess) were very popular in Ireland, particularly for the entertainments provided at the Castle, and the generosity of his table and cellar. In 1787 the duke undertook a three-month tour of Ireland, enjoying the hospitality of the well-heeled.

However, his excessive eating and drinking proved too much for the duke: on his return he collapsed, and died of liver failure three days later, at the age of thirty-three.

Some of the entertainments at the Castle were remarkable. In 1733, during the lord lieutenancy of Lionel Sackville, first duke of Dorset (1730–7 and 1750–5), he and his duchess arranged for a special celebration for the soldiers at the Castle on the king's birthday. After the departure of their guests, *Faulkner's Dublin Journal* reported that 'five sirloins of Beef roasted, weighing 48 pounds each, 8 Turkey Cocks, and 30 Sixpenny Loaves to be given to the Soldiers on Guard, which was served up to them on long Tables in the Castle-Yard, with two Barrels of Ale, and a Hogshead of Wine and Wax Tapers burning to light them at their Repast'; it also reported that 'several Hogsheads of Wine plaid from a Fountain, made for that purpose, among the Populace, who catched it, and drank their Majesty's and the Royal Family's Healths, with loud Huzzas and Acclamations of Joy'.[25] The earl of Orrery shared his view of Dorset with a friend in 1735:

> Our Vice-Roy is much belov'd: We pay our Duty at the Castle with loyal Hearts: We have no mental Reservation when we assure him of our Attachment to his Person and Government: He lives magnificently, and pleases all Sorts and Sizes of his subjects, from diminutive Dick Tighe up to the gigantic Baron of Kingston.[26]

That was not the first time that wine literally flowed among the populace; in 1665, on the occasion of the arrival of the duke of Ormond as lord lieutenant, 'a conduit was placed in the Corn-market, from which wine flowed in abundance'.[27] Similarly, Lord Chesterfield (1745–7), for the celebration of George II's birthday, arranged that the Castle's supper room be transformed into a Temple of Minerva, from which a continuous flow of wine spouted from statues, some of which was similarly piped into the yard.[28] A variation of this was held by the earl of Harrington (1747–50) to celebrate the birthday of the Prince of Wales in 1748: a ball was held 'in the new room designed by Lord Chesterfield (St Patrick's Hall)', and after the dancing, the company retired to

> a long gallery where, as you passed slowly through you stopped by the way at shops elegantly formed where was cold eating and all sorts of wine and sweetmeats, and the whole most beautifully disposed with transparent painting through which shade was cast like moonlight. Flutes and other soft instruments were playing all the while but, like the candles, unseen. At each end of the long building were placed fountains of lavender water, constantly playing that diffused a most grateful odor through this amazing fairy scean [scene] ...[29]

6.4 Duke of Clarence, 'The death of Clarence', from William Howitt & J.F. Smith (eds), *John Cassell's illustrated History of England*, vol. II (London, 1858), p. 15.

Largesse such as this had two aims: to woo members of parliament to vote with the government, and to divert the attention of the public away from politics. With a number of celebratory days in the Dublin calendar these were availed of to keep the people happy with food, drink and magnificent displays. The largesse was not new: in 1554 the mayor of Dublin, Patrick Sarsfield, informed a friend that he had 'spent that year in housekeeping twenty tuns of claret, over and above white wine, sack, malvoisie, Malmsey, muscadell, &c.'[30] Incidently, Malmsey was the wine in which George, the duke of Clarence, was drowned in 1478, for plotting treason against his brother, Edward IV, according to Shakespeare's *Richard III*: it was said that he was first stabbed, then drowned in a butt (a large vat) of Malmsey (plate 6.4). In a portrait in the National Portrait Gallery, London, purported to be of Margaret Pole, Clarence's daughter, she wears a bracelet on her right wrist from which dangles a barrel. 'Malmsey' was used to describe any sweet, strong wine, and was eventually used specifically for the sweetest style of Madeira, particularly that made from the Malvasia grape.[31]

6.5 *The Cunning and Happy Family,* print by Lewis Marks (–1855), London, 1822. Lady Conyngham sits on a sofa with George IV on her lap, kissing her, flanked by her daughters; her son on the right pockets coins from a purse, while on the left, sitting on a chamber pot filled with coins, is her husband, Henry Conyngham. Public domain via Wikimedia commons.

A consignment of wine that arrived in Dublin in preparation for Dorset's arrival at the Castle in 1751 was found to be less than satisfactory. In a letter to Lord George Sackville from George Stone, archbishop of Armagh, Stone describes how he arranged, in his own home and in the company of a select group of eight or nine others, a tasting of these wines, which were found to be 'not what could be wished',

> I have tasted all the different wines and find to my great concern that there is nothing but the claret which can be made to answer any purpose. Of the two sorts of champagne, that sealed with yellow wax might go off at balls, if there were a better kind for select meetings. The red wax is too bad for an election dinner at Dover. The four parcels of Burgundy are almost equally bad. If there is any difference that sealed with black wax and falsely and impudently called Vin de Beaune is the worst, and is indeed as bad as the worst tavern could afford ... I know how unhappy his Grace and you would be to see the tables so provided ... You have been most scandalously abused ...

6.6 James Gillray (1756–1815), *A voluptuary under the horrors of digestion* (1792), a caricature of George, prince of Wales (later George IV), showing the effects of his self-indulgence. Under the overflowing chamber pot at his elbow are unpaid bills and, on the shelf above, potions and remedies for his numerous ailments, including venereal disease and haemorrhoids. Courtesy of the Metropolitan Museum of Art, gift of Adele S. Gollin, 1976.

He judged the Château 'Margoux' as 'excellently good' and the La Tour 'very good', but was 'confident that not a drop of the wine so called was ever in the province of Burgundy'.[32]

The wines selected for the visit of King George IV to Ireland in August 1821 included red and white Hermitage, hock, claret (Leoville and Lafite), Madeira, Frontignac, Sillery champagne, sherry, burgundy, vin de Graves and Sauterne. These were served at Dublin Castle and at the viceregal lodge in Phoenix Park where the king stayed during his visit.

For the royal yacht at Dunleary there was a similar list of wines and, in addition, rum, brandy and port.[33] In a letter to a Mrs Taylor about the king's arrival in Ireland,

Lady Glengall reported that 'the king was dead drunk' when he landed; apparently he and his party 'drank all the wine on board the steamboat, and then applied to the whiskey punch, till he could hardly stand'.[34]

The king was, of course, impatient to join his mistress, the 'well-upholstered' Elizabeth, Marchioness Conyngham at Slane Castle, Co. Meath (plate 6.5), where they enjoyed four days together, and she apparently stayed with him at the Phoenix Park. Totally infatuated with the over-fifty-year-old, it was said that the main road from Dublin to Slane was straightened in order that the king could reach the castle in the shortest possible time. A rhyme suggests some of what they might get up to:

> 'Tis pleasant at seasons to see how they sit,
> First cracking their nuts, and then cracking their wit,
> Then quaffing their claret – then mingling their lips,
> Or tickling the fat about each other's hips.[35] (plate 6.6)

The duke of Shrewsbury's tenure as lord lieutenant was short; from September 1713 to September 1714: it was said that his Italian-born wife had persuaded him to accept the post as she wanted to 'play at being queen'. She apparently regaled her guests with a description of her toes 'from which, she claimed, growths protruded resembling thumbs'. Her husband was charming and entertained expansively, so much so, that following a robust celebration commemorating King William, he received a 'public rebuke from the bishop of Cork, who pronounced the drinking of toasts to the dead to be a wicked custom savouring of popery'.[36] An interesting document lists the sources of 'His Graces Entertainment money as Lord Lieut' as follows:[37]

£18. 1. 3 per Diem for 365 Days amounts to the summe of	£6,593.6.8
Port Corn money per annum farm'd by Mr Thompson of the	
Custom house att £250 per annum due the 2nd of Feb. 1713/14	
payable at 2 Severall paymts the first to be paid in Novr 1714,	
the other the 25th March 1715	£250
The Import of Wine Custom free £76 per annum payable by	
Mr Tucker of the Custom House	£76
By Wooll Licences granted computed to be worth about £5,000 per	£5,000
For the graizing of cows and horses in the Phoenix Park computed	
about £100 per annum to be accounted by John Crosthwaite Baylife	
(bailiff) of the said Park	£100
Total	**£12,019.6.8**

Another part of this document shows 'Allowance of Wine on State Days' to staff as follows: 'The King at Arms and Heralds' receive 9 bottles; 'Gunners and [?]' (8);

'Mace Bearers' (3); 'Battle Axes' (6); 'The Footmen' (6); 'The Maids' (4). Expenses of beer for one week was 'Small Beer – 9 barrels: Ale – 4 barrels'. The wine allowances on 'Public Days' were:

The Gentlemen at Large	6 bottles
Musick & Trumpets	do.
Music whilst playing	2
The Trumpet that sounds	1
The Porter every Sunday his Grace dines Publick	2
The Usher of the Hall the same	2
The Battle Axes Standing at the Door	
When His Grace dines publick	1
To the Keepers when they bring Venison	2
To the Chaplain Mr Harley's(?) per week	3
To the Musick on a Ball night	6
To the Trumpet and Kettle drum when	
His Grace goes to Church or parliament	3

On 'Private Days' the 'Steward's Table' was allowed eight bottles of wine, the 'Gentlewomen's' table – 3 bottles, the 'Clarke of the Kitchin' – 4 bottles, and the 'Cook & Confectioners Assistant' – 3 bottles. It is interesting to note that Anthony Julian, described as 'Yeoman of ye Wine-cellar and Butler', was paid £8 per annum, while John Ducomun, the 'Confectioner', was paid £30 per annum.[38]

The Castle cellar books dated between 1828 and 1833 show the types of wine served at the Castle and at the viceregal lodge:[39]

Port	Claret
Madeira	Sherry
Champagne, Dry	Champagne, Sweet
Hermitage Red	Hermitage White
Sauternes	Vin de Pauillac
Hock	Constantia
Verdia	Cyprus
Cote Rotie	Paxaretto
Cognac & Brandy	Arristo
Marcella	Cherry Brandy

Lords lieutenant were often happy to accept invitations from those outside the immediate circle of the Castle. In her novel *Ormond* Maria Edgeworth describes how during a lord lieutenant's visit to Castle Hermitage it was observed that 'till the company had drank a certain quantity of wine, nothing was said worth repeating, and afterwards, nothing repeatable'.[40] It has been suggested that Edgeworth modelled the aforesaid lord lieutenant on Townshend.[41] An invitation that was eagerly accepted was that to the home of Philip Tisdal, a judge of the Prerogative Court, in Stillorgan, Co. Dublin, who lived 'in a style of the greatest splendor and magnificence' and 'unbounded hospitality'; Townshend appreciated Tisdal's 'well-known cook and the company of an 8-bottle man as T[isdal] is said to have been'.[42]

Townshend described the Irish as a 'sociable, convivial people' and remarked that 'a social hour did no hurt sometimes to the King's service'.[43] On his visit to Ireland the Chevalier de Latocnaye tells how he had heard that it was in the power of the lords lieutenant to bestow a knighthood and describes how Townshend, in his cups, was so delighted with the music of a bagpipe player that he had him kneel before him and, using his sword, conferred a knighthood on him. On another occasion, the wine was so good at an inn and he had had so much of it that he did the same with the innkeeper. Next morning, remembering what had occurred, he explained that he had been 'acting the fool, that no more would be said about it'. The man didn't mind, but his wife was most put out.[44] Apparently many of Townshend's 'knights' carried on their normal occupations – selling soap and tobacco, noggins of whiskey, and farthing candles in different parts of the country.[45] *Faulkner's Dublin Journal* in September 1772 offered the following farewell to the outgoing marquis: 'Drunkards, pimps and whores go mourn/Townshend never shall return'.

A man who never did return was Jonah Barrington, after hosting a dinner party at his home for the lord lieutenant and the lord chancellor. He had previously pawned his family silver but invited the pawnbroker, John Stevenson, to join them and to bring with him the silver on the understanding that he would take it back at the end of the evening. His host plied Stevenson with so much wine that he fell asleep and, on awakening, he found that Barrington had disappeared, together with the silver. He fled to London in 1810 to escape his creditors.[46]

KNIGHTS OF ST PATRICK

After the political excitement of 'Grattan's parliament' in 1782, the lord lieutenant, Earl Temple (1782–3), decided to establish the Knights of St Patrick, based on the Scottish Order of the Thistle and the English Order of the Garter. It was a clever move: as Powell puts it, the Castle was 'short of cash', and with little patronage to spread among the elite, 'the Order was free, patriotic, it would connect the Castle to the leading nobility in Ireland, and would provide another avenue for the ceremonial' – and it succeeded.[47] For weeks prior to the ceremonies celebrating the event, weavers in the Liberties worked around the clock to produce two to three thousand yards of satin for the outfit which comprised a mantle of sky blue lined with white silk, with a hood on the right shoulder fastened with blue and gold

6.7 Insignia of the Knights of St Patrick.

tassels, undergarments of white silk trimmed with gold, a black velvet hat decorated with the Star of the Order and with red, white and blue ostrich feathers attached. The boots of white leather had turn-ups of sky blue, the spurs and sword hilt were gilded, the belt and scabbard were of crimson velvet, and among the insignia was a collar of gold with harps and roses linked with golden knots from which hung the gold badge of the Order (plate 6.7).[48] In their magnificent attire the proud knights-to-be processed in carriages to the Castle, where Lord Temple, the lord lieutenant, held a banquet in, appropriately, St Patrick's Hall (formerly known as the ballroom) (plate 6.8).[49] An installation ceremony to mark the foundation of the Order was held some days later, on 17 March 1783 (St Patrick's Day), in St Patrick's Cathedral in

6.8 John Keyse Sherwin (1751–90), engraver, *The installation banquet of the Knights of St Patrick in St Patrick's Hall, Dublin Castle*. Photograph by Davison & Associates, courtesy of the Office of Public Works, Dublin Castle.

Dublin, where the knights had been given their own chapel in the old choir, where their arms were affixed to individual stalls with their banner overhead. Among the 'principles of the Order' were the following: entertainments were to be paid for jointly, but there was a restriction on the amount of alcohol that could be consumed on such occasions: 'the union shall always dissolve, after a bottle of wine a man, or a similar portion of any other liquor'.[50] The following evening, a ball and a supper took place, this time in the Rotunda, part of the complex attached to the Lying-in Hospital (now called the Rotunda Hospital). It was said that 'dissatisfaction had long been felt with the suitability of [Dublin Castle] as a venue for elegant gatherings', and it possibly helped that the duke of Leinster, one of the newly installed knights, was chairman of the Board of the Rotunda.[51] The same duke opened the ball with the Countess Temple, after which over eight hundred guests enjoyed a supper which, in the usual hyperbole of the press at the time, 'consisted of every delicacy that art could produce ... the elegance of the viands and confectionary, and the richness of the wines, gave general satisfaction'.[52] On his return to Ireland as lord lieutenant (1787–8), Temple (now marquis of Buckingham) commissioned new ceiling panels for St Patrick's Hall at the Castle where, in the central painting, an allegorical representation of George III, the king is flanked by Britannia carrying a flag and Hibernia in a green dress; one group of putti hold the crown over George's head, while another hold a plumed hat and a ceremonial sword, part of the knights' ceremonial costume.[53]

Undoubtedly, the eighteenth-century lords lieutenant of Ireland were a motley, often colourful bunch, about whom many entertaining stories, true and false, were told. Dublin, in the eighteenth century, was known as 'the second city of the Empire', a capital busy with a social life centred around the court at the Castle and at the town houses of the aristocracy and gentry. As a result of the Act of Union with Britain in 1801, the latter category retreated to their rural estates in the country and in their place came the commercial and professional middle class, as prosperous merchants, doctors and lawyers moved into the town houses previously owned, or rented during the season by the ascendancy. These were the new elite, who quickly took their places on the Castle's guest lists. Maria Edgeworth caught the mood in her book *The Absentee*:

> ... most of the nobility and many of the principal families among the Irish commoners, either hurried in high hopes to London, or retired disgusted and in despair to their houses in the country. Immediately, in Dublin, commerce rose into the vacated seats of rank; wealth rose into the place of birth. New faces and new equipages appeared: people, who had never been heard of before, started into notice, pushed themselves forward, not scrupling to elbow their way even at the castle; and they were presented to my lord-lieutenant and to my lady-lieutenant; for their excellencies might have played their vice-regal parts to empty benches, had they not admitted such persons for the moment to fill their court.[54]

CHAPTER 7

The role of the monasteries

'Beer is made by men: wine by God', Martin Luther

THE BIBLE MAKES CLEAR THAT WINE was a gift from God in which as a drink, and the vine as a plant, it is frequently mentioned. Noah, in the Book of Genesis, planted a vineyard and became the first winemaker and probably the first drunkard: 'And he drank of the wine and was drunken' (Gen. 9:20–21). In the New Testament, Luke says 'No man also, having drunk old wine, straightaway desireth new; for he saith, "The old is better"' (Luke 5:39) – as it would have been sealed in an amphora. Jesus's first miracle was at the wedding at Cana where, when wine was running short, he changed water into wine (plate 7.1). After the master of the feast tasted the new wine, he said to the bridegroom, 'Everyone serves the good wine first, and when people have drunk freely, then the poor wine. But you have kept the good wine until now' (John 2:10). It indicates that wine is for joyful occasions, for feasting, and sharing. There are numerous patron saints of wine: each wine-producing country, if not area, has its own. St Killian is the patron saint of winegrowers in Germany. Every year in Bordeaux, for example, the feast of the fourth-century Vincent of Zaragossa, patron saint of winemakers, and protector of vineyard labourers, is celebrated on 22 January. This claim to fame is apparently due to his having 'vin' in his first name.[1] Martin Luther (1482–1552), called after another patron saint of wine, St Martin of Tours, received payment in wine for some of his preaching in Wittenberg; he enjoyed drinking it daily and had a substantial wine and beer cellar. While he called monks 'fleas on the fur coat of the Almighty', he conveniently forgot that some of these monks were responsible for that wine.[2] However, he condemned drunkenness and the abuse of alcohol and exhorted believers to accept responsibility for their behaviour.[3]

The requirement of wine by Christian communities to celebrate the Eucharist was possibly one of the main reasons why viniculture and winemaking survived in Western Europe after the fall of Rome in AD 476. Much credit, therefore, is due to the monastic orders, particularly in France and Germany, in the Middle Ages, for the crucial part they played in the history of wine and in the development of vineyards.[4] Bordeaux, for example, as the centre of the wine trade, is prominently mentioned in early Irish texts, according to one writer, and the Latin version of the name, *Burdigala*, was borrowed into Irish in the form *bordgal*, meaning in an eighth-century text, 'meeting-place, or city'.[5]

7.1 Marten de Vos (1532–1603), *The marriage feast at Cana* (1596). Public domain, via Wikimedia Commons.

Because of the use of red wine in the daily celebration of the Eucharist, monasteries frequently had vineyards attached to supply this need. Théophile Gautier, in his book *A romantic in Spain* (1845), claims that to facilitate the celebration of the 500 Masses that were being said daily at the twenty-four altars in the cathedral of Seville, a total of 4,687 gallons of wine per annum was required, which seems quite excessive. In medieval Catholicism, according to Eamon Duffy, the special position of the priest gave him 'access to mysteries forbidden to others: only he might utter the words which transformed bread and wine into the flesh

7.2 Ernst Nowak (1851–1919), *A good swig* (Ein guter Schluck), (by 1919) (attd).
Public domain via Wikimedia Commons.

and blood of God incarnate'– also called transubstantiation. And when a layperson 'drank the draught of unconsecrated wine [i.e., wine that has not been transformed into the Blood of Christ] which they were given after communion to wash down the host and ensure they had swallowed it, they had to cover their hands with the houseling-cloth, for the virtue of the Host and blood affected even the dead metal of the chalice.'[6] St Columbanus urged care was to be taken when drinking wine from the chalice and anyone found biting it (meaning, presumably, priests or monks) would be given a severe penance.It was even said that 'whooping cough could be cured by getting a priest to give one a threefold draught of water or [unconsecrated] wine from his chalice after Mass' as it was believed that 'power leaked from the Host and the blood'.[7]

According to one writer, a lack of evidence prevents any attempt to analyse who exactly received the wine – was it exclusively for ecclesiastics? Was it possible for lay persons to receive it at all or on special occasions? And how often was it distributed? If monks could not be trusted not to bite the chalice, it may seem unlikely that lay people would be allowed the opportunity to do so. Furthermore, from an economic point of view, it could be a challenge if wine was expected for every participant at every ceremony.[8] For producers of sacramental wine, however, there are rules to be followed, according to the *Ecclesiastical Record* (1907):

> The wine must be the fermented product of the ripe grape; the juice that has been expressed from the grape by the process of fermentation and which has not become corrupted and undrinkable, or otherwise substantially vitiated … The taste and colour, being mere accidents which depend on the quality of the particular grape and on certain slight modifications in manufacture, are immaterial. …while red wine is more expressive in its symbolism the white has this advantage that it leaves no stain on altar-linens. If wine becomes soured and converted to vinegar, it ceases to be valid; should the wine become undrinkable it will be invalid as it implies essential vitiation. While the addition of water reduces the quality of the wine, theologians agree that if the amount of water added exceeds, or is equal to, the quantity of wine – the resulting liquid is invalid. Furthermore, to render wine suitable, the 'must' (the unfermented juice of the grape) should be fermented, as it contains lees (dead yeast cells, grape seeds, pulp) and dregs (faeces) that are not fit for consecration.[9]

For those purchasing altar wine in the eighteenth century, it was recommended that samples should be analysed from time to time, and the advice was to go to a reliable Catholic merchant who will import the wine from a house or firm that has ecclesiastical recognition and the ability to guarantee its purity.[10]

The Dublin firm of William Thompson of 85 Lower Gardiner Street would probably answer the description of a 'reliable Catholic merchant'. In a 'memorandum' (dated June 1865) in the Dublin Diocesan Archive, Thompson informs (the diocese) that he has procured a large stock of 'the purest Wines for the use of the altar', and pledges 'my honour and reputation as a merchant to such of the Bishops and Clergy as may favour me with their orders, that the Wines having my brand on the corks are free from the slightest adulteration'. In the event of any doubt about the wine's suitability, he attaches a 'written testimony' from 'Professor Sullivan of the Catholic University', who declares them 'to be the purest Wines he has ever analysed'. He offers the following wines and prices: 'Rich Pale Malaga – 26s. per dozen; Dry Pale Malaga – 16s. per dozen, and Dry Rhenish Wine – 28s. per dozen (all inclusive of bottles, packages and carriage in any quantity not less than six dozen)'.[11] A wine label of Thompson's, headed 'Altar Wine', is displayed in the Museum of Wine in Malaga on which they guarantee the purity of the wine. Another company, T.W. & J. Kelly (the 'Oldest House for Pure Altar Wines'), who established themselves in 1824 in Dublin, advertised their wine regularly in *Irish Monthly*, a Catholic magazine founded in 1873, and John Rearden & Son of Great George's Street in Cork were appointed agents by the Dominican Fathers of the College of Corpo Santo, Lisbon, for supplying altar wine from their vineyard 'to the Clergy of Ireland'.[12]

It is obvious that the Church in Ireland would be obliged to ensure the purity of their wine, but it is equally obvious that it was an area that could be open to the unscrupulous in the eighteenth century and also later. In the mid-twentieth century in New York, for example, an enterprising Irish businessman, already in the fruit business in the south of Ireland, came into contact with an American who had a thriving business in sacramental wine, importing red port from the Douro Valley in Portugal for this purpose. The red port was expensive but he discovered that if he used white port, which was far cheaper, it was possible to colour the white port red with the addition of elderberry concentrate. The Irishman, on his return, got into the business of supplying elderberries, which were cooked, and the juice put through a vacuum evaporator, before it was canned into American gallon cans, 'crudely pasteurized by heating in a warm bath, before being packed, six to a cardboard carton'. A warning was stencilled on the packages, 'New York – Stow away from boiler', because if there was too much heat, they would ferment and burst their packaging. All went well for a number of years, until the scam was discovered.[13]

Monasteries and monks played a major part in the history of wine: bishops and monasteries in parts of Europe had substantial vineyards, granted to them by members of the nobility and, during the Crusades, donated by wealthy landowners seeking atonement for their sins, and a safe passage to the afterlife. The latter's generosity had another side to it – the tracts of land handed over were sometimes of poor soil, and unproductive but, as the monks discovered, it was fine for vine-growing. Two of the earliest vineyards were those of the Benedictines at Cluny (who followed the Rule of St Benedict), in the hills behind Macon, and a splinter group

7.3 Thomas Rowlandson (1757–1827), *The holy friar* (1807). Courtesy of the Elisha Whittelsey Collection, Metropolitan Museum of Art.

from that order, the Cistercians at Citeaux in the forests opposite Nuits-Saint-Georges. Both were aware of the value of vines and of wine, to use for themselves, but also to trade. In Burgundy, between the twelfth and early fourteenth century, the

Cistercians acquired, by purchase or donation, land in need of much clearing and planting, which became known as Clos du Vougeot; by 1336 the 120-acre plot was complete and enclosed by stone walls on all sides. The order remained in possession of this until the French Revolution, when all clerical estates were confiscated. Dom Goblet, the appropriately named monk who was responsible for both the vineyards and the wine, managed to hold on to his position for a while, due to his excellent reputation.[14] The monks there

> set to work to minutely understand and define every tiny parcel of vineyard land, painstakingly plotting the good and bad points of their geology and microclimate, and then comparing and defining their different flavours. Each plot was delineated, and the 'cru' system by which each batch of wine is kept separate and named separately... was started by the Cistercians at Vougeot.[15]

Throughout the period of the popes' residence in Avignon (1309–76) gifts of wine were sent there on a regular basis as the popes often protected the abbeys in disputes, and this in turn and in time developed into purchases by the papal court. In 1740 the Benedictines of the Abbey of Ste-Croix in Bordeaux bought Carbonnieux and made a good profit out of this Graves estate (plate 7.3).[16] One of the monks, Dom Perignon (1639–1715), achieved fame as the inventor of the sparkling wine that we know as champagne. This assertion was disputed, as the small town of Limoux, in the foothills of the eastern Pyrenees near Carcassonne, claimed that, since 1531, the nearby Benedictine Abbey of Saint-Hilaire had been producing a white wine that sparkled naturally after a second fermentation in the spring. The wine is called Blanquette de Limoux, and is still being made in the area.

While there were no Benedictine houses in Georgian Ireland, St Benedict, the founder of the order, made the following points in his *Rule* about monks drinking wine, which are relevant:

> 'Every one hath his proper gift from God, one after this manner and another after that' (1 Cor 7:7). It is with some hesitation, therefore, that we determine the measure of nourishment for others. However, making allowance for the weakness of the infirm, we think one hemina [half a pint] of wine a day is sufficient for each one. But to whom God granteth the endurance of abstinence, let them know that they will have their special reward. If the circumstances of the place, or the work, or the summer's heat should require more, let that depend on the judgment of the Superior, who must above all things see to it, that excess or drunkenness do not creep in. Although we read that wine is not at all proper for monks, yet, because monks in our times cannot be persuaded of this, let us agree to this, at least, that we do not drink to satiety, but sparingly; because 'wine maketh even wise men fall off'. But where the

poverty of the place will not permit the aforesaid measure to be had, but much less, or none at all, let those who live there bless God and murmur not.[17]

The clergy in Ireland could have benefited from a similar rule in the twelfth century when Giraldus Cambrensis said of them: 'You will not find one who, after all his rigorous observance of fasts and prayer, will not make up at night for the labours of the day, by drinking wine and other liquors beyond all bounds of decorum.'[18]

In the sixth century, 'wine from Gaul' was brought up the River Shannon to the community at Clonmacnoise, according to an account of the life of St Ciarán, the first abbot of Clonmacnoise. Much of Ireland's wine came through the port of Waterford due to its geographical position and safe harbour, and its easy access inland along the Barrow, Nore and Suir rivers. It was probably in this way, according to O'Neill, that Matthew O'Mukian, 'the unedifying abbot of Holy Cross, Co. Tipperary', who in 1488 was reproached for his involvement in the wine trade, received his goods, via the River Suir, on which his abbey was situated'.[19]

The work of the monks in making wine did not escape the attention of artists who were unable to resist depicting these men sneaking down to the monastery's cellar to have a glass or two. One was the German, Eduard von Grutzner (1846–1925), whose genre images of rotund and rosy-cheeked monks were popular (for a similar image see plate 7.2). So too was a German student song, called 'Brother Jerome', some of which went as follows:

> 'Where is Brother Jerome – Jerome?'
> The burly abbot said, 'He wasn't at vespers, vespers,
> Can he have gone to bed?'
> To the cell of Brother Jerome – Jerome,
> The abbot did then repair; But his crucifix, crucifix,
> Was all that he saw there!
> 'Where is Brother Jerome – Jerome?' The abbot asked once more;
> The sacristan pointed, pointed, To the open cellar door!
> They lighted a candle, candle
> And tottered down the stairs …
> Why he wasn't at vespers, vespers,
> There was no need to ask: He was sleeping and snoring, snoring,
> Beside the abbot's cask!
> He had emptied his tankard, tankard,
> And against the wall had sunk: The truth was Burschen, Burschen,
> That Brother Jerome was drunk![20] (plate 7.4)

In Tudor England vineyards were attached to monasteries, mostly in the south of the country, and grapes were grown on estates like that at Hatfield House in

7.4 Thomas Rowlandson, *Monks carousing outside a monastery.* Courtesy of the Yale Center for British Art, Paul Mellon Collection.

Hertfordshire. This house had been the residence of the bishops of Ely and it was likely that, as the Abbey of Ely was famous for its vines, they were also planted at Hatfield. It was to here in the early seventeenth century that the new owner, Robert Cecil, first earl of Salisbury, had 30,000 vines sent to him from France for his vineyard, a project that was ultimately unsuccessful.[21] The Dissolution of the Monasteries by King Henry VIII from 1536 put an end to the viniculture practised with much success by the monks in England, and so the art of tending vines there disappeared.[22]

Apart from its use in the celebration of Mass, wine was served to visiting dignatories and guests, it was drunk by the monks, given to the poor, and sold for the benefit of the monastery. It was also important, as has been seen, as a 'cure' in the case of illness, and looked upon as a remedy for those monks who were elderly, ill, or frail. In the twelfth century, according to St Laurence O'Toole's biographer, the saint used to entertain his guests with various kinds of wine but he drank only water 'slightly coloured with wine'.[23] Wine was enjoyed by the religious in the Priory of the Holy Trinity in Dublin (now Christ Church) in the mid-fourteenth century. It was permitted on great feast-days (approximately twelve per year), in the refectory, when 15*d*. worth of wine was allowed (15*d*. would buy about three gallons) among the dozen or so religious. Wine specifically for the Prior's Chamber was purchased on most days, sometimes two or three times and usually costing 2*d*. per gallon, but when he had visitors it could be more; in 1343 they paid 6*d*. a gallon for white wine when the archbishop of Dublin visited, and large purchases were made from Stephen de Gascoyne: 'for wines £6', and 'for 2 tuns, 35*s*.'.[24] However, as the Priory was just a few steps from the street of wine shops, Winetavern Street, it was not too inconvenient.[25] In fact, it may have only involved going down to the cellar of the church, as in the sixteenth century many wine taverns and vintners' cellars were described as being located 'under Christ Church, from the Dean and Chapter of which they were held', from one end of the minster to the other: in 1548 the Cathedral leased to a wine merchant called Arland Ussher 'the wine-tavern under the said church which the said Arland then enjoyed'.[26] In 1332 wine was being stored in these cellars at a rental of four shillings for sixteen days.[27] A letter dated 1633 from the lord deputy to the archbishop of Canterbury refers to his concerns that 'the vaults underneath the church itself turned all to ale houses and tobacco shops', and another account refers to these 'tippling rooms for beer, wine and tobacco, demised all to Papish recusants and by them and others … frequented in time of divine service, that, though there is no danger of blowing up the assembly above their heads, yet there is of poisoning them with the fumes'.[28]

While stories, cartoons and images of monks 'knocking back' surreptitious glasses of wine in the cellars of religious orders are amusing, the legacy of their experiments in the making of wine is enormous. They were major landowners in Europe: the Benedictines held as many as six monasteries in the diocese of Rheims and numerous vineyards elsewhere in the country. In Germany they owned and tended large vineyards in which they successfully cultivated the German Riesling grape. Cistercians, too, owned many vineyards in Europe; in France, according to Jancis Robinson, their Abbey of Clairvaux had extensive vineyards in Champagne, and the order was, apparently, the first to plant the chardonnay vine in Chablis.[29] It was their patience and hard work, their dedication, their scientific scrutiny of the land and its cultivation, that has played such a large part in our enjoyment of wine.

CHAPTER 8

Wine: the oldest medicine

FROM ANCIENT TIMES AND THROUGHOUT the eighteenth century, wine played a major part in medicine and in religious practices. The Greek Hippocrates (*c.*450 BC) was the first recognized practitioner who, having experimented with different wines for various ailments, recommended wine as a disinfectant, a medicine and part of a healthy diet. The Good Samaritan, after all, poured wine (and oil) into the wounds of the traveller that he encountered. The Roman physician Galen (second century AD) found through his experience of treating wounded gladiators that wine was the most effective disinfectant for wounds; the Talmud states that 'wine is the foremost of all medicines: wherever wine is lacking, medicines become necessary'; and wine was a feature in the worship of Bacchus, the god of wine.[1] In the thirteenth century, Roger Bacon, the philosopher and writer on alchemy and medicine, suggests that wine could (plate 8.1)

> preserve the Stomach, strengthen the Natural Heat, help Digestion, defend the Body from Corruption, carry the Food to all the Parts, and concoct the Food till it be turned into very Blood: It also cheers the Heart, tinges the Countenance with Red, makes the Tongue voluble, begets Assurance, and promises much Good and Profit.

'But', he warns, 'If it be over-much guzzled, it will on the contrary do a great deal of Harm: For it will darken the Understanding, ill-affect the Brain … beget shaking of the Limbs and Bleareyedness.'[2]

John Dymmok, an Englishman who came to Ireland possibly in the service of Lord Essex, in his *Treatise of Ireland* (1600), tended to blame the climate in Ireland for the amounts of wine and other liquors that were drunk:

> The cuntry lyeth very low, and therefore watrish and full of marishes, boggs and standing pooles, even in the highest mountaynes, which causeth the inhabitants, but especially the sojourners there, to be very subject to rheumes, catarrs, and flixes [*sic*] for remedy whereof they drinke great quantity of hott wynes, especially sackes and a kind of aqua vitae, more dryinge and less inflamynge, than that which is made in England.[3]

In the Tudor era when a man got drunk at home, a doctor's advice was to 'take a vomit with water and oil, or with a feather, or a rosemary branch, or else with his finger, or else let him go to bed to his sleep'.[4] In his book published in 1654,

8.1　Medical bag (possibly Irish?). Courtesy of the Wellcome Collection.

The tree of humane life; the blood of the grape, Tobias Whitaker stated that 'wine was one of the most important components in medical treatments meant to remove excess humours. It was called for in numerous remedies meant to provoke the body into emptying itself of any unwanted humours'. He further believed that wine was 'neerest to the nature of the Gods and their nature is incorrupt'; that those who regularly imbibed wine could be 'faire, fresh, plumpe, and fat'.[5] The humoural theory or system, elaborated by the physicians Hippocrates and Galen, taught that the human body was essentially composed of, and governed by, four liquids or 'humours' that balanced the body: black bile, yellow bile, blood and phlegm.

These humours were said to exist on two axes, moist-dry and cold-hot. Blood, for example, was moist and warm, while black bile was dry and cold. Each humour was associated with a different element, season and organ, and each contributed its character to the overall composition of the human body and each person's physical health and emotional temperament. In the event of a perceived imbalance, the remedies prescribed were bloodletting, that included leeches and cutting a vein, and purging by the use of emetics to encourage vomiting or laxatives to empty the bowels (plate 8.2).[6]

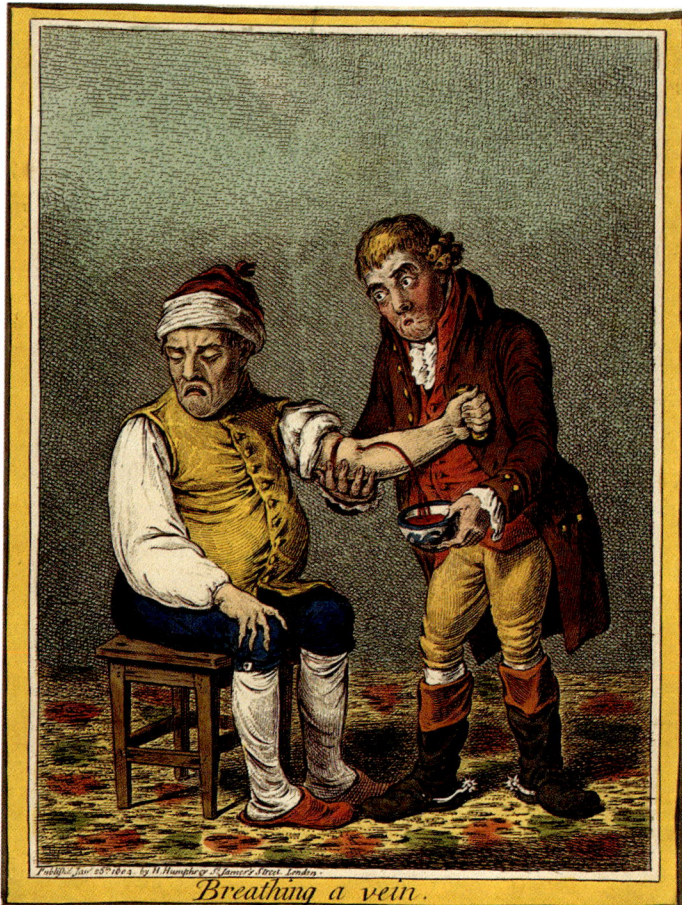

8.2 *Breathing a vein* (or, *An ill man being bled by a surgeon*), etching after J. Gillray, 1804. Courtesy of the Wellcome Collection. Blood was usually drawn from a vein in the arm and caught in a bowl or cup.

Even prior to Shakespeare's time, Dr William Vaughan, in his book *Approved directions for health* (1600), warned that 'sacke doth make men fat and foggy' though it 'comforteth the spirits marvellously'. Up to the 1540s, sack could be obtained only in apothecaries' shops, and was used solely for medicinal purposes.[7] In the early seventeenth century, and after a long and cold journey on his horse, Josias Bodley, an English military engineer, was offered wine containing burnt sugar, nutmeg and ginger, to warm him; and another military man, Sir William Brereton, was given 'cinnamon in burnt wine claret' to ward off 'the flux'.[8] A popular winter warmer, 'burnt' wine was achieved by plunging a hot poker into spiced wine. An almanac of 1686, entitled *Rider's British Merlin* – with a subtitle, 'Bedeckt with many delightful varieties and useful verities' – recommends in the month of June, 'Scurvey-Grass Ale, and Worm-wood Beer' as 'wholesome drinks', and advises, in August, 'Forbearing to sleep presently after meat' and 'Red wine and Claret are excellent Remedies for Children, against the Worms'.[9]

8.3 Lithograph by C.J. Winter, 1869, after T. Rowlandson, *Three doctors in close discussion, their patient being nursed in the next room.* Courtesy of the Wellcome Collection.

In the eighteenth and nineteenth centuries people were not shy about discussing their health with each other, probably doing so in the hope that a cure or panacea would be recommended. From correspondence it can be seen that they kept themselves informed regularly regarding complaints, sometimes checking up to see how an illness might be progressing or otherwise, constantly giving advice and sending recipes (or 'receipts') of 'cures' that they had experienced or of which they had been informed. In fact, it was expected that everyone had their store of medical 'cures', especially women, and those who did not were frowned upon, seen as being similar to a woman who was unable to bake, sew or manage the servants. A collection of recipes and cures written into or collected in a notebook was an important item in every household. Until the late eighteenth century, most doctors in Ireland were quacks with some exceptions, one being Lord Trimleston from Co. Meath, a distinguished botanist who had studied medicine in Paris. Surgery was extremely dangerous and often did not work, so bloodletting and blistering were frequently the treatments that were applied. As one doctor put it in a letter to a colleague in 1818, 'The superiority of bloodletting over wine, wine over bloodletting, will be successfully established two or three times in the course of every century'.[10] Daniel O'Connell remarked that 'almost all the diseases of persons in the upper classes do at middle life arise from repletion or over-much food in the stomach', which was probably true.[11] Among the upper classes, however, gout was the major health problem, particularly for men (plate 8.3).

'Irish hospitality' had another meaning for Lord Orrery, who commented in a letter to a friend: 'Lord Thomond is laid up with the Gout: the Irish Hospitality has broke out in his Feet, and pins him down to a great Chair and a slender Meal'.[12] Orrery would have agreed with William Buchan who was of the opinion in *Domestic Medicine* (1784) that excessive alcohol and idleness can be the causes of gout.[13] In his book, *A Treatise on the Gout* (1760), Charles Louis Liger wrote that 'in Great Britain there are perhaps as many if not more victims to this excruciating distemper than in any other part of the world'.[14] It would seem fairly obvious that, given the amounts of wine consumed in Ireland during the eighteenth and nineteenth centuries, there would be numerous health problems, among them gout, about which the barrister Jonah Barrington had this to say:

> I have heard it often said that, at the time I speak of, every estated gentleman in the Queen's County [Laois] was *honoured* by the gout ... its extraordinary prevalence was not difficult to be accounted for, by the disproportionate quantity of acid contained in their seductive beverage, called rum-shrub, which was then universally drunk in quantities nearly incredible, generally from supper-time till morning, by all country gentlemen, as they said, to keep down their claret.[15]

Barrington's grandfather was one of these gentlemen, and every season 'horse-loads' of boxes of oranges and lemons arrived at his house, Cullenaghmore, Co. Laois. As soon as word got around of this delivery, the colonel and his friends, night after night and in various neighbouring houses, enjoyed the pleasures of claret, followed by rum-shrub (see recipe below), made with the freshest of fruit. Eventually, as Barrington recalls, 'the gout thought proper to put the whole party *hors de combat* – having the satisfaction of making cripples for a few months such as he did not kill'.[16] (plate 8.4)

How effective rum-shrub was in 'keeping down their claret' is doubtful but drinkers obviously felt that it had some medicinal benefit, and this will be looked at later in the chapter. But to return to remedies for gout – paradoxically, Lord Molesworth recommended to his wife 'a large glass of strong wine' to be taken

8.4 Thomas Rowlandson (1757–1827), *Serving punch*. Courtesy of the Yale Center for British Art.

'pretty frequently'.[17] Conscious of his health, Jonathan Swift found wine essential for his disorders, 'and absolutely necessary to support me'; he wrote to Stella, 'I dined today with Mr Secretary St John, and staid till seven' yet 'would not drink his champaign and burgundy, for fear of the gout'.[18] (plate 8.5) A Dr Wright, in 1795, recommended Madeira as 'one of the most useful and best [remedies] for elderly persons in gouty habits', but Lord Chesterfield (1694–1773), who was sent an inferior bottle of it to help his complaint, wrote by return: 'Sir, I have tried your sherry and prefer the gout'.[19] (plate 8.6) In a letter to a doctor friend, Richard Lovell Edgeworth wrote that he could not understand how 'the entire class of middling people in this country, who drink intemperately of whiskey-punch, are exempt from the gout, gravel, and stone … and … they live to an old age … The gentlemen who drink wine, and eat luxuriously, are … afflicted with all the demons of disease, and flock to Bath and Spa, like regular birds of passage, every autumn'.[20] Apparently, the essayist Joseph Addison took exercise while composing: he would

8.5 James Gillray (1756–1815), *Punch cures the gout,–the colic,–and the 'Tisick'* or *Three people drinking punch as a cure for (right to left) gout, colic, and phthisis.* 1799. Courtesy of the Wellcome Collection.

walk up and down the long gallery in his London home, Holland House, at each end of which was placed an open bottle of wine, both of which were duly consumed in the process.[21] Pole Cosby's son wrote that his father's gout was attributed to the 'violent exercises' of his youth, 'for he strained his joynts and whole body so much that ye gout was knotted more in knobs with him than it would otherwise have done'. Such a description is perhaps not too surprising when he reveals the nature of these exercises:

> he wo'd vault over anything that he co'd reach to lay the first joints of his fingers on. Five horses set close standing by one another he wo'd lay his hand on the first horses neck, and vault into the saddle on the fifth horse, he wo'd commonly and make nothing of leaping over a fishpond 21 feet wide, he would

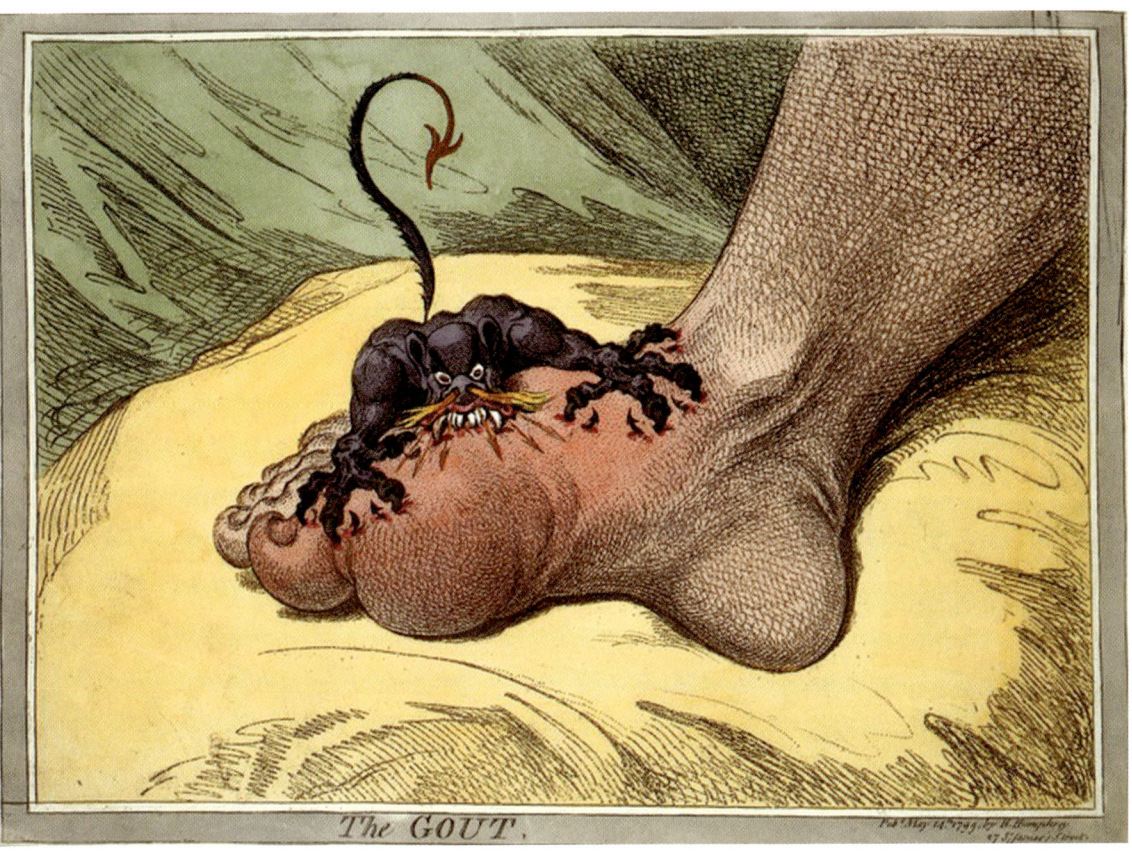

The GOUT.

8.6 James Gillray (1756–1815), *The Gout* [or] *A swollen and inflamed foot: gout is represented by an attacking demon.* 1799. Courtesy of the Wellcome Collection.

leap 24 feet on plain ground, he would follow a pack of fleet Hounds from morning till night and keep closer in with ye hounds than anyone on horseback, he danced on the roaps as well as any roap dancer that ever was ...[22]

In her 'Cooking recipes and medical cures', Mary Ponsonby has a couple of remedies for gout: one was for 'three grains of musk in a glass of Madeira or Tent sweetening it with sugar', while the recipe for the other sounds quite dramatic and required some muscle to prepare:

Take one pound of stone Brimstone pound in fine and pour one Gallon of Boiling water upon it in a stone jar, shake it several times a day for 2 or 3 days then draw it off for use, take half a pint every morning an hour before breakfast. The jar to be kept close stop'd.[23]

Tent, a sweet, dark, unfortified dessert wine from southern Spain, was enjoyed by Samuel Pepys; it was humorously referred to as a 'rich wine, drank generally as a stomachic'. It later became, incidentally, the wine used by the Church of England for communion.[24]

Drinking wine in moderation was generally considered to be therapeutic and to have health benefits, including nutrition. British soldiers in hot climates were recommended 'to moisten pretty frequently with Madeira, there is not such a Medicine in the whole Pharmacopaeia for a West India climate used *moderately*'.[25] An officer in the British army, Dr John Buchanan, writing in 1746, discounted the common (but correct) opinion that drinking strong, sweet wines encouraged gout: he states that 'Gouty Officers avoid drinking French wines, for fear of giving them the Gout, but in Flanders it's the only wine they drink, particularly Burgundy, Hermitage & acknowledge they never were so healthy. & in our Dutch cantonment French claret was drunk dayly & that freely, yet I don't remember many Gouty complaints'. His formula for maintaining health was quite standard: 'Spare dyet with good exercise & light wines seems to be the best preservative from Distempers'.[26] Katherine Conolly of Castletown, Co. Kildare, believed that 'when gout gets to the stomach nothing is found better than a spoonful or two of the juice of tansy [a flowering herbaceous plant with a history of medicinal use] in a glass of any strong wine and repeated'.[27]

Lady Kildare's problem was somewhat different. Before going to a ball in 1762 she had consumed an amount of wine, with her husband's approval. He counselled her afterwards: 'I think you were right in drinking near a pint before your ball, but should have advised Madeira rather than hock lest the effect might have occasion'd your going-forth oftener than you would have chosen upon such a day'.[28]

Advice and 'prescriptions' such as this on health matters were handed out like – well, glasses of claret. In the 1750s, Sir Edward O'Brien of Dromoland was advised by a friend to confine his drinking to three pints of wine instead of 'bumping away all night' with a gallon, while in 1783 a friend of William Conyngham's wrote to sympathize with his recent illness,

> occasioned by your being a Desciple of that foolish Dr Cadogan. It is not fit for you and me at our Time of Life to drink Water etc. He was a drunkard. We never were. Sometimes we have exceeded, as who of a good-natured Temper have not often. I beseech you not to drink less than a Bottle of good claret in condition after your Dinner and a Pint of old Port after your Supper.[29]

While the drinking of 'the sober gallon of claret' consumed by many was considered to be utterly excessive, doctors too believed in the positive health aspects of wine. Daniel O'Connell, suffering from 'a slow nervous fever', was advised by his doctor in 1794 to drink a bottle of port per day to cure it.[30] Thomas Jefferson said, 'I have lived temperately … I double the doctor's recommendation of a glass and half of wine each day and even treble it with a friend'.[31] For his daughter in her final illness in 1804, he recommended sherry: writing to his son-in-law who was with his wife at Monticello, 'The sherry at Monticello is old and genuine, and the Pedro Ximenes much older still and stomachic. Her palate and stomach will be the best arbiters between them'.[32] In France a major commercial spat occurred between the French regions when Louis XIV's physician recommended that the king should drink burgundy rather than champagne for his health.[33] In Dublin, Mrs Katherine Bayly's daughter-in-law gave her a present of hock when she was 'ill of the jaundice', as it was considered helpful in curing it; and the actor Tate Wilkinson, on his first visit to Dublin in the winter of 1757/8, took ill with a fever which lasted three weeks, from which he, too, recovered, he believed, by drinking hock; 'Mr Chaigneau often used to joke and say what an expensive guest I was to him, in old hock; the quantity I drank in whey, by his account, was incredible'.[34] Lord Byron recommended hock and soda-water as a hangover remedy, and Richard Brinsley Sheridan, regarding claret, insists in *School for Scandal* that 'women give headaches, this don't'.[35] The earl of Chesterfield's treatment, recommended by his doctor for an unspecified illness, involved 'the consumption of substantial amounts of mercury and burgundy' which he called 'my two most constant friends'.[36] Richard Lovell Edgeworth had his head shaved by his local barber in Edgeworthstown so that his wig would fit snugly, and whether it was the result of this, or perhaps to cure a condition like ringworm, he had his head treated with brandy.[37]

Even though drinkers and medical practitioners in the eighteenth century were fully aware that gout was a direct result of too much wine, it seemed to make little or no difference to their habit nor to the frequency with which they imbibed. A book such as *The juice of the grape, or, wine preferable to water* (1724) did not help. The author points out that, taken in moderate quantities, wine had the answer to every complaint: it has 'the power to sudden Refreshment, to warm the Stomach, gently stimulate its Fibres, promote Digestion, raise the Pulse, rarify the Blood, add to its Velocity, open Obstructions, forward Excretions, greatly promote insensible Perspiration, increase the natural Strength, and enlarge the Faculties both of Body and Mind'. Further, he believes that men 'of a good Constitution, whose Parts are sound and Vitals untainted', suffer no ill-effects from 'a continual debauch or excess in this exhilarating fluid, for a long series of Years; but always appear florid and gay, vigorous and lusty'.[38] The physician Sir Edward Barry was more measured in describing the effects of wine:

> When taken in just proportion, it surprisingly strengthens and excites the spirits; and in an increasing quantity gives a quick succession of agreeable ideas, banishes grief and fear and exalts the latent virtues or vices of the mind: But when too far increased, disturbs, and weakens all the functions of the

mind and body; ends at length in ebriety [inebriety?], insensibility, and all appearances of a temporary *Apoplexy* ...[39]

Barry tells of a patient of his own who, at about seventy years old, 'became leucophlegmatic [dropsical], his legs began to swell, and his appetite and digestion to be depraved'; he recommended a diet that included 'a pint of the best French claret every day' as his only drink, and he recovered.[40] Another patient, who had been ill for some days, was living on a daily ration of 'a Quart of Brandy, a Gallon of Milk and three new-laid Eggs': Barry advised him not to exceed the quart, as the patient admitted that 'he has no other way of banishing Melancholy Thoughts'.[41] The attitude reflects the belief in the 'humours' of the body, that a regulated intake of alcohol, either alone or with added ingredients, could be beneficial.[42] Soldiers who, when returning from Flanders to England and Ireland, often brought fevers with them, but when treated in hospital with 'the prudent use of Old Hock diluted with water, which is less inflammatory than any other Wine of the same strength, and the most grateful and septic cordial in putrid diseases', recovered well.[43] In eighteenth-century Britain, four wines were routinely stocked in shops for medicinal purposes: Mountain (a fortified wine from Malaga), Canary or sack, Rhenish (hock) and port: red wines were considered astringent, and white wine regarded as a mild laxative. As an antiseptic wine was widely used by military doctors to prevent conditions such as gangrene.[44]

The 'previously unpublished' diary of John Scott, first earl of Clonmell (1739–98), lord chief justice of the king's bench, appeared in print in 1880.[45] Jonah Barrington said of Scott that 'his passions were his slave, and his cunning was his instrument'.[46] He ate and drank excessively, becoming grossly overweight and was known by the nickname of 'Copper-faced Jack' on account of his red face (plate 8.7). His diary shows that he made many attempts to reduce his drinking and improve his way of living. It appears that he was 'helplessly drunk every night, [and] that a couple of able-bodied lackeys regularly came at twelve o'clock to carry his Lordship to bed'. In 1774 under a heading 'Good Resolutions' Scott writes 'I have given up wine'. He goes on, revealingly, worried about his career, 'The pains of the damned are not equal to the horrors of going to court unprepared, and the fact of losing your reputation and going down in it', and he exhorts himself to 'give up every object, pursuit, pleasure, avocation, diversion; banish everything from your mind but business, the business of your profession ... shun wine as a pest to business or if you may drink wine be sure to drink water with it'.[47] Scott died just before his sixtieth birthday and, as will be seen below, Jonah Barrington's grandfather and his friends were hale and hearty when probably in their sixties and seventies, though suffering from gout, having spent most of their lives imbibing wine. Jonah himself, another disciple of Bacchus, lived well into his seventies. Theobald Wolfe Tone (1763–98), one of the founding members of the United Irishmen, and leader of the

8.7 Gilbert Stuart (1755–1828), Portrait of John Scott, first earl of Clonmell (1739–98), otherwise known as 'Copper-faced Jack'. Public domain, via Wikimedia Commons.

1798 Rebellion, had, like Scott, a tendency to berate himself for his drinking habits in his journal with phrases such as 'Bad! Bad!', 'very drunk', 'wakened very sick' and 'generally very drunk – bed. God knows how', appearing frequently, as were his deliberations on 'leaving off the use of wine altogether'. By the mid-1790s, and living in France, however, he had sobered up, 'having retrenched my quantity of wine one half'.[48]

Drawn & Etched by Theodore Lane.   Engᵈ by Geo. Hunt.

CHAMPAIGN DRIVING AWAY REAL PAIN.

Wine Cures the Gout, the Colic and the Phthisic.
Wine it is to all men the very Best of Physic.

Published by Thoˢ. McLean. 26. Haymarket. London. 1827.

8.8 Aquatint by G. Hunt, *Champaign driving away real pain*, 1827, after Theodore Lane
(1800–28). Courtesy of the Wellcome Collection.

Following a dinner with colleagues in London, the Scottish diplomat and
politician Sir Gilbert Elliot (1722–77) wrote to a friend, 'I find the least quantity
of claret always affects my stomach, and consequently sinks my spirits instead of
the usual effect of wine, which I believe in this age is an advantage, for the men
of all ages drink abominably'; and he wonders how 'men of business and the
great orators of the House of Commons, contrive to reconcile it with their public
exertions'.[49] Richard Cumberland, the dramatist and civil servant, greatly enjoyed
the company of the publisher George Faulkner in Dublin, at whose house he dined.

He was impressed with the 'good meat and excellent claret in abundance; I sat at his table once from dinner till two in the morning, whilst George swallowed immense potations with one solitary sodden strawberry at the bottom of the glass, which he said was recommended to him by his doctor for its cooling properties'.[50] Concerned at the amount of alcohol that was being drunk in Ireland, a clergyman, Dr William Henry, appealed to the young, to those who had not started to drink, in fairly descriptive language, to

> cast your eyes on the habitual dram drinker, with his limbs decrepid by the gout; his veins and bladder tortured with the stone, the great glands full of putrifying sores; his schirrous liver swollen to an enormous load; his dropsical belly protuberant like a tun; his asthmatic lungs panting for breath; his shrivelled ghastly countenance discoloured into a blackish yellow by jaundice ...[51]

Jonathan Swift tended to blame champagne for illness: 'Your former comrades once so bright,/With whom you toasted half the night,/Of rheumatism and pox complain,/And bid adieu to dear Champaign'.[52] He wrote to Stella in 1711, 'Dined with Mr Domville ... I drank three or four glasses of champagne ... though it is bad for my pain; but if it continue, I will not drink any wine without water till I am well.[53] (plate 8.8) Swift wrote a poem for 'Stella's birthday' when 'a great bottle of wine, long buried, being that day dug up. 1722–3':

> Behold the bottle, where it lies
> With neck elated toward the skies!
> The god of winds and god of fire
> Did to its wondrous birth conspire;
> And Bacchus for the poet's use
> Pour'd in a strong inspiring juice.
> It drags behind a spacious womb,
> And in the spacious womb contains
>   A sovereign medicine for the brains.[54]

RECIPES FOR CURES

Well-run households had a book of recipes and remedies (sometimes referred to as 'receipts'), used by the family and very often handed down from one generation to the next. A number of these can be found in family archives in the National Library of Ireland, and other places, and they make for interesting reading. From these it is obvious that women exchanged recipes with friends whose names were noted in the recipe titles, or they would have read about recipes and/or cures and copied them into their book. Included in these were remedies for a multitude of illnesses, such as for 'the Plague', 'Hystericks' or 'To relieve the common Irish complaint of a pain about ye Heart' – for the latter 'strong tea made of peppermint or penny royal, add to this a little wine of any sort with some sugar, and take 3 spoonfuls a dose'. For a sore throat – gargle with '3 table spoonfuls of Claret, one of Vinegar, half a spoonful of Honey, a teasp of salt, a pinch of Alum, boil and scum it'; for a stomach pain – 'Half an ounce of rhubarb, a quarter of a nutmeg grated in a quart of Madeira – take a small wine glass going to bed'.[55]

It should be noted that there was no threshold age for children to be introduced to taking alcohol, as it was routinely used in both cooking and medicine. Mrs Mary Delany had a home-grown remedy for a little girl's cough – 'two or three snails boiled in her barley-water, or tea-water, or whatever she drinks, might be of great service to her' – and she offered 'two *infallible receipts*' to cure 'ague' (a fever or shivering fit) in children: one was 'pounded ginger, made into a paste with brandy, spread on sheep's leather, and a plaister of it laid over the navel'. The other was 'a spider put into a goose-quill, well sealed and secured, and hung about the child's neck as low as the pit of his stomach. Either of these I am assured will ease'.[56] These were 'external cures' which were fine for children, albeit odd, but Lady Morgan's sister, unwell as a child, was given 'four glasses of wine every day for ten days' by her father who remained convinced that it had 'done her much good'.[57] Bishop Synge told his daughter that when he was young and had toothache, his remedies were 'toasted figs to the Swell'd Gums, and Syrrup of Onions in the Ear'. As Alicia Synge's servant was recuperating from illness, claret was recommended by her father, the bishop, 'as long and as much as the Doctor pleases'.[58] Lord Robert Ponsonby Tottenham (1773–1850), bishop of Clogher and owner of Woodstock in Co. Wicklow, suffered from a skin condition and was recommended to immerse himself in a bath of red wine every evening. Unknown to the bishop, after his bath his enterprising servant duly decanted the contents of it into bottles and sold it in the local village.[59]

Katherine Conolly mentions numerous 'cures' in her letters from 1707 to 1747. She was disappointed to hear, in April 1731, that her sister Jane had stopped taking 'Assis [asses'] milk … till May is advanced'; this consisted of hartshorn shavings and water, milk, wine, rum or brandy and was recommended to be taken as a tonic after a long fever. She was a believer in garlic as a remedy for colic, rheumatism and asthma – a clove or two of bruised garlic in a glass of sack to be taken night and morning.[60] For asthma, Thomas Sheridan's cure also included garlic, but mixed with whiskey, bitter orange, gentian root, snake root and wormwood.[61] In another letter to Jane in 1739, Conolly is pleased that her sister is again taking the milk, and hopes she is enjoying the wine that she recently sent to her: 'I hope you will not be too sparing of it on yourself for 2 or 4 glassis a day will nather do you nor me hurt, for that is my stint at dinner. At night I never taste wine but a glass or 2 of punch which agrees better with me than any wine at night'.[62] It is interesting to note her preference for whiskey punch at night, and the regularity with which she took wine. So too with Richard Lovell Edgeworth who, advising the 'indisposed' Josiah Wedgwood in 1788 that he found, when unwell, that 'by relaxation, and by increasing my quantity of daily stimulus in the form of three or four glasses of claret, not port, and half a glass of porter', he restored himself to health.[63] Nicholas Peacock from Co. Limerick wrote in his diary in April 1741 that he gave Jon, his servant, 1*s*. 1*d*. to buy wine for himself as 'his illness hinders ye flow.'[64] Something that might have worked well for Jon was a remedy described as 'an excellent Diuretick' from an early eighteenth-century publication, in which it was recommended to 'Take 4 Pound of live Millepedes, infuse them cold in 8 Pints of White Wine for 14 Days; then strain for Use'.[65]

To twenty-first-century eyes some of these remedies are quite bizarre, but perhaps anything was worth trying and, at the time, they were possible lifelines. Women took pride in their collections of remedies, frequently to be found written in notebooks together with their recipes. The recipes make for some interesting reading as will be seen from the examples below.

HOME-MADE WINES, SHRUB AND SYLLABUB

In 'Big Houses', wine for cooking was given to the cook on application to the butler. However, there was no shortage of recipes to make wine at home. Hannah Glasse published *The art of cookery made plain and easy* in 1747, using, as she put it, plain language so that servants could understand it: it was a bestseller and hugely influential. In this, she offers recipes for making numerous types of wine: from raisins, elder, oranges, oranges with raisins, gooseberries, currants, cherries, birch, quince, cowslip or clary, raspberries and even turnip wine. Incidentally, Mrs Anne Donnellan, in a letter to her friend, the blue-stocking Mrs Elizabeth Montagu, remarks how 'few people are aware that a claret glass of cowslip wine before going to bed is an innocent and generally successful soporific'.[66] Mrs Glasse assures the reader that her elder-flower wine is 'very like Frontiniac'. The cost and the ingredients for 'Ten Gallons of Raisin Wine' are listed in an 1829 recipe book as follows: '2 lb Raisins @ 11*d*. per pound; a Stone Sugar 9*s*. 4*d*.; Lemons 1*s*. 8*d*.; A Gallon of Whiskey 6*s*. 8*d*.'[67] Wine was not held back in her recipes – most of her meat, game and poultry dishes contain it. A recipe for ginger wine compiled by the Pope family in Waterford in the early nineteenth century includes such a volume of ingredients that one wonders how they were able to physically make the wine, for example, twelve gallons of water and 28 pounds of brown sugar – both of which, along with other ingredients, including 12 ounces of bruised ginger, were to be 'boiled together for half an hour', then strained, and poured onto the rinds of 12 lemons.[68] And included in Henry Sandford's 'commonplace book' (see Chapter 2) is a recipe for 'Red Port' in which ten gallons of 'Coniac' brandy are added to '100 gallons of best and strong Syder, one pound of Allum powder'd fine', half a pound of Cochineal (the latter to be dissolved thoroughly in the brandy before being added), 'then mix all together, shaking them for some Days, keep it at least a year, or 2 years it's best'.[69]

'Shrub' or 'rum-shrub' has been mentioned already as the drink much-enjoyed by Jonah Barrington's grandfather and his friends; it was a popular drink between 1775 and 1825, and a favourite also with Thomas Jefferson, whose personal recipe for 'Orange Shrub' is as follows:

> To a Gallon of Rum two Quarts of Orange Juice and two pound of Sugar – dissolve the Sugar in the Juice before you mix it with the Rum – put all together in a Cask shake it well – let it stand 3 or 4 Weeks it will be very fine fit for Bottling – when you have Bottled off the fine pass the thick thro' a Philtring Paper put into a Tunnell – that not a drop may be lost.[70]

It has been said that shrub owes its existence to the smuggling of rum and brandy: the casks would be dropped strategically into the sea prior to the ship's landing, to be retrieved later.[71] When tainted by seawater, fruit peel and sugar would be added to the liquor to obscure the taste. In his book about the family wine and provisions firm, Alex Findlater mentions that they sold shrub, raspberry being a popular flavor, priced in 1827 at seven or eight shillings a gallon.[72] Shrub was sometimes served from its own decanter. According to Robin Butler, coloured decanters (blue, sometimes green) were thought to hold spirits. In half-bottle size, they usually came in sets of three – with gilded or engraved labels for Brandy, Rum and Hollands (gin). When there was a fourth decanter in the set, it was usually for Shrub.[73]

Sack posset was a custard-like drink, made from sack, ale and cream, sweetened and flavoured with nutmeg, and was a favourite pick-me-up of Sir Walter Raleigh's. Sack was, apparently, another wine that had health benefits: a Dr Shaw reported in 1724 that 'Mountain (a sweet wine from the Malaga region), excellent in the collick also banishes fever, gout and all sorts of ailments'. The health merits of sack were extolled by a seventeenth-century versifier:

> It comforts aged persons
> And seems their youth to render,
> It warmes the braines, it fils the veynes,
> And fresh bloud doth ingender.[74]

Syllabub was one of the very popular desserts of the period (see Chapter 3). Because of its festive appearance, it was a suitable dish for any celebration. The ingredients were whipped cream, whipped egg whites, white wine, sugar, lemon or orange juice and the zest of the fruit. The important thing was that the cream and egg white mixture should sit on top of the wine and fruit juice, and that it should be served in a wide-topped glass with a spoon, on a salver. It was also suggested that one might alternate red and white wine in the glasses to make it look even more attractive (see p. 83, plate 3.7). The frothier the top was, the better, and the best way to achieve that was to spray milk straight from the cow's udder (as that has a natural froth) into the wine. Such a recipe for syllabub using beer rather than wine appears in Elizabeth Raffald's book, *The experienced English housewife* (1769):

> To make a Syllabub under the cow:
> Put a bottle of strong beer and a pint of cider into a punch bowl, grate in a small nutmeg and sweeten it to your taste. Then milk as much milk from the cow as will make a strong froth and the ale look clear. Let it stand an hour, then strew over it a few currants well washed, picked and plumped before the fire. Then send it to the table.[75]

In a verse relating to the hawkers of Dublin who made their living selling their wares on the streets, Jonathan Swift wrote of an orange seller:

> Come, buy my fine Oranges, Sauce for your Veal,
> And charming when squeez'd in a Pot of brown Ale.
> Well roasted, with Sugar and Wine in a Cup,
> They'll make a sweet Bishop when Gentlefolks sup.[76]

Obviously, this drink was, as Swift asserts, consumed by the upper classes. 'Sweet Bishop', or 'smoking bishop' as Scrooge called it in Dickens' *A Christmas Carol*, was so called because the bitter oranges were roasted until the rind was blackened releasing the aromatic oils, the wine spiced with cloves, and sugar, then served hot: Lord Orrery, who asked Swift for the recipe, remarked that 'certainly the best oranges are the produce of your table'. It appears that 'bishop' refers to one of a group of drinks known as 'ecclesiasticals', named after various orders in the Catholic Church: if port is used instead of claret it is called a 'smoking cardinal'; if champagne replaces claret it is a 'smoking pope'.[77]

Food, its quantity and its effect on a person's health, did not seem to be of any real importance compared with the drinking of wine, which could and did cause ill-health but, according to the medical profession at the time, was also the remedy. Those who professed to be medical doctors were frequently charlatans, often caricatured by people like Rowlandson and Cruikshank. Women frequently died in childbirth: aristocratic and gentry women tended to hand their newborn babies to a wet nurse, so as not to get too emotionally close to the child as infant mortality was high, and smallpox common. On that very point, however, one of the revolutionary achievements in medical science took place in the eighteenth century – immunization, and the successful use of a vaccine against smallpox. Perhaps less spectacular, but of interest regarding the subject of this book, was another medical discovery – percussion, a method of investigating diseases of the chest. Apparently, the physician who discovered it, whose father was an innkeeper, conceived the idea of tapping the chest with his fingers as he had used this method when he was younger to gauge the level of the wine in his father's casks.

Epilogue

THERE CAN BE NO DOUBT THAT in Ireland an extraordinary amount of alcohol, particularly whiskey among the lower classes, and wine among the upper classes, was consumed in the eighteenth century. Neither is there any doubt about the gargantuan amounts of food provided for guests on the dining tables of the numerous Big Houses, as related by visitors and natives alike. It is fair to say, however, that alcohol abuse was fairly rampant in England at the same time. Samuel Johnson recalled that, when he was a child, 'all the decent people in Lichfield got drunk every night, and were not the worse thought of', and in the 1730s, George Edward Pakenham, after a 'delightful' season of hunting in Co. Westmeath, remarked that 'the fox hunters [in Ireland] live much after the same manner in England and drink as hard'.[1] The drinking culture of eighteenth-century Ireland, however, owed much to the need for British interests to maintain the political adherence of the uncertain loyalties of the Irish at the time. It was a fairly oppressive protestant century for the most part and everyone – including Swift – had to be quick on their political feet between the Williamite wars and the more liberal expressions of the 1790s.

From the latter decades of the eighteenth century the amounts of both alcohol and food taken were less excessive, something that was remarked upon by many observers, like Philip Luckombe who wrote in 1779 that he had been 'happily disappointed; the bottle is circulated freely, but not to that excess we have heard it was, and I of course dreaded to find'. Arthur Young agreed, noting that at dinner everyone drank as much or as little as they pleased, 'nor have I ever been asked to drink a single glass more than I had an inclination for' and he asserted that 'hard drinking is very rare among people of fortune'.[2] As early as 1769, George Faulkner informed Lord Chesterfield (who, as has been seen, was highly critical of Ireland's drinking habits in the 1740s) that 'drinking is a good deal lessened'; and Richard Twiss observed in 1775 that 'hospitality and drinking went formerly hand in hand, but since the excesses of the table have been so judiciously abolished, hospitality is not so violently practised as heretofore'.[3] According to Powell, 'in the 1720s, 12.4m gallons of wine were consumed in Ireland. This had increased by 15 per cent by 1791, but in the intervening period the population had actually doubled,' and Clarkson and Crawford note that 'during the long eighteenth-century the gentry of Ireland ate and drank in ways that that were not greatly different from those of the gentry in England'.[4] It should be mentioned, however, that while the consumption of wine was in decline in Ireland, the gap was partly filled by an increase in the consumption of beer and whiskey.

9.1 *L'après-dinée des Anglais*. From *Scènes Anglaises dessinées à Londres, par un français prisonnier de guerre.* Hand-coloured etching, France, 1814. © Trustees of the British Museum. Six men in varying stages of intoxication surround a low, cloth-covered dining table (not bare as was customary for dessert), on which are a big punchbowl, bottle, and glasses. One lies on the floor clasping a bottle and shouting, his chair overturned. Two pairs converse affectionately; an elderly man, his elbows on the table, supports his head, registering anguish. A seventh stands at a sideboard with a chamber pot taken from a cupboard in the sideboard.

So, what brought about the change?

It had much to do with the abolition of Grattan's parliament and the Act of Union in 1800, after which the status of Dublin as a capital city and the nucleus of the social and political life of Ireland was reduced. The Protestant ascendancy retreated to their country estates or departed to England. The houses on the graciously-laid-out squares and streets of the capital were sold and were now occupied by doctors and lawyers, as a middle class emerged, particularly after Catholic Emancipation in 1829. Maria Edgeworth, writing in 1819, noted a change in the lifestyles or the 'manners' of the gentry between the 1770s and 1820s, including the disappearance of the 'desperately tiresome formal dinners' at which guests consumed 'more than they could eat and twenty times more than they should drink'. In her book *The Absentee,* set after the Union, the hero Lord Colombre found 'in all its warmth' the hospitality of which his father had boasted, 'but meliorated and refined; less convivial, more social; the fashion of hospitality had improved. To make the stranger eat or drink to excess, to set before him old wine and old plate, was no longer the sum of good breeding'; and the statistician Edward Wakefield noted in 1812 that, in his experience, gentlemen did not begin to drink until after the post-meal tea and coffee were served and nor was there any compulsion for them to drink at all.[5]

Some of this positive change might be put down to the temperance movements of the time, allied to an increase of evangelical activity, both of which would have helped to put a stop to some of the activities of the more notorious clubs in the country. Temperance societies were firmly established in Ireland by 1829, and having some success. This is underlined by a letter from a Wexford man, John Cooney, to his wine merchant in Dublin in 1840 informing him that he will not order any more spirits or wine until his stock reduces, as 'Temperance is the order of the day here & drinking going quite out of fashion'.[6] The medical profession was much to the fore in promoting the movement even though it would have a negative effect on their earnings, a point made by Dr John Cheyne, physician-general to the army in Ireland, who acknowledged that 'numerous diseases, from rheumatism to insanity, were either brought on or considerably worsened by drinking'.[7]

Eighteenth-century Ireland is an interesting place in so many ways. Emerging from the wars of the previous century, peace allowed politics to operate (to a limited degree) and a class of people emerged, eager to copy the habits of the country that ruled them, in their buildings, possessions and manners. The historian R.B. McDowell puts it well:

> in considering the Irish way of life, two factors should be taken into account. In it the landed world enjoyed a greater social predominance than in any part of the British Isles, and its attitudes to expenditure, contempt for close account-keeping and quick competitiveness in expansive living, went almost unchallenged. Moreover, the living standards of both upper- and middle-class Irishmen tended, to some extent at least, to be fixed by those of the more prosperous country with which Ireland had close ties.[8]

But while they may have aped much of what England possessed, the Irish did not follow their fashion in drink: they left port to the English, and remained faithful to their beloved claret (plate 9.1).

In some ways one can perhaps understand how French wine, claret, in particular, found so much favour in eighteenth-century Ireland with the aristocracy, gentry and the type of 'Irish' gentry described by Jonah Barrington in 1827 as 'half-mounted' gentlemen – in his opinion, those who did not possess the full complement of horses, carriage, etc. to be a *real* gentleman. After the wars of the previous century, it was safe to build houses that were not fortified on their estates, trees (badly needed after the wars) were planted, and many had money to furnish their houses with the best they could afford, including monogramed silverware and tableware. That accomplished, the entertaining began.

Historically the Irish have been hospitable – welcoming, feeding and enjoying company. That resulted, as has been seen, to use Lord Orrery's term, in 'gargantuan feasts' where claret was always served. Then there were the strong, familial and indeed ancient links with Bordeaux to all parts of Ireland. France was a Catholic country, often at war with England; and when taxes became prohibitive between those two countries, while the very wealthy English remained largely faithful to claret, port became the substitute drink of preference there. Drunkenness was omnipresent, from the Castle in Dublin, to the newly formed clubs and fraternity gatherings that became so fashionable, to the dinner parties in the houses of the aristocracy and the gentry. It brought about illnesses, especially gout or, to borrow Orrery's term for the complaint, 'the Irish hospitality' and, perhaps unsurprisingly, remedies for this included a bottle of claret before retiring. It begged the question posed by Bishop Berkeley: 'Whether it be really true that such wine is best as most encourages drinking, *i.e.* that must be given in the largest dose to produce its effect? And whether this holds with regard to any other medicine?'[9] Berkeley and Samuel Madden were concerned about the vast sums of money being spent on French wine: Madden did not hold back in his criticism of the gentleman who 'feeds an idle crowd of Eaters and Drinkers at his table and swills their Gutts there with French wine, that is, with the Blood of his Country'.[10]

It is perhaps apposite to end with this quote from Samuel Madden. The quote above comes from his book published in 1738, at a time when the demand in Ireland for French wine was not exceptionally high when compared with the later acceleration in import figures from the 1750s, and the continued growth in demand upwards to the figures quoted in Chapter 1. In hindsight, perhaps it was better for Madden that he was spared the need to comment on this.

Notes

INTRODUCTION

1   Quoted in Elizabeth Malcolm, *'Ireland sober, Ireland free': drink and temperance in nineteenth-century Ireland* (Dublin, 1986), p. 39.
2   Thomas Cromwell, *Excursions through Ireland: province of Leinster* (London, 1820), i, p. 50.
3   William H.A. Williams, *Creating Irish tourism: the first century, 1750–1850* (Cambridge, 2010), pp 31–2.
4   E. Melville, *Sketches of society in France and Ireland, years, 1805–6–7* (Dublin, 1811), p. 139.
5   Laurence Whyte, 'The Parting Cup, or, The Humours of *Deoch an Doruis* …', *Original poems on various subjects, serious, moral, and diverting* (Dublin, 1742, 2nd ed.), p. 94.
6   Clairet is a mix of white and red grapes fermented together. Small quantities of this dark pink wine are still being produced in Bordeaux under the appellation Bordeaux Clairet, which wine experts advise should be drunk 'as young as possible'.

CHAPTER I 'Their wine is chiefly claret'

1   The quotation that gives the title to this chapter is taken from J. Bush, *Hibernia Curiosa* (1769).
2   Elizabeth Malcolm, *'Ireland sober, Ireland free': drink and temperance in nineteenth-century Ireland* (Dublin, 1986), pp 1–2.
3   Ibid., p. 10.
4   *Dublin Penny Journal*, 24 (8 December 1832), i, p. 190.
5   Ted Murphy, *A kingdom of wine: a celebration of Ireland's wine geese* (Cork, 2005), p. 24.
6   Arthur Young, *A tour in Ireland* (London, 1780), vol. 2, p. 326.
7   Máirtín Mac Con Iomaire, 'Gastro-topography: exploring food-related placenames in Ireland', *Canadian Journal of Irish Studies*, 38:1/2 (2014), pp 126–57 at 131.
8   Murphy, *A kingdom of wine*, p. 30.
9   Thomas Wright (ed.), *Giraldus Cambrensis: the topography of Ireland* (tr. T. Forester) (Ontario, 2000), p. 13.
10 Finola O'Kane, *Landscape design in eighteenth-century Ireland* (Cork, 2004), p. 176.
11 Sara Paston-Williams, *The art of dining: a history of cooking and eating* (The National Trust, 1993, 1999 edn), p. 34. Verjuice is mentioned in many 'receipt' or recipe books in the National Library of Ireland.
12 Patricia McCarthy, 'Vails and travails: how Lord Kildare kept his household in order', *IADS*, 6 (2003), pp 120–39.
13 John Gilbert (ed.), *Calendar of ancient records of Dublin* (19 vols, Dublin, 1889–1944), 6, p. 364.
14 Peadar Livingstone, *The Fermanagh story* (Enniskillen, 1969), p. 122.
15 Toby Barnard, *Making the grand figure: lives and possessions in Ireland, 1641–1770* (London and New Haven, 2004), p. 38. 'Sack' was the name used from the sixteenth century for sherry and fortified wines from Spain. Much enjoyed by Shakespeare's Sir John Falstaff, it was often mixed with spice.
16 T. Barnard, 'The cultures of eighteenth-century Irish towns' in P. Borsay & L. Proudfoot (eds), *Provincial towns in early modern England and Ireland: change, convergence and divergence*. Proceedings of the British Academy, 108 (2002), pp 195–222.
17 Maria Edgeworth, *Castle Rackrent* (Oxford, 1980 ed.), p. 55.
18 Charles Ludington, *The politics of wine in Britain: a new cultural history* (London, 2013), p. 114.
19 Quoted in James Kelly, 'The consumption and sociable use of alcohol in eighteenth-century Ireland', *PRIA*, 115C (2015), pp 219–55 at p. 227.

20 L.M. Cullen, 'The Irish merchant communities of Bordeaux, La Rochelle and Cognac in the eighteenth century' in L.M Cullen & P. Butel (eds), *Négoce et industrie en France et en Irlande au xviii siecles* (Bordeaux, 1978, 1980 edn), pp 51–63 at p. 53.

21 James Kelly, 'The consumption and sociable use of alcohol', p. 227, and Malcolm, '*Ireland sober, Ireland free*', pp 28–9.

22 Richard Hayes, 'Liens Irlandais avec Bordeaux' in R. Hayes, C. Preston, J. Weygand, *Les Irlandais en Aquitaine* (Bordeaux, 1971), pp 3–18 at p. 18.

23 Martyn J. Powell, *The politics of consumption in eighteenth-century Ireland* (London, 2005), p. 11.

24 Online ref. GEO/MAIN/52878-79, gpp.royalcollection.org (accessed 9 September 2018).

25 Constantia Maxwell, *Dublin under the Georges, 1714–1830* (London, 1937, 1997 ed.), p. 102.

26 Barnard, *A new anatomy of Ireland, the Irish Protestants, 1649–1770* (London and New Haven, 2003), pp 78, 308.

27 Richard Hayes, 'Irish links with Bordeaux', *Studies: An Irish Quarterly Review*, 27:106 (1938), pp 291–306.

28 Edmund Penning-Rowsell, *The wines of Bordeaux* (London, 1969, ed. 1973), p. 193.

29 Murphy, *A kingdom of wine*, p. 49.

30 Penning-Rowsell, *The wines of Bordeaux*, p. 152. Benicarlo, a strong and full-flavoured wine, was exported to France for mixing with claret.

31 *A Frenchman's walk through Ireland, 1796–7*, translated from the French of De Latocnaye by John Stevenson (Dublin, 1917), p. 147.

32 Penning-Rowsell, *Wines of Bordeaux*, p. 155.

33 Murphy, *A kingdom of wine*, p. 41.

34 Penning-Rowsell, *Wines of Bordeaux*, p. 156.

35 Robinson, *The Oxford companion to wine*, pp 37, 82. The 2017 Chateau Mouton Rothschild, for example, is a mix of 90 per cent Cabernet Sauvignon, 9 per cent Merlot and 1 per cent Petit Verdot.

36 Ludington, *The politics of wine in Britain* (London, 2013), pp 82–3.

37 *Letters written by the late Jonathan Swift, DD, Dean of St Patrick's, Dublin, and several of his friends. From the year 1710 to 1742* (London, 1769), v. p. 253.

38 Quoted in Maxwell, *Dublin under the Georges*, pp 314–15.

39 Ludington, *The politics of wine in Britain*, p. 113.

40 *The diary of Samuel Pepys*, entry 20 January 1661/62, www.pepysdiary.com, accessed 29 August 2018.

41 Jonathan Swift, *Journal to Stella*, letter 16, February 1710–11, p. 149. Online Project Gutenberg e-book ed. Accessed 26 March 2020.

42 Thomas Sheridan (ed.), Letter to Sir Charles Wogan in Spain, 1735, *The works of the Revd Jonathan Swift, DD* (London, 1801, revised ed.), xiii, p. 210.

43 Jon Hurley, *A matter of taste, a history of wine drinking in Britain* (Stroud, 2005), p. 148.

44 Barnard, *Making the grand figure*, pp 331–2.

45 J. Bush, *Hibernia curiosa: a letter from a gentleman in Dublin to his friend at Dover in Kent* (Dublin, 1769), p. 26.

46 Ludington, *The politics of wine in Britain*, p. 83.

47 The diary of Samuel Pepys, entry for Friday, 10 April 1663 in www.pepysdiary.com, accessed 8 February 2019; Hurley, *A matter of taste*, p. 131.

48 Quoted in Tara Kellaghan, 'Claret, the preferred libation of Georgian Ireland's elite', Submission for DIT Dublin Gastronomy Symposium 2012, pp 1–13.

49 Robinson, *The Oxford companion to wine*, p. 173.

50 'Claret and London; hedonism and claret', accessed online 15 May 2019, www.economist.com/christmas-specials/2009/12/17/hedonism-and-claret

51 Robinson, *The Oxford companion to wine*, pp 693–4.

52 Edward McParland, unpublished paper on Provost Andrews at a Trinity Monday discourse in 2010 (IAA). My thanks for permission to use it.

53 George Mott, 'Eating and drinking habits in Ireland two hundred years ago', *Irish Ancestor*, 5:1 (1973), pp 7–11.

54 F. Power Cobbe, *Life of Frances Power Cobbe as told by herself* (London, 1904 ed.), pp 16–17.
55 PRONI, D3044/F/13, volume compiled by Lord Clanwilliam marked on cover 'Fragmentary, August 1795–June 1850'.
56 Charles A. Read (ed.), *The cabinet of Irish literature* (London, 1884), ii, p. 89.
57 Marie-Louise Legg (ed.), *The Synge letters, 1746–1752* (Dublin, 1996), letter 106, 3 August 1750.
58 Penning-Rowsall, *Wines of Bordeaux*, p. 105.
59 Hurley, *A matter of taste*, p. 111.
60 Penning-Rowsall, *Wines of Bordeaux*, pp 437–8.

CHAPTER 2 Wine cellars, merchants and links with Bordeaux

1 Sir Edward Barry, *Observations, historical, critical, and medical, on the wines of the ancients* (London, 1775), pp 477–8.
2 Finola O'Kane, *Landscape design in eighteenth-century Ireland: mixing foreign trees with the natives* (Cork, 2004), p. 43.
3 T.C. Barnard, 'Gardening, diet and "improvement" in later seventeenth-century Ireland', *Journal of Garden History*, 10 (1990), pp 71–85, at p. 77.
4 Vandra Costello, *Irish demesne landscapes, 1660–1740* (Dublin, 2016), pp 89–90.
5 Alexander Henderson, *The history of ancient and modern wines* (London, 1824), p. 277.
6 Barry, *Observations*, p. 68.
7 Leon Battista Alberti, *De re aedificatoria*, Book 5, Chapter 17, p. 150.
8 Barry, *Observations*, pp 70–1.
9 Hugh Johnson, *World atlas of wine* (London, 1985 ed.), p. 48.
10 Barry, *Observations*, p. 10; Erik Larsen, *The devil in the white city* (London, 2004), p. 40; Robinson, *The Oxford companion to wine*, p. 416.
11 Heinz-Gert Woschek (ed.), *Wine and architecture* (Birkhäuser, 2013), p. 10.
12 *The Dublin Journal*, 26–9 October 1734.
13 My thanks to Dr Conor Lucey for this reference.
14 PRONI, Earl of Erne Papers, D1939/2/24/4, Crom Castle, wine cellar, plan and sections.
15 Johnson, *World atlas of wine*, p. 49.
16 Robin Butler, *Great British wine accessories, 1550–1900* (Suffolk, 2009), p. 17.
17 Sir John Dalrymple, *Memoirs of Great Britain and Ireland* (Dublin, 1773), App., Pt. II, 59.
18 Pat Rogers, *The life and times of Thomas, Lord Coningsby: the Whig hangman and his victims* (London, 2011), pp 53–4.
19 Butler, *Great British wine accessories*, p. 14.
20 John Hailman, *Thomas Jefferson on wine* (Jackson, MI, 2006), p. 4.
21 Caroline Le Mao, 'A pioneer institution in the capital of wine: Mitchell glassware 18th century'. http://www.verre-histoire.org/colloques/innovations/pages/p401_01_lemao.html#anbp3, accessed 6 March 2021.
22 From www.verre-et-cristal.com/pierre_mitchell.php, accessed 3 August 2019.
23 https://www.decanterchina.com/en/knowledge/producers/chateau-du-tertre, accessed 3 August 2019.
24 Eliza was a sister of Count Jean-Baptiste Lynch, mayor of Bordeaux. www.verre-et-cristal.com/pierre_mitchell.php, accessed 3 August 2019.
25 M.S.D. Westropp, *Irish glass: an account of glass-making in Ireland from the XVIth century to the present day* (London, 1921), p. 51.
26 Andre L. Simon, *Bottlescrew days: wine drinking in England during the eighteenth century* (London, 1926), p. 234.
27 Butler, *British wine accessories*, p. 26.
28 Ibid., pp 28, 34.
29 My thanks to Dr Conor Lucey for images of these labels.
30 National Archives of Ireland, Accession 99/10, Lamphier/Lanphier Estate, 2/17, Renewal of lease for lives by The Rt Hon Lodge Redmond Viscount Frankfort de Montmorency to John

Pennefather Lanphier, Kilkenny City of The White Hart Inn, 2 January 1830. My thanks to Aideen Ireland for this information.

31 Jack Kenny, 'Ancient label history' on www.labelandnarrowweb.com, 14 July 2017, accessed 18 January 2020.

32 PRONI, Villiers Stuart Papers, MS T3131/C/5/61, letter from Maurice Ronayne to Grandison, London, 9 August 1730. My thanks to Dr Anne Casement.

33 Marie-Louise Legg, '"Irish wine": the import of claret from Bordeaux to provincial Ireland in the eighteenth century' in Raymond Gillespie & R.F. Foster (eds), *Irish provincial cultures in the long eighteenth-century: making the middle sort: essays for Toby Barnard* (Dublin, 2012), pp 93–105 at 94–5.

34 Legg (ed.), *The Synge letters, 1746–1752* (Dublin, 1996), letter 55: 4 July 1749.

35 Hock is the generic term for white wine from the Rhine regions (also called Rhenish wines), or sometimes for German wines in general. Robinson, *Oxford companion*, p. 346; Legg, '"Irish wine"', pp 93–105; Legg, *The Synge letters*, letter 191: 27 June 1752.

36 Legg, *The Synge letters*, letter 6: 19 May 1747; letter 138: 11 June 1751; letter 180: 22 May 1752; letter 173: 4 October 1751.

37 NLI, Townley Hall Papers, MS 9540, account book of (unnamed) wine merchant in Drogheda, 1773–85,

38 hazelwoodheritagesociety.com, accessed 3 August 2019.

39 *The diary of Samuel Pepys*, 20 January 1661/2, www.pepysdiary.com, accessed 29 August 2018.

40 A.P.W. Malcomson, *John Foster: the politics of the Anglo-Irish ascendancy* (Oxford, 1978), pp 18–19.

41 PRONI, D562/9265, letter from John Page, Dundalk, to John Foster, Collon, dated 27 August 1814.

42 PRONI, T2519/4/1006, Foster Massereene Papers, letter from Sneyd & Co. to John Foster, 8 November 1808.

43 Terence Dooley, 'Copy of the marquis of Kildare's household book, 1758', *Archivium Hibernicum*, 62 (2009), pp 183–220 at 215.

44 *Mrs Beeton's book of household management* (1982 ed.), p. 963.

45 PRONI, MIC170, Lord Dacre/Barrett-Lennard family (Clones) papers.

46 H.F. Berry, 'Notes from the diary of a Dublin lady in the reign of George II', *Journal of the Royal Society of Antiquaries of Ireland*, 8:2 (30 June 1898), pp 141–54 at 141–2.

47 NLI, Clonbrock Papers, MS 19,503, Cellar book of Luke and Robert Dillon, 2nd and 3rd Barons Clonbrock (1808–27), pp 3–5.

48 PRONI, Shannon Papers, D2707/A/1/11/16, letter undated.

49 Paston-Williams, *The art of dining*, p. 219.

50 NLI, MS 2548, Ormond Papers, 'House book with accounts of stores & provisions'.

51 J.L. McCracken, 'The social structure and social life, 1714–60' in T.W. Moody & W.E. Vaughan, (eds), *A new history of Ireland*, iv: *Eighteenth-century Ireland, 1691–1800* (Oxford, 1986, 2009 ed.), pp 31–56 at p. 39.

52 Ted Murphy refers to those who fled to France and Spain as the 'wine geese' in his book, *A kingdom of wine*.

53 J.G. Simms, 'The Irish on the Continent, 1691–1800' in Moody & Vaughan (eds), *A new history of Ireland*, iv, pp 629–56 at p. 647.

54 Barnard, *A new anatomy*, p. 308.

55 Antoin E. Murphy, *Richard Cantillon: entrepreneur and economist* (Oxford, 1986), p. 25.

56 Louis Cullen, 'The Irish merchant communities of Bordeaux, La Rochelle and Cognac in the eighteenth-century' in L.M. Cullen & P. Butel (eds), *Négoce et industrie en France et en Irlande aux XVIII e et XIXe siècles* (Bordeaux, 1978), pp 51–63 at p. 53.

57 Murphy, *A kingdom of wine*, p. 41.

58 Penning-Rowsell, *Wines of Bordeaux*, pp 151–2.

59 T.P. Whelehan, *The Irish wines of Bordeaux* (Dublin, 1990), p. 25.

60 Ibid., pp 157–8.

61 Murphy, *A kingdom of wine*, p. 45.

62 Correspondence with Keith MacCarthy Morrogh, 22 July 2019.

63 Cullen, 'The Irish merchant communities of Bordeaux, La Rochelle and Cognac' in Cullen & Butel (eds), *Négoce et industrie en France et en Irlande*, pp 51–63 at p. 57.

64 Report by Dave Pollock, Ormond Castle, Carrick on Suir, Co. Tipperary; building remains in the middle/lower yard, May/June 2017, and email to author, 3 July 2018.

65 Henry Blackall, 'The Galweys of Munster', *JCHAS*, 71:213/14 (1966), pp 138–58 at pp 140–1.

66 Simms, 'The Irish on the Continent, 1691–1800' in Moody & Vaughan (eds), *A new history of Ireland*, iv, pp 629–56 at 649; Cullen, 'The Irish merchant communities of Bordeaux, La Rochelle, and Cognac' in Cullen & Butel (eds), *Négoce et industrie en France et en Irlande*, pp 51–63 at 58.

67 Correspondence with Keith MacCarthy Morrogh, 22 July 2019, in author's possession.

68 PRONI, Wilmot Papers, T3019/5342, Waite, Dublin Castle to Wilmot, 14 October 1766, & T3019/5343, George Boyd, Abbey Street, Dublin to Waite on same date.

69 Kelly, 'The consumption and sociable use of alcohol in eighteenth-century Ireland', pp 232–3.

70 Louis Cullen, 'The Boyds in Bordeaux and Dublin' in Thomas M. Truxes (ed.), *Ireland, France and the Atlantic in a time of war: reflections on the Bordeaux–Dublin letters 1757* (London, 2017), pp 51–69 at p. 57.

71 Paloma Fernández Pérez, *El rostro familiar de la metrópoli. Redes de parentesco y lazos mercantiles en Cádiz, 1700–1812* (Madrid, 1997), p. 166.

72 Margaret Murphy & Michael Potterton, *The Dublin region in the Middle Ages: settlement, land use and the economy* (Dublin, 2010), p. 456.

73 Liam Murphy, *Waterford merchants and their families on distant shores* (Dublin, 2018), p. 26.

74 Kevin Down, 'Colonial society and economy' in Art Cosgrove (ed.), *A new history of Ireland*, ii: *Medieval Ireland, 1169–1534* (Oxford, 1987), pp 439–91 at 489; Timothy O'Neill, *Merchants and mariners in medieval Ireland* (Dublin, 1987), p. 44; Andre Simon, *The history of the wine trade in England*, p. 227.

75 Richard Hayes, 'Irish links with Bordeaux', *Studies: An Irish Quarterly Review*, 27:106 (June 1938), pp 291–306 at p. 293.

76 Liam Murphy, *Waterford merchants and their families*, p. 220.

77 Legg, '"Irish wine"', p. 97. In Waterford, a large number of pottery wine jugs from Bristol, Bruges and Bordeaux were discovered in city centre excavations. E. McEneaney, 'When Waterford was the wine capital of Ireland' (text from Waterford Treasures Museum).

78 Timothy O'Neill, *Merchants and mariners*, pp 51, 56.

79 Hurley, *A matter of taste*, p. 202

80 Patrick Walsh & A.P.W. Malcomson, *The Conolly archive* (IMC, Dublin, 2010), MSS 717, letter to Conolly, 17 March 1781, p. 176.

81 http://www.historyofparliamentonline.org/volume/1820-1832/member/sneyd-nathaniel-1767–1833, accessed 12 April 2018.

82 NLI, De Vesci Papers, MS 38,921, 1799–1806, Letters & bills from Sneyd & Blackwood 1804–6 to Viscount de Vesci.

83 PRONI, Abercorn Papers, D623/A/96/10, letter from James Hamilton Jnr, Strabane to Marquess of Abercorn, 25 February 1804 regarding payment of £72 13s.1d. (online); John S. Powell, Documents on Portarlington, No. 3, 'The Emo Estate, 1798–1852', purchases in 1826, 1832 and 1833; PRONI, D562/15574, letter to John Foster from Nathaniel Sneyd re order for wine, December 1812. Foster's niece, Ann, was married to a member of the Sneyd family.

84 Cobbe Family Archive, 'A document of extracts from the Cobbe Family Papers at Newbridge House, Co. Dublin re: wine, drinks, vintners and merchants', compiled by C. Dowd Smith, 2017.

85 John Russell (ed.), *Memoirs, journal and correspondence of Thomas Moore* (London, 1853), vol. 4, p. 129.

86 Angela Byrne (ed.), *John (Fiott) Lee in Ireland, England & Wales, 1806–07* (Oxford, 2018), p. 304.

87 Carlow County Library, Vigors Papers, Box no. 1.

88 C.H. Holland (ed.), *Trinity College Dublin and the idea of a university* (Dublin, 1991), p. 81.

89 Trinity College Dublin, Catalogue of Muniments, Series P4 Bursar's Vouchers, MUN P1 series.

90 NLI, Mansfield Papers, MS 9629, Letterbook of Walter Woulfe, 15 May 1765.

91 Rhenish became known as Hock in the eighteenth century.

92 NLI, O'Hara Papers, MS 36,375/4; Cellar book of Chas King O'Hara [?] 1840–54; letter from B M Tabuteau, wine merchant, and consul to the Netherlands.

93 NLI, Inchiquin Papers, MS 14,833–5, Accounts of Sir Lucius O'Brien 1837–57.

94 Ibid., MS 45,602/1, letters to Edward Donough O'Brien, fourteenth Baron Inchiquin from B M Tabuteau, wine merchant, 1878–89.

95 Legg, '"Irish wine"', p. 96.

96 Ibid., p. 104.

97 Barnard, *A new anatomy of Ireland*, p. 275.

98 Legg, ' "Irish wine"', p. 105.

99 Barnard, *Making the grand figure*, p. 291.

100 Erasmus D. Borrowes, 'The French settlers in Ireland, Nos. 5, 6 and 8: the Huguenot colony at Portarlington, in the Queen's County', *UJA*, Ser. 1, 3 (1855), pp 56–67, 213–31; 6 (1858), pp 327–46.

101 King's Inns, Bill books, salaries, cash, wine, 1793–1806, E4/2/1.

102 Ibid., Wine memorandum book 1833–35, D6/4.

103 'King's Inns, List of wines', undated. My thanks to Robert Towers.

104 King's Inns, Committee Minute Book, B2/1/2: Meeting of Wine Committee June 7th 1861.

105 Bartholomew Duhigg, *History of the King's Inns* (Dublin, 1806), pp 97, 590. My thanks to Robert Towers.

106 University of London, Senate House Library, Headfort Estate Papers MS 937/6, Bills Book. My thanks to Dr Conor Lucey for this.

107 Edmund Joyce, *Borris House, Co. Carlow, and elite regency patronage*, Maynooth Studies in Local History, 108 (Dublin, 2013), p. 40.

108 Kelly, 'The consumption and sociable use of alcohol', p. 239.

109 Borrowes, 'The French settlers in Ireland', *UJA*, http://anextractofreflection.blogspot.com/2014/03/the-french-settlers-in-ireland-no-8-pt3.html, accessed 27 May 2021.

110 RIA, MR/17/G/9(12), Handbill for furniture auction, by Charles Sharpe, auctioneer, 1838.T.

111 *Leinster Express*, 27 November 1841.

112 After the recovery of tartrates and alcohol, lees are usually returned to the vineyard, where they serve to add some nitrogen to the soil. Robinson, *The Oxford companion to wine*, p. 398.

113 Legg, '"Irish wine"', p. 105.

114 John H. Gebbie (ed.), *An introduction to the Abercorn letters (as relating to Ireland, 1736–1816)* (Omagh 1972), letter from John James Burgoyne (agent) to marquis of Abercorn, dated 28 June 1807.

115 Rebecca M.R. Campion, 'Reconstructing an ascendancy world: the material culture of Frederick Hervey, the earl bishop of Derry (1730–1803)' (PhD, NUIM, 2012).

116 Anthony Powell (ed.), *Barnard letters, 1778–1824* (London, 1928), p. 83.

117 De Latocnaye, *A Frenchman's walk through Ireland, 1796–7* (Belfast, 1917), p. 20.

118 Hurley, *A matter of taste*, p. 130.

119 Legg, '"Irish wine"', p. 105.

120 NLI, Conolly Papers, MS 14,339, Ledgers of miscellaneous accounts of Lady Louisa Conolly.

121 NLI, Powerscourt Papers, Facsimile 12. My thanks to Dr Brian Dornan for this reference.

122 PRONI, Abercorn Papers, T2541/1A/4/9/31, letter from Sir J.J. Burgoyne, Strabane, to marquis of Abercorn, 9 October 1816.

123 PRONI, Castlereagh Papers, D3030/1648, 'Draft inventory of wines in Castlereagh's cellars in Dublin 18 March 1801'.

124 PRONI, Shannon Papers, D2707/A/3/3/189, letter, Shannon to Boyle, 25 February 1802; D2707/A/3/3/89, letter, Shannon to Boyle [18 June 1798].

125 Penning-Rowsell, *Wines of Bordeaux*, pp 408, 409.

126 Hailman, *Thomas Jefferson on wine*, p. 116.

127 Hogsheadwine.wordpress.com, accessed 6 October 2020.

128 James Kelly, 'The consumption and sociable use of alcohol in eighteenth-century Ireland', p. 227, footnote 21.

129 *Dublin Esdall Newsletter*, 17 February 1752.

130 *Nenagh Guardian*, 3 November 1852.

131 *Dundalk Democrat*, 27 August 1859.

132 My thanks to Dr Edward McParland for pointing this out.

133 Quoted in Murphy, *A kingdom of wine*, p. 32.

134 Constantia Maxwell, *The stranger in Ireland* (Dublin, 1954, 1979 ed.), p. 271.

135 Information kindly supplied by Freddie O'Dwyer, email to author, 2 March 2019.

136 L.M. Cullen, 'The smuggling trade in Ireland in the eighteenth century', *PRIA*, 67 (1968–9), pp 149–75 at p. 164.

137 Cullen, 'Five letters relating to Galway smuggling in 1737', *JGAHS*, 5:27 (1956/7), pp 10–25 at p. 14.

138 Cullen, 'Economic development, 1691–1750' in Moody & Vaughan (eds), *A new history of Ireland*, iv, pp 123–95 at p. 139.

139 Woolley (ed.), *The correspondence of Jonathan Swift*, vol. 4, p. 273, letter to Sir Charles Wogan, 1735.

140 Ada Kathleen Longfield, *Anglo-Irish trade in the 16th century* (London, 1929), p. 142.

141 Correspondence to author from Keith MacCarthy Morrogh, 22 July 2019.

142 Legg, '"Irish wine"', p. 102.

143 Cullen, 'The smuggling trade in Ireland', p. 169.

144 Murphy, *A kingdom of wine*, p. 32

145 Legg, '"Irish wine"', p. 102.

146 The National Archives Kew, T 1/331/32, Report of an incident from the Collector of Customs at Portsmouth, 1748.

147 Ludington, '"To the king o'er the water"' in Holt (ed.), *Alcohol: a social and cultural history*, pp 163–84 at 175.

148 F.G. James, 'Irish smuggling in the eighteenth century', *IHS*, 12:48 (September 1961), pp 299–317 at p. 303.

149 De Latocnaye, *A Frenchman's walk through Ireland, 1796–7* (Belfast, 1917), p. 164.

150 Quoted in Kelly, 'The consumption and sociable use of alcohol', pp 219–55 at p. 229.

151 O'Kane, *Ireland and the picturesque: design, landscape, painting and tourism 1700–1840* (New Haven & London, 2013), p. 35, and footnotes 18 and 19 on p. 202.

152 W.H. Maxwell, *Wild sports of the West* (Dublin, no date), xii.

153 O'Kane, *Ireland and the picturesque*, p. 35.

154 NAI, CSO/RP/1824/2194, letter from James Crosbie, magistrate, Ballyheige Castle, County Kerry.

155 NAI, CSO/RP/SC/1821/1626, letter from Major George Warburton, concerning disturbances and smuggling in counties Clare and Kerry, 11 November 1821.

156 T. Crofton Croker (ed.), *Killarney legends; arranged as a guide to the lakes* (London, 1853), pp 150–1.

157 Antoin E. Murphy, *Richard Cantillon* (Oxford, 1986), p. 20.

158 John Ainsworth (ed.), *The Inchiquin manuscripts* (Dublin, 1961), p. 162. Letter dated 4 March 1748/49.

159 Jonah Barrington, *Personal sketches of his own times*, vol. 2, p. 116.

160 Joe Varley, 'Smuggling in the eighteenth and early nineteenth century', *Journal of Research on Irish Maritime History*, www.lugnad.ie, accessed 7 August 2020.

161 NLI, MS 2191, Commonplace book by Henry Sandford, No. 1 Royal Crescent, Bath, England, 1780–1783, vol. 2, p. 39. My thanks to Valerie Brouder, Michael Sandford and Tom Wills-Sandford.

162 Franklin Denham, 'Timoleague Abbey', *JCHAS*, 1 (1892), pp 173–8.

163 Robert Cochrane, 'Timoleague Friary, County Cork', *JCHAS*, 18 (1912), pp 14–25.

164 Ibid.

165   Nigel Surry, 'Two early Georgian wine merchants: the correspondence of James Brydges, 1st duke of Chandos (1674–1744) with Edward Hooker and Gilbert Wavell 1720–*c*.1730', *Proceedings of the Hampshire Field Club Archaeological Society*, 40 (1984), pp 91–8.

166   Penning-Rowsell, *The wines of Bordeaux*, p. 105; Surry, 'Two early Georgian wine merchants', pp 91–8.

167   Hurley, *A matter of taste*, p. 197.

168   Penning-Rowsell, *The wines of Bordeaux*, p. 97.

169   Robinson, *The Oxford companion to wine*, p. 88.

170   Penning-Rowsell, *The wines of Bordeaux*, p. 93.

171   R. ffolliott, 'The burglary at William Leeson's house, Bolingbroke, Co. Tipperary in 1785', *Irish Ancestor*, 16:2 (1984), pp 118–121.

172   *Hibernian Chronicle*, 15 December 1777.

173   [Bishop Joseph Stock] 'A narrative of what passed at Killalla, in the county of Mayo during the French invasion in 1798 by an eye-witness [Stock]' (Dublin, 1800), p. 76.

CHAPTER 3 Dining and wining

1   Katharine Simms, 'Guesting and feasting in Gaelic Ireland', *JRSAI*, 108 (1978), pp 67–100, at p. 95.

2   Quoted from David Dickson, *Dublin, the making of a capital city* (Dublin, 2014), p. 35.

3   Quoted in Malcolm, '*Ireland sober, Ireland free*', p. 9.

4   M. Mac Con Iomaire & T. Kellaghan, 'Royal pomp: viceregal celebrations and hospitality', 2011 Oxford, Symposium on Food and Cookery.

5   Charles Smith, *The ancient and present state of the county and city of Cork* (Dublin, 1774), vol. ii, book iv, p. 243.

6   Quoted in Patricia McCarthy, *Life in the country house in Georgian Ireland* (New Haven & London, 2016), p. 91.

7   Quoted in Maxwell, *Dublin under the Georges*, p. 101.

8   John Knightley, draft Chapter 6 of study on Sir William Godfrey, p. 14, kindly sent to author.

9   *Dublin Penny Journal*, 1:4 (21 July 1832), 32.

10   *Dublin Penny Journal*, 2:65 (28 September 1833), 98.

11   Quoted by John Knightley, draft chapter, as above, p. 11.

12   Quoted in Robinson, *The Oxford companion to wine*, p. 254.

13   J.T. Gilbert (ed.), 'The streets of Dublin, No. 6', *IQR*, 3:1 (Dublin, 1853), p. 274.

14   'A Pilgrimage to Quilca in the Year 1852 in a letter to Anthony Poplar Esq.', *Dublin University Magazine*, 40:239 (November 1852), pp 509–46.

15   The Countess of Cork and Orrery (ed.), *The Orrery Papers* (London, 1903), vol. 1, p. 215, letter to Baron Waynright, Cork, 12 April 1737.

16   Alison FitzGerald, 'Taste in high life: dining in the Dublin town house' in Christine Casey (ed.), *The eighteenth-century Dublin town house* (Dublin, 2010), pp 120–7.

17   Bowood Archives, v. 5, 1769–70, extracts from the diary of Sophia, countess of Shelburne, 1 August 1769. My thanks to the late Knight of Glin for the transcription.

18   John Burns, *An historical and chronological remembrancer of all remarkable occurrences from the Creation to this present year of Our Lord, 1775* (Dublin, 1775), p. 283.

19   Noreen Casey, 'Architecture and decoration' in Ian Campbell Ross (ed.), *Public virtue, public love: the early years of the Dublin Lying-in Hospital the Rotunda* (Dublin, 1986), p. 93.

20   Ibid., p. 94.

21   *Dublin Journal*, 31 October 1809.

22   F. Elrington Ball, *A history of the County Dublin – Howth and its owners* (Dublin, 1917), p. 132.

23   Walter Scott (ed.), *The works of Jonathan Swift* (Edinburgh, 1814), vol. xii, 'The duty of servants at inns', pp 461–5.

24   British Library, 'Discovering literature: Restoration & 18th century'; an introduction to *She Stoops to Conquer* first performed in London in 1773. www.bl.uk. Accessed 8 July 2019.

25 Robert Oresko (ed.), *The works in architecture of Robert and James Adam* (London, 1975), p. 48.

26 Quoted in McCarthy, *Life in the country house*, p. 152.

27 'Anecdotes of Thomas Mathew, Esq., of Thomastown in the County of Tipperary', *Walker's Hibernian Magazine, or Compendium of entertaining knowledge, for January 1796*, pp 32–7.

28 McCarthy, *Life in the country house*, p. 91.

29 Oresko (ed.), *The works in architecture*, p. 48.

30 Three ceilings from Mespil House were acquired by the Office of Public Works in 1952 when the house was demolished: two were installed in Dublin Castle, the third in Áras an Uachtaráin.

31 Paston-Williams, *The art of dining*, p. 249.

32 Thomas Cosnett, *A footman's directory and butler's remembrancer* (London, 1823), pp 78–9.

33 Butler, *Great British wine accessories*, p. 120

34 Cosnett, *A footman's directory*, p. 64.

35 John Trusler, *The honours of the table* (London 1788, ed. 1791), p. 8.

36 Copies kindly given to the author by the late Knight of Glin, December 2004.

37 Paston-Williams, *The art of dining*, p. 256.

38 Frances Gerard, *Some celebrated Irish beauties of the last century* (London, 1895), p. xvii; Stephen R. Penny, *Smythe of Barbavilla: the history of an Anglo-Irish family* (privately published, 1974), p. 40.

39 McCarthy, *Life in the country house*, pp 100–1.

40 Paston-Williams, *The art of dining*, p. 260.

41 Frances Power Cobbe, *Life of Frances Power Cobbe. By Herself*, 2 vols (Cambridge, 1894), i, p. 19.

42 Butler, *Great British wine accessories*, p. 222.

43 NLI, Hamilton of Hamwood Papers, MS 49,155/3/1, Notebook containing a fair copy of the poem, 'A Country Dinner', by Caroline Hamilton, 1805. My thanks to Professor Andrew Carpenter for this reference.

44 Quoted in McCarthy, *Life in the country house*, p. 149.

45 Jean Marchand (ed.), *A Frenchman in England 1784* (Cambridge, 1933 ed.), p. 29; quoted in McCarthy, *Life in the country house*, p. 91.

CHAPTER 4 The paraphernalia of wine-drinking

1 *Finn's Leinster Journal*, 1788, quoted in Alison FitzGerald and Conor O'Brien, 'The production of silver in late-Georgian Dublin', *IADS*, 4 (2001), 8–47.

2 Philippa Glanville, *Silver in England* (London & New York, 1987, 2006 ed.), p. 88.

3 NLI, Powerscourt Papers, MS 19,302, Inventory of plate at Powerscourt, 1885.

4 In Irish furniture inventories of the period they are often called 'gardevins' [*gardes de vins*].

5 Knight of Glin & James Peill, *Irish furniture* (New Haven & London, 2007), pp 185, 188. '*Tôle*' is tin plate, which can be lacquered, painted or enamelled.

6 Edmund Joyce, *Borris House, Co. Carlow, and elite regency patronage*, Maynooth Studies in Local History, No. 108 (Dublin, 2013), pp 45–7.

7 Alison FitzGerald, *Silver in Georgian Dublin* (Oxford, 2017), pp 90–1.

8 Philippa Glanville, *Silver in England* (London & New York, 1987), p. 89.

9 James Howley, 'Icehouses' in *Art and architecture of Ireland*, vol. iv, *Architecture 1600–2000* (New Haven and London, 2014), pp 378–9.

10 NLI, Rochfort Papers, MS 8682(3), 'Inventory of the furniture of Clogrenan Lodge', n.d.

11 Butler, *Great British wine accessories*, pp 214–16.

12 Royal Archives, Collection George IV's Bills, GEO/MAIN/25407–25408, letter from Edward Thomason, 4 September 1826.

13 http://collections.vam.ac.uk/item/O11704, accessed 10 November 2021.

14 Jane Fenlon, *Goods & chattels: a survey of early household inventories in Ireland* (The Heritage Council, 2003), p. 77.

15 NLI, MS 33,575, An inventory of the Rt Honble Nath. Clements plate, 1775; Alison FitzGerald, *Silver in Georgian Dublin*, p. 143.

16 Alison FitzGerald, 'A sterling trade: making and selling silver in Ireland' in William Laffan & Christopher Monkhouse (eds), *Ireland: crossroads of art and design, 1690–1840* (Chicago, 2015), pp 174–9.

17 Fenlon, *Goods & chattels*, p. 130.

18 W.H. Maxwell, *Wild sports of the West* (1832, London, 1843 ed.), p. 243.

19 M.S.D. Westropp, *Irish glass: an account of glass-making in Ireland from the XVIth century to the present day* (London [1920]), p. 20; Fenlon, *Goods & chattels*, p. 21.

20 *Lloyd's News Letter*, October and November 1713. Quoted in M.S.D. Westropp, *Irish glass*, p. 41.

21 Mary Boydell, *Irish glass*, The Irish Heritage Series 5 (Dublin, 1976), unpaginated.

22 My thanks to Cathal Dowd Smith, Cobbe Family Archivist at Newbridge House, Co. Dublin, for information on this item.

23 Boydell, *Irish glass*, unpaginated.

24 NLI, Townley Hall Papers, MS 10,279, under heading 'Glassware' in Inventory February. 1741.

25 Simon, *Bottlescrew days*, p. 229.

26 Antoine Giacometti, 'Rathfarnham Castle Glass: 2014 Excavation Report for Office of Public Works, dated 10 June 2016', pp 6, 62, 66.

27 J. Bush, *Hibernia curiosa: a letter from a gentleman in Dublin to his friend at Dover in Kent* (London, 1767), p. 22.

28 Butler, *Great British wine accessories*, p. 242.

29 Ibid., pp 156–7.

30 NLI, Powerscourt Papers, MS 19,302, Inventory of plate at Powerscourt, 1885.

31 Mary Boydell, *Irish glass* (Dublin 1976) (not paginated).

32 According to Paston Williams, 'wines were preferred as cold as possible', p. 191.

33 Glanville, *Silver in England*, p. 89.

34 NLI, Townley Hall Papers, MS 10,279, Weight of plate by Mr Thomas Walker, February 1741.

35 Joseph McDonnell, 'Irish rococo silver', *Irish Arts Review*, 13 (1997), pp 78–87, note 22.

36 Newbridge House, Co. Dublin, 'An account of the bishops plate as it was given to me by his sister Betty, October 1730'. My thanks to C. Dowd Smith.

37 Butler, *Great British wine accessories*, pp 110, 112.

38 Beth Carver Wees, *English, Irish & Scottish silver at the Sterling and Francine Clark Art Institute* (Manchester, VT, 1997), p. 116.

39 Simon, *Bottlescrew days*, p. xii.

40 For information on this tree, see www.powo.science.kew.org (accessed 23 July 2018). Thomas Jefferson, third president of the United States and an oenophile, found it difficult to obtain corks, so had cork oak trees planted on his estate at Monticello, in Virginia, but with no success as the climate was found to be too cold (Hailman, *Thomas Jefferson on wine*, p. 5).

41 Robinson, *The Oxford companion*, p. 200.

42 Sir Herbert Maxwell, *Half-a-century of successful trade, being a sketch of the rise and development of the business of W & A Gilbey, 1857–1907* (London, 1907), pp 20–2.

43 Butler, *Great British wine accessories*, p. 42.

44 Murphy, *A kingdom of wine*, p. 114.

45 Simon, *Bottlescrew days*, pp xii, xiii.

46 Butler, *Great British wine accessories*, p. 48.

47 St Patrick's University Hospital Archives, MS A22: 'An inventory of the household goods belonging to the Rev Docr Jonathan Swift Dean of St Patrick's Dublin; in the Deanery house'.

48 Conor O'Brien, 'Dean Swift's and some early Irish labels', *Journal of the Wine Label Circle*, 9:3 (June 1992), pp 54–60.

49 A.C. Elias Jr. (ed.), *Memoirs of Laetitia Pilkington*, 2 vols (London, 1997), vol. 1, p. 31.

50 Murphy, *A kingdom of wine*, pp 114–15.

51 George Dalgleish, 'The silver travelling canteen of Prince Charles Edward Stuart' in Alexander Fenton & Janken Murdal (eds), *Food & drink & travelling accessories: essays in honour of Gösta Berg* (Scotland, 1988), pp 168–84.

52 Maurice Healy, *Stay with me flagons* (London, 1952), p. 99.

53 Robinson, *The Oxford companion*, p. 385.

54 Conor O'Brien, 'Dean Swift's and some early Irish labels', pp 54–60. The earl of Orrery was a biographer of Swift. In an inventory of Swift's household goods, these were referred to as '5 silver scroles & chain to mark wine', St Patrick's University Hospital Archives, MS A22.

55 Cosnett, *The footman's directory*, p. 79.

56 Glanville, *Silver in England*, p. 88

57 Alison FitzGerald, *Silver in Georgian Dublin: making, selling, consuming* (London, 2017), p. 109.

58 Ida Delamer & Conor O'Brien, *500 years of Irish silver* (Dublin, 2005), p. 123.

59 Butler, *Great British wine accessories*, pp 181, 184, 186. In the National Museum of Ireland is a label 'T' for Teneriffe, a fortified wine.

60 *The Dublin Journal*, 30 June–2 July 1778.

61 Alison FitzGerald & Conor O'Brien, 'The production of silver in late-Georgian Dublin', *IADS*, 4 (2001), pp 8–47. See also Claudia Kinmonth, *Irish country furniture* (New Haven and London, 1993).

62 Delamer & O'Brien, *500 years of Irish silver*, p. 115.

63 Isaac Butler, 'A journey to Lough Derg', *JRSAI*, 22 (1892), pp 132–3.

64 *Dublin Penny Journal*, 2:84 (8 February 1834), pp 249–50.

65 Douglas Bennett, 'Eighteenth-century table silver', *Irish Arts Review*, 2 (1985), pp 29–31.

66 NLI, MS 19,302, Inventory of plate at Powerscourt, 1885.

67 Jane Fenlon, *Goods & chattels*, pp 13–14; Newbridge House Collection, 'Account book of Dorothea Rawdon and (later) of her second husband Charles Cobbe inscribed Feb 15th 1723 & An account of the bishop's plate, 1730'.

68 Benson Earle Hill, *Recollections of an artillery officer* (London, 1836), 2 vols, i, p. 110.

69 Quoted in Hurley, *A matter of taste*, p. 101.

70 Account returned by Sheriff of Co. Monaghan of sale at Dawson Grove, 1827. NLI MS 741.

71 Paston-Williams, *The art of dining*, p. 262.

72 Christopher Christie, *The British country house in the eighteenth century* (Manchester, 2000), p. 257.

73 J.D. Herbert, *Irish varieties for the last fifty years* (London, 1836), p. 159.

74 Hailman, *Thomas Jefferson on wine*, pp 291–2.

75 Ibid., p. 291.

76 McCarthy, *Life in the country house*, p. 75.

CHAPTER 5 Male bonding and toasting

1 Quoted in McCarthy, *Life in the country house*, p. 151.

2 Countess of Minto (ed.), *Life and letters of Sir Gilbert Elliott* (London, 1874), vol. 1, p. 189.

3 Simon, *Bottlescrew days*, p. 46.

4 Frances Power Cobbe, *The life of Frances Power Cobbe by herself* (London, 1894, 1904 ed.), p. 18.

5 Maria Edgeworth, *Castle Rackrent, an Hibernian tale* (London, 1800 ed.), pp 9, 6.

6 Henry French, 'Getting drunk soberly: elite masculinity and drinking culture in eighteenth-century England', accessed on academia.edu 3 February 2019, p. 7. This might explain why chamber pots were kept openly in the corner of the dining room, or discreetly within the sideboard, as in many Irish houses.

7 Lena Boylan, 'The Conollys of Castletown', *QBIGS*, 11:4 (October–December 1968).

8 Quoted in Maxwell, *Country and town in Ireland under the Georges* (Dundalk, 1949), p. 23.

9 James Kelly, 'The consumption and sociable use of alcohol in eighteenth-century Ireland', *PRIA*, 115C (2015), pp 219–55 at p. 249.

10 Rebecca Rupp, 'Cheers: celebration drinking is an ancient tradition', *National Geographic*, 26 December 2014.

11 John Bernard, *Retrospections of the stage* (London, 1830), vol. 1, pp 328–9.

12 Charles Ludington, *The politics of wine in Britain: a new cultural history* (London, 2013), p. 204.

13 Quoted in Maxwell, *Country and town in Ireland* (Dundalk, 1949), p. 21.

14   J. Bush, *Hibernia curiosa: a letter from a gentleman in Dublin to his friend at Dover in Kent* (London, 1769), p. 21.

15   Barnard, *Making the grand figure*, p. 244.

16   Sir Edward Sullivan (ed.), *Buck Whaley's memoirs* (London, 1906), p. 271.

17   Maria Edgeworth, *Ormond: a tale* (Dublin, 1972 ed.), p. 1.

18   Edgeworth, *Ormond: a tale*, p. 353.

19   Sir James Prior, *Life of Edmond Malone, editor of Shakespeare* (London, 1860), vol. 1, p. 78.

20   TCD, Conolly Papers, MS 3974–84/1433.

21   Catriona Kennedy, '"Our separate rooms": Bishop Stock's narrative of the French invasion of Mayo, 1798', *Field Day Review*, 5 (Dublin, 2009), pp 94–107.

22   'Sir Josias Bodley's visit to Lecale 1602' in C.L. Falkiner, *Illustrations of Irish history and topography, mainly of the 17th century* (London, 1904), p. 333.

23   Rupp, 'Cheers: celebration drinking is an ancient tradition', *National Geographic*, 26 December 2014.

24   Martyn J. Powell, 'Political toasting in eighteenth-century Ireland', *Journal of the Historical Association*, 91:304 (October 2006), pp 508–28 at 512.

25   Lucy Worsley, *If walls could talk: an intimate history of the home* (London, 2011), p. 303.

26   Eamonn Ó Ciardha, *Ireland and the Jacobite cause, 1685–1766* (Dublin, 2002), p. 170.

27   Powell, *The politics of consumption in eighteenth-century Ireland*, p. 23.

28   Powell, 'Political toasting', p. 509.

29   Kelly, 'The consumption and sociable use of alcohol in eighteenth-century Ireland', p. 245.

30   Ian McBride, *Eighteenth-century Ireland: the isle of slaves* (Dublin, 2009), pp 308–9.

31   British Library, Egerton Manuscripts, MS 917, f. 235, 'A list of the healths that were drank on her Majesty's birth day at the Royall Hospital' [undated, but *c*.1712]. I am grateful to Dr Edward McParland for bringing this to my attention, and for transcribing it.

32   'Old Dublin Inns', *Saturday Herald*, 29 March 1913.

33   Powell, *The politics of consumption* (2005), p. 87.

34   John Gilbert, *History of the city of Dublin*, vol. 1, p. 44.

35   Maxwell, *Dublin under the Georges*, p. 119.

36   David Ryan, *Blasphemers and blackguards: the Irish Hellfire Clubs* (Dublin, 2012), p. 36.

37   Quoted in William Laffan, 'Clubs, pubs & parties' in Brendan Rooney (ed.), *A time and a place: two centuries of Irish social life* (Dublin, 2006), pp 123–5.

38   Ryan, *Blasphemers and blackguards*, p. 72.

39   Ibid., p. 35.

40   Ibid., p. 155.

41   Pertaining to the worship of Aphrodite, whose cult was on the island of Cyprus.

42   J.T. Gilbert (ed.), 'The streets of Dublin', *IQR*, 2 (Dublin, 1852), p. 529.

43   Maxwell, *Country and town in Ireland under the Georges*, pp 21–2.

44   T. Mooney & F. White, 'The gentry's winter season' in David Dickson (ed.), *The gorgeous mask: Dublin, 1700–1850* (Dublin, 1987), pp 1–16.

45   Maxwell, *Country and town in Ireland*, pp 34–5.

46   Lisa-Marie Griffith, '"Never let the facts interfere with a good story": the origin of the Ouzel Galley Society', *History Ireland*, 20:2 (March–April 2012), pp 24–5.

47   George A. Little, *The Ouzel Galley* (Dublin, 1953), pp 33, 31, 43.

48   My thanks to Keith MacCarthy Morrogh.

49   C.J. Woods, *Travellers' accounts as source-material for Irish historians* (Dublin, 2009), p. 73.

50   Mairtín Mac Con Iomaire, 'Public dining in Dublin: the history and evolution of gastronomy and commercial dining, 1700–1900', *International Journal of Contemporary Hospitality Management*, 25:2 (2012), pp 227–46.

51   J.T. Gilbert, *A history of the city of Dublin* (Dublin & London, 1861), vol. 1, p. 44.

52   Royal Irish Academy, M. 24 E 37, Minute book of the Florists' Club [Dublin].

53   E. Charles Nelson, 'The Dublin Florists' Club in the mid-eighteenth century', *Garden History*, 10:2 (Autumn, 1982), pp 142–8.

54 Review of Leo Damrosch, *The Club: Johnson, Boswell and the friends who shaped an age* (London, 2019), in *Sunday Times*, 21 April 2019.

55 Hailman, *Thomas Jefferson on wine*, p. 203.

56 Eric Gillett (ed.), *Elizabeth Ham by herself, 1783–1820* (London, 1945), p. 75.

57 Quoted in Paston-Williams, *The art of dining*, p. 258.

58 Anthony Trollope, *Framley Parsonage* (London, 1906), p. 191.

59 James Boswell, *Life of Samuel Johnson, comprehending an account of his studies and numerous works in chronological order* (London, 1847), p. 417.

60 Richard Valpy French, *Nineteen centuries of drink in England: a history* (London, 1884), p. 51.

61 *The diary of Samuel Pepys*, 19 June 1663. www.pepysdiary.com, accessed 30 May 2019.

62 Henry French, 'Getting drunk soberly: elite masculinity and drinking culture in eighteenth-century England', p. 6, accessed on academia.edu, 3 February 2019.

63 Quoted in Simon, *Bottlescrew days*, p. 177.

64 Maxwell, *Dublin under the Georges*, p. 107.

65 Hailman, *Thomas Jefferson on wine*, p. 60.

66 *Recollections of Sir Jonah Barrington*, https://archive.org/details/recollectionsofjoobarriala/, 43–45 –, accessed 11 January 2020.

67 Kelly, 'The consumption and sociable use of alcohol', p. 255.

68 'The itinerary of Fynes Morrison' in C.L. Falkiner, *Illustrations of Irish history and topography, mainly of the 17th century* (London, 1904), pp 225–230. Susan Flavin, 'Consumption and material culture in sixteenth-century Ireland' (PhD, University of Bristol, 2011), p. 169.

69 Quoted in Susan Flavin, 'Consumption and material culture', p. 169.

70 Sighle Ní Chinneide (ed.), 'A Frenchman's impressions of Limerick, town and people, in 1791', *North Munster Antiquarian Journal*, 5:4 (1948), pp 96–101.

71 T.M. MacKenzie, *Dromana: the memoirs of an Irish family* (Dublin, 1907), p. 210.

72 Toby Barnard, *The abduction of a Limerick heiress: social and political relations in mid-eighteenth-century Ireland*, Maynooth Studies in Local History, No. 20 (Dublin, 1998), pp 22, 26.

73 L.A. Clarkson & E. Margaret Crawford, *Feast and famine: food and nutrition in Ireland, 1500–1920* (Oxford, 2001), p. 56.

74 'A journey to Lough Derg by Isaac Butler *c.*1741', *JRSAI*, 5th series, 2 (1892), pp 126–36.

75 PRONI, T/2855/1, Volume entitled 'Miscellaneous observations on Ireland, 1759–60' by Lord Chief Baron Willes.

76 Thomas Clarkson, *A portraiture of Quakerism* (London, 1807), vol. 1, pp 159–60.

77 Henry French, 'Getting drunk soberly: elite masculinity and drinking culture in eighteenth-century England', www.academia.edu, accessed 4 March 2020.

CHAPTER 6 Nothing but the best at Dublin Castle

1 J.L. McCracken 'The political structure 1714–60' in Moody & Vaughan (eds), *A new history of Ireland*, iv (Oxford, 1986), pp 57–83 at 58.

2 Martyn J. Powell, *The politics of consumption in eighteenth-century Ireland* (London, 2005), p. 151.

3 M. Mac Con Iomaire & T. Kellaghan, 'Royal pomp: viceregal celebrations and hospitality in Georgian Dublin'. Oxford symposium on food and cookery, St Catherine's College, Oxford, 2011, pp 1–15 at 1.

4 W. Pinkerton, 'Lord Deputy of Ireland's household expenses (circa 1580)', *Ulster Journal of Archaeology*, 1st series, 8 (1860), pp 27–34.

5 Joseph Robins, *Champagne & silver buckles: the viceregal court at Dublin Castle, 1700–1922* (Dublin, 2001), p. 6.

6 Charles K. O'Mahony, *The viceroys of Ireland: the story of a long line of noblemen and their wives who have ruled Ireland and Irish society for over seven hundred years* (London, 1912), p. 131.

7 PRONI, Wilmot Papers, T3019/908, letter from Clements to Edward Weston, chief secretary 1746–50, 23 June 1747.

8   PRONI, Wilmot Papers, T3019/1014, letter from Sir Richard Wolseley, Mount Wolseley, to Wilmot, Dublin Castle, 2 April 1748.

9   John Kirwan (ed.), *The chief butlers of Ireland and the house of Ormond* (Dublin, 2018), p. xxvi.

10 Robins, *Champagne & silver buckles*, p. 6.

11 Much of this paragraph is taken from 'The book of vice regal ceremonies' quoted in Sir Bernard Burke, *The rise of great families, other essays and stories* (London, 1873), pp 235–8.

12 Robins, *Champagne & silver buckles*, p. 100.

13 NLI, Eyre Matcham MSS, letter from earl of Halifax to Lord Melcombe, Dublin Castle, 28 April 1762.

14 NLI, Ormond Papers, MS 2548, House book with accounts of stores & provisions from June 1701 to July 1703.

15 Barnard, *Making the grand figure*, p. 12.

16 Ibid., p. 11.

17 PRONI, Wilmot Papers, T3019/3208, letter from Richard Rigby, Woburn, to Wilmot, Dublin Castle, 15 July 1757; ibid., T3019/3223, letter from ditto to ditto, 7 August 1757.

18 Francis Hardy, *Memoirs of the political and private life of James Caulfield, earl of Charlemont* (London, 1812), vol. 1, p. 317.

19 PRONI, Wilmot Papers, T3019/5343, letter from George Boyd, Abbey Street, to Robert Wilmot, Dublin Castle, 11 October 1766.

20 Derbyshire Record Office, D3155/C2081 'Total bills for wine laid down in the cellars of Dublin Castle for the use of the Duke of Bedford dated 4 Oct 1757', and PRONI, Wilmot Papers Summary, T3019. The Green Room, called the Board of Green Cloth in medieval times, was traditionally (in British Royal houses) where the records of household expenses were examined.

21 Mac Con Iomaire & Kellaghan, 'Royal pomp: viceregal celebrations and hospitality in Georgian Dublin', Oxford 2011, pp 1–15; Kellaghan, 'Claret: the preferred libation of Georgian Ireland's elite', Submission for DIT Gastronomy Symposium, pp 1–13; Robins, *Champagne & silver buckles*, p. 72.

22 Robins, *Champagne & silver buckles*, p. 72. Sillery and Hautvillers are among the 300 villages from which modern champagne continues to be made. My thanks to Keith MacCarthy Morrogh for this information.

23 Nathaniel William Wraxall, *Posthumous memoirs of his own times*, 3 vols (London, 1836), ii, p. 350.

24 National Archives, PRO 30/70/3/145, Duke of Rutland to Lord Chatham, 14 February 1785.

25 Quoted in Powell, *The politics of consumption*, p. 155.

26 Countess of Cork and Orrery (ed.), *The Orrery Papers* (London, 1903), vol. 1, p. 144.

27 John Gilbert, *The history of the city of Dublin*, vol. 1, p. 255.

28 Robins, *Champagne & silver buckles*, p. 27

29 The McCarthy Mor, *Ulster's Office, 1552–1800; a history of the Irish Office of Arms from the Tudor Plantations to the Act of Union* (Arkansas, 1996), p. 161.

30 Gilbert, *A history of the city of Dublin*, vol. 1, p. 150.

31 Robinson, *The Oxford companion to wine*, p. 422.

32 *Report on the Manuscripts of Mrs Stopford-Sackville of Drayton House, Northamptonshire* (London, HMSO, 1904–10), vol. 1, p. 170.

33 NLI, MS Joly 41, Wine orders for George IV during his visit to Dublin, August 1821.

34 Sir Herbert Maxwell (ed.), *The Creevey Papers: a selection from the correspondence and diaries of Thomas Creevey, MP* (London, 1904), letter from the Countess of Glengall to Mrs Taylor, August 27th, pp 29–30.

35 www.turtlebunbury.com/history accessed 9 January 2019.

36 Robins, *Champagne & silver buckles*, p. 16.

37 Royal Irish Academy, MS 24/H/22, 'The Establishment of his Grace the Duke of Shrewsbury's Household at Dublin Castle ye year 1713'. My thanks to Edward McParland for this reference.

38 Ibid. The discrepancy might be due to the artistry required and involved in confectionery and table display and, his name might indicate that he was French, an added cachet.

39 PRONI, D619/35/C/1 and D619/35/C/2, Cellar Books for Dublin Castle and Viceregal Lodge, 1828–33.

40 Maria Edgeworth, *Ormond*, in *Tales and novels by Maria Edgeworth* (London, 1833), vol. 18, p. 229.

41 Powell, *The politics of consumption*, pp 147–8.

42 Francis Elrington Ball, *A history of the Co. Dublin*, vol. 1 (Dublin, 1902), p. 127.

43 Quoted in Powell, *The politics of consumption*, pp 147–8.

44 de Latocnaye, *A Frenchman's walk through Ireland*, pp 94–5.

45 John Gamble, *Sketches of history, politics and manners in Dublin and the north of Ireland in 1810* (London, 1810), p. 59.

46 William J. O'N. Daunt, *Personal recollections of the late Daniel O'Connell M.P.* (London, 1848), vol. 1, pp 108–10.

47 Powell, *The politics of consumption*, p. 169.

48 Robins, *Champagne & silver buckles*, pp 90–1.

49 Roisin Kennedy, *Dublin Castle art* (Dublin, 2010), p. 23.

50 HMC, Charlemont, ii, 'Public Principles of the Order of St Patrick', p. 404.

51 Noreen Casey, 'Architecture and decoration' in Ian Campbell Ross (ed.), *Public virtue, public love: the early years of the Dublin Lying-in Hospital* (Dublin, 1986), p. 77.

52 *Hibernian Magazine,* March 1783, pp 166–7.

53 Kennedy, *Dublin Castle art,* p. 22.

54 Maria Edgeworth, *The Absentee* (Oxford, 2001 ed.), p. 83.

CHAPTER 7 The role of the monasteries

1 Bordeaux.com, accessed 19 December 2019.

2 Gisela H. Kreglinger, *The spirituality of wine* (Grand Rapids, MI, 2016), pp 53–4.

3 Ibid., p. 182.

4 Wine was also required for Jewish religious ceremonies.

5 Quoted in N.X. O'Donoghue, *The Eucharist in pre-Norman Ireland* (Notre Dame, ID, 2011), p. 184.

6 Eamon Duffy, *The stripping of the altars: traditional religion in England, c.1400–1580* (New Haven & London, 1992), p. 110.

7 Ibid.

8 O'Donoghue, *The Eucharist in pre-Norman Ireland*, pp 184–5.

9 P. Morrisroe, 'The altar and its ornaments', *Ecclesiastical Record*, 4:21 (June 1907), pp 590–602 at 592–5.

10 Morrisroe, 'The altar and its ornaments', p. 602.

11 Dublin Diocesan Archive, MS 48 P5/4b. A wine label of Thompson's is displayed in an exhibition in the Wine Museum in Malaga, Spain, seen November 2018.

12 *Strattens' guide to Dublin Cork and South of Ireland: a literary, commercial and social review* (1892), p. 202.

13 Thanks to Nicholas Grubb for this, email 28 August 2019.

14 Jancis Robinson, *The Oxford companion to wine*, p. 184.

15 Oz Clark, *The history of wine in 100 bottles* (London, 2015), p. 30.

16 Penning Rowsell, *The wines of Bordeaux*, p. 104.

17 *The Holy Rule of St Benedict by Saint Benedict, Abbot of Monte Cassino*, Ch XL http://www.documentacatholicaomnia.eu/03d/04800547,_Benedictus_Nursinus,_Regola,_EN.pdf – accessed 25 February 2019.

18 Richard Valpy French, *Nineteen centuries of drink in England: a history*, https://onlinebooks.library.upenn.edu, accessed 15 May 2020.

19 Timothy O'Neill, *Merchants and mariners in medieval Ireland* (Dublin, 1987), pp 44, 55–6.

20 R.H. Stoddard, 'In the Cloister Cellar', *The Aldine*, 7:4 (April 1874), 84. Poem translated by Stoddard.

21 Alicia Amherst, *A history of gardening in England* (London, 1896), pp 155–6.

22 Paston-Williams, *The art of dining*, p. 105.

23   Gilbert, *A history of the city of Dublin*, vol. 1, p 101.
24   John Mills (ed.), *Account roll of the Priory of the Holy Trinity, Dublin, 1337–1346* (Dublin, 1891), p. 171; the editor's note observes, 'judging by his name, the wine must be claret'.
25   Mills (ed.), *Account roll of the Priory of the Holy Trinity*, p. xv.
26   Gilbert, *A history of the City of Dublin*, vol. 1, p. 53.
27   O'Neill, *Merchants and mariners*, p. 53. In the 1820s, the vaults of the Catholic Pro-Cathedral in Dublin, which was in the process of being built, were leased to the commissioners of Inland Revenue for the storage of wines and spirits, generating much-needed funds for the building. My thanks to David Griffin for this information.
28   J.T. Gilbert (ed.), *The streets of Dublin* (Dublin, 1852), *IQR*, 368.
29   Jancis Robinson, *The Oxford companion to wine*, p. 449.

CHAPTER 8 Wine: the oldest medicine

1   Robinson (ed.), *The Oxford companion to wine*, p. 433.
2   Roger Bacon, *The cure of old age and preservation of youth* (London, 1683), p. 107.
3   Quoted in Longfield, *Anglo-Irish trade in the 16th century*, p. 133.
4   Lucy Worsley, *If walls could talk: an intimate history of the home* (London, 2011), p. 313.
5   Quoted in Louise Hill Curth & Tanya M. Cassidy, '"Health, strength and happiness": medical constructions of wine and beer in early modern England' in Adam Smyth (ed.), *A pleasing sinne: drink and conviviality in seventeenth-century England* (Cambridge, 2004), pp 143–60.
6   https://www.nlm.nih.gov/exhibition/emotions/balance.html accessed 11 June 2021.
7   Quoted in Paston-Williams, *The art of dining*, p. 105; Pinkerton, 'Lord Deputy of Ireland's household expenses', *Ulster Journal of Archaeology*, 1st Series, 8 (1860), pp 27–34.
8   Malcolm, *'Ireland sober, Ireland free'*, pp 4, 5.
9   Accessed online 9 February 2021.
10   Royal College of Physicians in Ireland, Archive MS/20b, letter from Dr Cheyne to Dr Edward Percival, 2 December 1818. My thanks to Dr John Wallace for this quote. An Irish silver 'bleeding bowl' (into which the blood was drained from the patient), dated 1699, was advertised in Adam's auction on 15 October 2019.
11   Quoted in Tony Farmar, *Patients, potions & physicians: a social history of medicine in Ireland (1654–2004)* (Dublin, 2004), p. 68.
12   Countess of Cork and Orrery (ed.), *The Orrery Papers*, vol. 1 (London, 1903), p. 183.
13   William Buchan MD, *Domestic medicine: or, the family physician* (Edinburgh, 1769), p. 455.
14   Charles Louis Liger, *A treatise on the gout* (London, 1760), p. vii.
15   *Recollections of Jonah Barrington, with introduction by George Birmingham* (Dublin & London, 1918) https://archive.org/details/recollectionsofjoobarriala/, p. 4.
16   Ibid., p. 5.
17   James Kelly, 'Domestic medication and medical care in late early modern Ireland' in James Kelly & Fiona Clark (eds), *Ireland and medicine in the seventeenth and eighteenth centuries* (London, 2010), pp 109–35 at 113.
18   David Woolley (ed.), *The correspondence of Jonathan Swift, D.D.* (Frankfurt, 2007), p. 273, letter to Sir Charles Wogan from Swift, 1735; *Journal to Stella* (March 10th 1710–11), p. 202, Sir Walter Scott, *The works of Jonathan Swift: Journal to Stella*, accessed online: www.books.google.ie, 11 Jan. 2020.
19   Hurley, *A matter of taste*, pp 114, 60.
20   Quoted in Valerie Pakenham, *The Big House in Ireland* (London 2000), pp 122–3.
21   Quoted in Mark Girouard, *A country house companion* (Leicester, 1992 ed.), p. 72.
22   Quoted in Valerie Pakenham, *The Big House in Ireland*, pp 119–20.
23   NLI, MS 5606, Mary Ponsonby, 'Cooking recipes and medical cures', p. 323.
24   Hurley, *A matter of taste*, p. 107.
25   Anthony Powell (ed.), *Barnard letters, 1778–1824* (London, 1928), p. 61.

26 John Buchanan, MD, *Regimental practice; or, A short history of diseases to His Majesties own Royal Regiment of Horse Guards when abroad* (1746), pp 163, 311.

27 Marie-Louise Jennings & Gabrielle M. Ashford (eds), *The letters of Katherine Conolly, 1707–1747* (IMC, Dublin, 2018), letter from Katherine Conolly to Jane Bonnell, 25 November 1740, p. 201.

28 Powell, *The politics of consumption*, p. 13.

29 Leslie Clarkson & Margaret Crawford, *Feast and famine: food and nutrition in Ireland, 1500–1920* (Oxford 2001), p. 56.

30 James Kelly, 'Domestic medication and medical care in late early modern Ireland', p. 113.

31 Quote from drinkwhatyoulike.wordpress.com, '30 days of Thomas Jefferson on wine – day 9', accessed 3 July 2019.

32 Hailman, *Thomas Jefferson on wine*, p. 302.

33 Robinson, *The Oxford companion to wine*, p. 433.

34 H.F. Berry, 'Notes from the diary of a Dublin lady in the reign of George II', *JRSAI*, 5th Series, 8:2 (30 June 1898), pp 141–54.

35 Quoted in Robinson, *The Oxford companion to wine*, p. 254.

36 Malcolm, '*Ireland sober, Ireland free*', p. 41.

37 Barnard, *Making the grand figure*, p. 275.

38 Peter Shaw, *The juice of the grape; or, Wine preferable to water* (London, 1724), p. 9.

39 Barry, *Observations*, p. 12.

40 Ibid., *Observations*, pp 392–3.

41 Cork & Orrery (ed.), *The Orrery Papers*, letter from Dr Barry to Lord Orrery, 26 December 1736, vol. 1, p. 186.

42 James Kelly, 'The consumption and sociable use of alcohol', p. 241.

43 Barry, *Observations*, p. 417.

44 Paul E. Kopperman (ed.), *Theory and practice in eighteenth-century medicine: 'Regimental Practice' by John Buchanan, M.D.* (Oregon, 2012), p. 648.

45 William J. Fitz-Patrick, *Curious family history: or Ireland before the Union: including Lord Chief Justice Clonmell's unpublished diary* (1867, Dublin, 1869 ed.), p. 41.

46 Barrington, *Recollections*, p. 195.

47 FitzPatrick, *Curious family history*, pp 22–3.

48 Malcolm, '*Ireland sober, Ireland free*', pp 53–4.

49 Countess of Minto (ed.), *Life and letters of Sir Gilbert Elliot, first earl of Minto from 1751 to 1806* (London, 1874), vol. 1, p. 189.

50 *Memoirs of Richard Cumberland, written by himself* (Boston, 1806), p. 99. (online) Cumberland, dramatist and civil servant, came to Ireland as under secretary in 1761, under Lord Halifax as lord lieutenant.

51 Malcolm, '*Ireland sober, Ireland free*', p. 43.

52 Quoted in Simon, *Bottlescrew days*, p. 175.

53 *Journal to Stella*, letter xliv, 22 March 1711–12, p. 434, accessed online 10 February 2020, project Gutenberg, ed. George A. Aitken.

54 *The works of Jonathan Swift, DD, with memoir of the author, by Thomas Roscoe* (London, 1870), p. 686.

55 NLI, MS 5606, Mary Ponsonby, Cooking recipes and medical cures, pp 14, 339, 6.

56 Quoted in Valerie Pakenham, *The Big House in Ireland* (London, 2000), pp 116, 120–1.

57 *Lady Morgan's memoirs, autobiography, diaries and correspondence* (London, 2000), pp 120–1.

58 Legg, *Synge letters*, letter 209, 29 August 1752; letter 154, 29 July 1751.

59 www.tottenham.name, Bishop of Clogher, accessed 29 May 2019.

60 Marie-Louise Jennings & Gabrielle M. Ashford, *The letters of Katherine Conolly, 1707–1747* (IMC, Dublin, 2018), Katherine Conolly to Jane Bonnell, 12 April 1731; 12 March 1735/6.

61 Kelly, 'The consumption and sociable use of alcohol', pp 219–55, at 241.

62 Jennings & Ashford, *The letters of Katherine Conolly*, 8 August 1739.

63 Kelly, 'The consumption and sociable use of alcohol', p. 241.

64   Marie-Louise Legg, *The diary of Nicholas Peacock, 1740–51: the worlds of a County Limerick farmer and agent* (Dublin, 2005), p. 61.

65   Henry Banyer, *Pharmacopoeia pauperum; or, The hospital dispensatory* (London, 1721 ed.), p. 59.

66   Elizabeth Robinson Montagu, Emily Jane Climenson, *Elizabeth Montagu, the queen of the Bluestockings: her correspondence from 1720 to 1721*, vol. 1 (London, 1906), pp 71–2.

67   NLI, Mansfield Papers, MS 42,105, 'A manuscript "Receipt Book" compiled by an unknown hand', 1811–31.

68   NLI, MS 34,932/1–3, Culinary and medical recipe books, possibly compiled by members of the Pope family of Waterford.

69   NLI, MS 2191, vol. 2, p. 128, Commonplace book by Henry Sandford, No 1 Royal Crescent, Bath, England, 1780–1783.

70   Hilaire Dubourcq, *Benjamin Franklin book of recipes* (2004), p. 174.

71   scottishantiques.com/shrub-decanter (accessed 29 November 2018).

72   Alex Findlater, *Findlaters – the story of a Dublin merchant family, 1774–2001* (Dublin, 2001), p. 29.

73   Butler, *Great British wine accessories*, p. 132.

74   Hurley, *A matter of taste*, p. 59.

75   Information from britishfoodhistory.com, January 3, 2013, accessed 29 May 2019.

76   Quoted in William Laffan (ed.) *The cries of Dublin: drawn from the Life by Hugh Douglas Hamilton, 1760* (Dublin, 2003), p. 86.

77   https://britishfoodhistory.com/category/eighteenth-century-2/. Accessed 11 March 2021.

EPILOGUE

1   Kelly, 'The consumption and sociable use of alcohol', p. 245.

2   Maxwell, *Dublin under the Georges*, pp 107, 315.

3   Malcolm, *'Ireland sober, Ireland free'*, p. 45.

4   Powell, *The politics of consumption*, pp 12–13.

5   Malcolm, *'Ireland sober, Ireland free'*, p. 49; Maria Edgeworth, *The Absentee* (2001 ed.), pp 81–2; Edward Wakefield, *An account of Ireland, statistical and political*, 2 vols (London, 1812), vol. ii, p. 787.

6   NLI, MS 50,377, letter from John Cooney, Wexford, to Kelly, wine merchants, Lr. Gardiner Street, Dublin, 24 February 1840.

7   Malcolm, *'Ireland sober, Ireland free'*, p. 65.

8   R.B. McDowell, 'Ireland in 1800' in Moody and Vaughan (eds), *A new history of Ireland*, iv, pp 657–712 at 685.

9   *Bishop Berkeley's Querist, republished with notes showing how many of the same questions still remain to be asked, respecting Ireland* (London, 1829), p. 65.

10   Samuel Madden, *Reflections and resolutions proper for the gentlemen of Ireland, as to their conduct for the service of their country* (Dublin, 1738), p. 20.

Select bibliography

Ainsworth, John (ed.), *The Inchiquin manuscripts* (Dublin, 1961).

Amherst, Alicia, *A history of gardening in England* (London, 1896).

Bacon, Roger, *The cure of old age and preservation of youth* (London, 1683).

Ball, F. Elrington, *A history of the county of Dublin: Monkstown, Kill-of-the-Grange, Dalkey, Tully, Stillorgan and Kilmacud* (Dublin, 1902).

Ball, F. Elrington, *A history of the county of Dublin: Howth and its owners* (Dublin, 1917).

Barnard, Toby, *Making the grand figure: lives and possessions in Ireland, 1641–1770,* (London & New Haven, 2004).

Barnard, T.C., 'The cultures of eighteenth-century Irish towns' in P. Borsay & L. Proudfoot (eds), *Provincial towns in early modern England and Ireland: change, convergence and divergence.* Proceedings of the British Academy, 108 (2002), pp 195–222.

Barnard, Toby, *The abduction of a Limerick heiress: social and political relations in mid-eighteenth-century Ireland* (Dublin, 1998).

Barnard, Toby, *A new anatomy of Ireland, the Irish Protestants, 1649–1770,* (London & New Haven, 2003).

Barnard, T.C., 'Gardening, diet and "improvement" in later seventeenth-century Ireland', *Journal of Garden History*, 10, (1990), pp 71–85.

Barrington, Jonah, *Personal sketches of his own times*, vol. 2 (London, 1832).

Barry, Sir Edward, *Observations, historical, critical, and medical, on the wines of the ancients* (London, 1775).

Bennett, Douglas, 'Eighteenth-century table silver', *Irish Arts Review*, 2 (1985), pp 29–31.

Bernard, John, *Retrospections of the stage*, vol. 1 (London, 1830).

Berry, H.F., 'Notes from the diary of a Dublin lady in the reign of George II', *JRSAI*, 8:2 (30 June 1898), pp 141–54.

Blackall, Henry, 'The Galweys of Munster', *JCHAS*, 71:213/14 (1966), pp 138–58.

Borrowes, Erasmus D.,'The French settlers in Ireland, Nos. 5, 6 and 8: The Huguenot colony at Portarlington, in the Queen's County', *UJA*, ser. 1, 3 (1855), pp 56–67, 213–31; 6 (1858), pp 327–46.

Boswell, James, *Life of Samuel Johnson, comprehending an account of his studies and numerous works in chronological order* (London, 1847).

Boydell, Mary, *Irish glass*, The Irish Heritage Series 5, (Dublin, 1976).

Bush, J., *Hibernia curiosa: a letter from a gentleman in Dublin to his friend at Dover in Kent* (Dublin, 1769).

Buchan, William M.D., *Domestic medicine: or, The family physician* (Edinburgh, 1769).

Butler, Isaac, 'A journey to Lough Derg by Isaac Butler *c.*1741', *JRSAI*, 5th series, 2:1 (1892), pp 13–24.

Butler, Robin, *Great British wine accessories, 1550–1900* (Suffolk, 2009).

Byrne, Angela (ed.), *John (Fiott) Lee in Ireland, England & Wales, 1806–07* (Oxford, 2018).

Casey, Noreen, 'Architecture and decoration' in Ian Campbell Ross (ed.), *Public virtue, public love: the early years of the Dublin Lying-in Hospital* (Dublin, 1986).

Christie, Christopher, *The British country house in the eighteenth century* (Manchester, 2000).

Clark, Oz, *The history of wine in 100 bottles* (London, 2015).

Clarkson, L.A., & E. Margaret Crawford, *Feast and famine: food and nutrition in Ireland 1500–1920* (Oxford, 2001).

Clarkson, Thomas, *A portraiture of Quakerism* (1870).

Cobbe, Frances Power, *Life of Frances Power Cobbe as told by herself* (London, 1894, 1904 ed.).

Cochrane, Robert, 'Timoleague Friary, County Cork', *JCHAS*, 18 (1912), pp 14–25.

Cork and Orrery, Countess of (ed.), *The Orrery Papers*, 2 vols (London, 1903).

Cosnett, Thomas, *A footman's directory and butler's remembrancer* (London, 1823).

Costello, Vandra, *Irish demesne landscape, 1660–1740* (Dublin, 2016).

Crofton Croker, T. (ed.), *Killarney legends; arranged as a guide to the lakes* (London, 1853).

Cromwell, Thomas, *Excursions through Ireland: province of Leinster* (London, 1820).

Cullen, L.M., 'The Irish merchant communities of Bordeaux, La Rochelle and Cognac in the eighteenth century' in L.M. Cullen & P. Butel (eds), *Négoce et industrie en France et en Irlande au xviiiᵉ siècles* (Bordeaux, 1978), pp 51–63.

Cullen, L.M., 'The Boyds in Bordeaux and Dublin' in Thomas M. Truxes (ed.), *Ireland, France and the Atlantic in a time of war; reflections on the Bordeaux–Dublin letters 1757* (London, 2017), pp 51–69.

Cullen, L.M., 'The smuggling trade in Ireland in the eighteenth century', *PRIA*, 67:5 (1968–9), pp 149–75.

Cullen, L.M., 'Five letters relating to Galway smuggling in 1737', *JGAHS*, 27 (1956/7), pp 10–25.

Cullen, L.M., 'Economic development, 1691–1750' in Moody & Vaughan (eds), *A new history of Ireland*, iv, pp 123–95.

Delamer, Ida, & Conor O'Brien, *500 years of Irish silver* (Dublin, 2005).

Denham, Franklin, 'Timoleague Abbey', *JCHAS*, 1 (1892), pp 173–8.

Dooley, Terence, 'Copy of the marquis of Kildare's household book, 1758', *Archivium Hibernicum*, 62 (2009), pp 183–220.

Down, Kevin, 'Colonial society and economy' in Art Cosgrove (ed.), *A new history of Ireland*, ii, *Medieval Ireland, 1169–1534* (Oxford, 1987), pp 439–91.

Duffy, Eamon, *The stripping of the altars: traditional religion in England, c.1400–1580* (London & New Haven, 1992).

Duhigg, Bartholomew, *History of the King's Inns* (Dublin, 1806).

Edgeworth, Maria, *Ormond* (reprint of 1st ed., London, 1972).

Edgeworth, Maria, *Castle Rackrent* (Oxford, 1980 ed.).

Edgeworth, Maria, *The Absentee* (Oxford, 2001 ed.).

Elias Jr., A.C. (ed.), *Memoirs of Laetitia Pilkington*, 2 vols (London, 1997).

Falkiner, C.L., 'The itinerary of Fynes Morrison', *Illustrations of Irish history and topography, mainly of the 17th century* (London, 1904), pp 225–30.

Fenlon, Jane, *Goods & chattels: a survey of early household inventories in Ireland* (The Heritage Council, Kilkenny, 2003).

ffolliott, R. 'The burglary at William Leeson's house, Bolingbroke, Co. Tipperary in 1785', *Irish Ancestor*, 16:2 (1984), pp 118–21.

FitzGerald, Alison, 'Taste in high life: dining in the Dublin town house' in Christine Casey (ed.), *The eighteenth-century Dublin town house* (Dublin, 2010), pp 120–7.

FitzGerald, Alison, *Silver in Georgian Dublin* (Oxford, 2017).

FitzGerald, Alison, 'A sterling trade: making and selling silver in Ireland' in William Laffan & Christopher Monkhouse (eds), *Ireland: crossroads of art and design, 1690–1840* (Chicago, 2015), pp 174–9.

Fitz-Patrick, William J., *Curious family history: or, Ireland before the Union: including Lord Chief Justice Clonmell's unpublished diary* (1867, Dublin 1869 ed.).

French, Henry, 'Getting drunk soberly: elite masculinity and drinking culture in eighteenth-century England', University of Exeter, www.academia.edu accessed 4 March 2020.

Gamble, John, *Sketches of history, politics and manners in Dublin and the north of Ireland in 1810* (London, 1810).

Gebbie, John H. (ed.), *An introduction to the Abercorn letters (as relating to Ireland, 1736–1816)* (Omagh, 1972).

Gerard, Frances, *Some celebrated Irish beauties of the last century* (London, 1895).

Gilbert, J.T., & R.M. (eds), *Calendar of ancient records of the city of Dublin*, 19 vols (Dublin, 1889–1944).

Gilbert, J.T., *A history of the city of Dublin*, vol. 1 (Dublin, 1854).

Gilbert, J.T. (ed.), 'The streets of Dublin, No. 6', *IQR*, 3:1 (Dublin, 1853), p. 274

Gillett, Eric (ed.), *Elizabeth Ham by herself, 1783–1820* (London, 1945).

Glanville, Philippa, *Silver in England*, (London & New York, 1987, 2006 ed.).

Glin, Knight of, & James Peill, *Irish furniture* (New Haven & London, 2007).

Hailman, John, *Thomas Jefferson on wine* (Jackson, MI, 2006).

Hardy, Francis, *Memoirs of the political and private life of James Caulfield, earl of Charlemont* (London, 1812).

Hayes, Richard, 'Liens Irlandais avec Bordeaux' in R. Hayes, C. Preston, J. Weygand, *Les Irlandais en Aquitaine* (Bordeaux, 1971), pp 3–18.

Hayes, Richard, 'Irish links with Bordeaux', *Studies: an Irish Quarterly Review*, 27:106 (1938), pp 291–306.

Healy, Maurice, *Stay with me flagons* (London, 1952).

Henderson, Alexander, *The history of ancient and modern wines* (London, 1824).

Herbert, J.D., *Irish varieties for the last fifty years* (London, 1836).

Hill, Benson E., *Recollections of an artillery officer* (London, 1836) 2 vols.

Holland, C.H. (ed.), *Trinity College Dublin and the idea of a university* (Dublin, 1991).

Hurley, Jon, *A matter of taste, a history of wine drinking in Britain* (Stroud, 2005).

James, F.G., 'Irish smuggling in the eighteenth century', *IHS*, 12:48 (September 1961), pp 299–317.

Jennings, Marie-Louise, & Gabrielle M. Ashford (eds), *The letters of Katherine Conolly 1707–1747* (IMC, Dublin, 2018).

Johnson, Hugh, *The world atlas of wine* (London, 1985 ed.).

Joyce, Edmund, *Borris House, Co. Carlow, and elite regency patronage*, Maynooth Studies in Local History 108 (Dublin, 2013).

Kellaghan, Tara, 'Claret, the preferred libation of Georgian Ireland's elite'. Submission for DIT Dublin Gastronomy Symposium 2012, pp 1–13.

Kelly, James, 'Domestic medication and medical care in late early modern Ireland' in James Kelly & Fiona Clark (eds), *Ireland and medicine in the seventeenth and eighteenth centuries* (Surrey, 2010), pp 109–35.

Kelly, James, 'The consumption and sociable use of alcohol in eighteenth-century Ireland', *PRIA*, 115C (2015), pp 219–55.

Kennedy, Catriona, '"Our separate rooms": Bishop Stock's narrative of the French invasion of Mayo, 1798', *Field Day Review 5* (Dublin, 2009), pp 94–107.

Kennedy, Roisin, *Dublin Castle art* (Dublin, 2010).

Kinmonth, Claudia, *Irish country furniture, 1700– 1950* (London & New Haven, 1993).

Kirwan, John (ed.), *The chief Butlers of Ireland and the house of Ormond* (Dublin, 2018).

Kopperman, Paul E. (ed.), *Theory and practice in eighteenth-century medicine: 'Regimental Practice' by John Buchanan, MD* (Oregon, 2012).

de Latocnaye, *A Frenchman's walk through Ireland 1796–7*, translated from the French of De Latocnaye by John Stevenson (Dublin, 1917).

Legg, Marie-Louise (ed.), *The Synge letters, 1746–1752* (Dublin, 1996).

Legg, Marie-Louise, '"Irish Wine": the import of claret from Bordeaux to provincial Ireland in the eighteenth century' in Raymond Gillespie & R.F. Foster (eds), *Irish provincial cultures in the long eighteenth-century: making the middle sort: essays for Toby Barnard* (Dublin, 2012), pp 93–105.

Liger, Charles Louis, *A treatise on the gout* (London, 1760).

Little, George A., *The Ouzel Galley* (Dublin, 1953).

Livingstone, Peadar, *The Fermanagh story* (Enniskillen, 1969).

Longfield, Ada Kathleen, *Anglo-Irish trade in the 16th century* (London, 1929).

Ludington, Charles C., '"To the King o'er the Water": Scotland and claret *c.*1660–1763' in Mack Holt (ed.), *Alcohol: a social and cultural history* (Oxford, 2006), pp 163–84.

Ludington, Charles C., *The politics of wine in Britain: a new cultural history* (London, 2013).

Maxwell, W.H., *Wild sports of the West* (Dublin, 191– , ed.).

Maxwell, Constantia, *Dublin under the Georges, 1714–1830* (London, 1937, 1997 ed.).

Maxwell, Constantia, *The stranger in Ireland* (1954, Dublin, 1979 ed.).

Maxwell, Constantia, *Country and town in Ireland under the Georges* (Dundalk, 1949).

Maxwell, Sir Herbert (ed.), *The Creevey Papers: a selection from the correspondence and diaries of Thomas Creevey, MP* (London, 1904).

McBride, Ian, *Eighteenth-century Ireland: the isle of slaves* (Dublin, 2009).

McCarthy, Patricia, *Life in the country house in Georgian Ireland* (London & New Haven, 2016).

McCarthy, Patricia, 'Vails and travails: how Lord Kildare kept his household in order', *IADS*, 6 (2003), pp 120–39.

Mac Con Iomaire, Máirtín, 'Gastro-topography: exploring food-related placenames in Ireland', *Canadian Journal of Irish Studies*, 38:1/2 (2014), pp 126–57.

Mac Con Iomaire, Máirtín, 'Public dining in Dublin: the history and evolution of gastronomy and commercial dining, 1700–1900', *International Journal of Contemporary Hospitality Management*. 25:2 (2012), pp 227–46.

Mac Con Iomaire, M., & T. Kellaghan, 'Royal pomp: viceregal celebrations and hospitality in Georgian Dublin', Oxford Symposium on Food and Cookery, 2011.

MacKenzie, T.M., *Dromana: the memoirs of an Irish family* (Dublin, 1907).

McCracken, J.L. 'The social structure and social life, 1714–60' in Moody & Vaughan (eds), *A new history of Ireland*: iv (Oxford, 1986, 2009 ed.), pp 31–56.

McCracken, J.L., 'The political structure 1714–60' in Moody & Vaughan (eds), *A new history of Ireland*: iv (Oxford, 1986, 2009 ed.), pp 57–83.

McDonnell, Joseph, 'Irish rococo silver', *Irish Arts Review*, 13 (1997), pp 78–87.

McDowell, R.B.,'Ireland in 1800' in Moody & Vaughan (eds), *A new history of Ireland*: iv (Oxford, 1986, 2009 ed.), pp 657–712.

Malcolm, Elizabeth, *'Ireland sober, Ireland free'; drink and temperance in nineteenth-century Ireland* (Dublin, 1986).

Malcomson, A.P.W., *John Foster: the politics of the Anglo-Irish ascendancy* (Oxford, 1978).

Melville, E., *Sketches of society in France and Ireland, years 1805–6–7* (Dublin, 1811).

Memoirs of Richard Cumberland, written by himself (Boston, 1806).

Mills, John (ed.), *Account roll of the priory of the Holy Trinity, Dublin, 1337–1346* (Dublin, 1891).

Moody, T.W., & Vaughan, W.E. (eds), *A new history of Ireland*: iv, *Eighteenth-century Ireland, 1691–1800* (Oxford, 1986, 2009 ed.).

Montagu, Elizabeth Robinson, Emily Jane Climenson, *Elizabeth Montagu, the queen of the Bluestockings: her correspondence from 1720 to 1721*, vol. 1 (London, 1906).

Mooney, T., & F. White, 'The gentry's winter season' in David Dickson (ed.), *The gorgeous mask: Dublin, 1700–1850* (Dublin, 1987), pp 1–16.

Mott, George, 'Eating and drinking habits in Ireland two hundred years ago', *Irish Ancestor*, 5:1 (1973), pp 7–11.

Murphy, Antoin E., *Richard Cantillon: entrepreneur and economist* (Oxford, 1986).

Murphy, Liam, *Waterford merchants and their families on distant shores* (Dublin, 2018).

Murphy, Ted, *A kingdom of wine: a celebration of Ireland's wine geese* (Cork, 2005).

Nelson, E. Charles, 'The Dublin Florists' Club in the mid-eighteenth century', *Garden History*, 10:2 (Autumn, 1982), pp 142–8.

Ní Chinnéide, Sighle, (ed.), 'A Frenchman's impressions of Limerick, town and people, in 1791', *North Munster Antiquarian Journal*, 5:4 (1948), pp 96–101.

O'Brien, Conor, 'Dean Swift's and some early Irish labels', *Journal of the Wine Label Circle*, 9:3 (June 1992), pp 54–60.

Ó Ciardha, Eamonn, *Ireland and the Jacobite cause, 1685–1766: a fatal attachment* (Dublin, 2002).

O'Donoghue, N.X., *The Eucharist in pre-Norman Ireland* (Indiana, 2011).

O'Kane, Finola, *Ireland and the picturesque: design, landscape, painting and tourism 1700–1840* (London & New Haven, 2013).

O'Kane, Finola, *Landscape design in eighteenth-century Ireland* (Cork, 2004).

O'Mahony, Charles K., *The viceroys of Ireland: the story of a long line of noblemen and their wives who have ruled Ireland and Irish society for over seven hundred years* (London, 1912).

O'Neill, Timothy, *Merchants and mariners in medieval Ireland* (Dublin, 1987).

Oresko, Robert (ed.), *The works in architecture of Robert and James Adam* (London, 1975).

Pakenham, Valerie, *The Big House in Ireland* (London, 2000).

Paston-Williams, Sara, *The art of dining: a history of cooking and eating* (The National Trust, 1993, 1999 ed.).

Penning-Rowsell, Edmund, *The wines of Bordeaux* (London, 1969, 1973 edn).

The diary of Samuel Pepys, www.pepysdiary.com.

Pinkerton, W., 'Lord Deputy of Ireland's household expenses (circa 1580)', *Ulster Journal of Archaeology*, 1st series, 8 (1860), pp 27–34.

Powell, Anthony (ed.), *Barnard Letters, 1778–1824* (London, 1928).

Powell, Martyn J., *The politics of consumption in eighteenth-century Ireland* (London, 2005).

Powell, Martyn J., 'Political toasting in eighteenth-century Ireland', *Journal of the Historical Association*, 91:304 (October 2006), pp 508–28.

Read, Charles A. (ed.), *The cabinet of Irish literature: selections from the works of the chief poets, orators and prose writers of Ireland*, 4 vols (London, 1879–80).

Robins, Joseph, *Champagne & silver buckles: the viceregal court at Dublin Castle, 1700–1922* (Dublin, 2001).

Robinson, Jancis (ed.), *The Oxford companion to wine* (Oxford, 1994, 2006 ed.).

Ryan, David, *Blasphemers and blackguards; the Irish Hellfire clubs* (Dublin, 2012).

Shaw, Peter, *The juice of the grape; or, wine preferable to water* (London, 1724).

Sheridan, Thomas (ed.), Letter to Sir Charles Wogan in Spain, 1735, *The works of the Revd Jonathan Swift, DD* (London, 1801, revised ed.).

Simms, J.G., 'The Irish on the Continent, 1691–1800' in Moody & Vaughan (eds), *A new history of Ireland*, iv (Oxford, 1986, 2009 ed.), pp 629–56.

Simms, Katharine, 'Guesting and feasting in Gaelic Ireland', *JRSAI*, 108 (1978), pp 67–100.

Simon, Andre L., *Bottlescrew days: wine drinking in England during the eighteenth century* (London, 1926).

Simon, Andre L., *The history of the wine trade in England*, vol. i (London, 1906–7).

Smith, Charles, *The ancient and present state of the county and city of Cork* (Dublin, 1774), vol. 11, book IV.

Sullivan, Sir Edward (ed.), *Buck Whaley's memoirs* (London, 1906).

Swift, Jonathan, *Journal to Stella*, letter 16, February 1710–11, p. 149. Online Project Gutenberg e-book ed.

Trusler, John, *The honours of the table* (London, 1788, ed. 1791).

Wakefield, Edward, *An account of Ireland, statistical and political*, 2 vols (London, 1812).

Walsh, Patrick, & A.P.W. Malcomson, *The Conolly archive* (IMC, Dublin, 2010).

Westropp, M.S.D., *Irish glass: an account of glass-making in Ireland from the XVIth century to the present day* (London, 1921).

Whelehan, T.P., *The Irish wines of Bordeaux* (Dublin, 1990).

Whyte, Laurence, 'The Parting Cup, or, The Humours of Deoch an Doruis ...', *original poems on various subjects, serious, moral, and diverting* (Dublin, 1742, 2nd ed.).

Williams, William H.A., *Creating Irish tourism: the first century, 1750–1850* (Cambridge, 2010).

Woods, C.J., *Travellers' accounts as source-material for Irish historians* (Dublin, 2009).

Woolley, David (ed.), *The correspondence of Jonathan Swift, DD* (Frankfurt, 2007).

Woschek, Heinz-Gert (ed.), *Wine and architecture* (Birkhäuser, 2013).

Wright, Thomas (ed.), *Giraldus Cambrensis: The topography of Ireland* (tr. T. Forester), (Ontario, 2000).

Young, Arthur, *A tour in Ireland* (London, 1780).

Index

Page references in **bold** refer to images or artists.